Code Name
Christiane Clouet

For Frieda and Russ
With great affection and admiration

[signature]

May 15, 1995

Claire
Chevrillon

*Code
Name
Christiane
Clouet*

A Woman

in the French Resistance

Translation by Jane Kielty Stott
Foreword by John F. Sweets

Texas A&M University Press

College Station

Library of Congress Cataloging-in-Publication Data

Chevrillon, Claire, 1907–
    Code name Christiane Clouet : a woman in the French
Resistance / by Claire Chevrillon ; translation by Jane Kielty
Stott ; foreword by John F. Sweets.
        p.   cm.
    Translation of an unpublished manuscript.
    Includes bibliographical references and index.
    ISBN 0-89096-628-1.—ISBN 0-89096-629-X (pbk.)
    1. Chevrillon, Claire, 1907–   .   2. World War, 1939–1945—Un-
derground movements—France—Paris.   3. World War, 1939–
1945—Cryptography.   4. World War, 1939–1945—Personal nar-
ratives, French.   5. Guerrillas—France—Paris—Biography.   6.
Paris (France)—History.   I. Title.
D802.F82P3743   1995
940.53′4436—dc20   94-33349
                                                                CIP

Contents

LIST OF ILLUSTRATIONS   VII

ACKNOWLEDGMENTS   VIII

TRANSLATOR'S NOTE   IX

TRANSLATOR'S ACKNOWLEDGMENTS   XII

FOREWORD, BY JOHN F. SWEETS   XIII

PREFACE   XVII

1.   The Phony War, August, 1939–May, 1940   3

2.   Invasion, May–June, 1940   8

3.   Port-Blanc, July–August, 1940   15

4.   Paris, Fall, 1940   22

5.   Paris, Fall, 1940—Continued   27

6.   Two Incidents Concerning My Parents, Port-Blanc, Fall 1940   31

7.   The Persecution of Jews, Fall, 1940–June, 1942   33

8.   Paris, Fall, 1940–42   36

9.   Paul's Captivity, September, 1940–May, 1944   39

10.   The Spirit of Resistance Grows, Summer, 1940–June, 1942   51

11.   Interlude: The Children at Orgeval, Winter, 1941–June, 1942   57

12.   The Persecution of Jews, Second Phase, July–October, 1942   58

13.   My Journey to the Free Zone, October–November, 1942   67

14.   Events in North Africa Seen from Home, November–December, 1942   70

15.   Our Team, December, 1942–March, 1943   72

16.   Arrests in Our Team, February–April, 1943   79

17.   My Arrest, April, 1943   84

18.   Fresnes, April–June, 1943   89

19.   Return from Fresnes, June, 1943   100

20.   An Eventful Summer, June–July, 1943   106

21.   The Gestapo on the rue de Grenelle, September, 1943   111

22.   Code Clerk, October, 1943–January, 1944   119

23.   Code Service, January–June, 1944   124

24.   Elation and Sadness, D-Day–July, 1944   138

25.   Port-Blanc, September, 1943–July, 1944   142

26.   Liberation in Brittany, July–August, 1944   151

27.   The Liberation of Paris, Late July–August 24, 1944   155

EPILOGUE 167

APPENDIXES

A   Charles Geoffroy-Dechaume's letter to Dr. Bernard Ménétrel,
     Advisor to Marshal Pétain 197
B   Two letters written by Charles Ferdinand-Dreyfus
     before his deportation 198
C   Two letters written from Jacqueline d'Alincourt
     to her family before her deportation 199
D   Letter from Dr. Cécile Dubost to Jean Ayral's father 200

NOTES 203
INDEX 215

List of Illustrations

The school at Bourg-Dun, 1940   43
Paul with Marie-France, André, and Françoise   44
Antoinette with André, Françoise, and Francis, 1940   45
German officers and soldiers at Café de la Paix, 1940   46
André and Clarisse, Port-Blanc, 1938   47
André braiding his granddaughter's hair   47
Antoinette and the children at Port-Blanc   48
Mme. Fabre   48
Pedicabs in Paris during the war   49
Paul in Oflag 4D   50
Charles before the war   130
Sylvie with Francis, 1942   131
The children at Port-Blanc, 1942   131
Jean Ayral   132
German sentry, Lyons, 1942   132
Daniel Ferdinand-Dreyfus   132
Geneviève Janin, 1943   133
Jacqueline d'Alincourt   134
Claire Chevrillon, 1943   135
Code on a silk handkerchief   136
Pierre Brossolette in London   137
Antoinette doing homework with André   185
Breton maquis   186
Welcoming Americans in Rennes   187
Barricades, Paris, 1944   188
German general at time of surrender   189
Victory parade, Champs-Elysées   190
Generals de Gaulle and Leclerc   191
Simone Lemoine, London, 1944   192
Charles Fassier after the war   192

Acknowledgments

My special gratitude goes to Dr. Geneviève Janin, without whose steady encouragement and practical help this work would never have been completed; to Madeleine Blondel, Curator of the Musée de la Vie Bourguignonne, who typed the manuscript in her free time; to Nicolette Picheral, Francis Fabre, Harriet Proudfoot, Nicolette Boillot, and Florence Hepp, for their pertinent suggestions; and, to Jane Kielty Stott, my translator, who inspired this English version, and whose perseverance made it possible.

Claire Chevrillon

Translator's Note

I met Claire Chevrillon (b. 1907) more than twenty-five years ago in Morocco where she was directing the French Cultural Center in Fez and I was teaching English at the American Library. She and I would play flute duets on Sunday afternoons in the hilly outskirts of the Old City. After we both left North Africa, Claire and I stayed in touch, and when I went to see her in Paris in 1987, she gave me a copy of a memoir she'd just finished writing about the Second World War that she was privately circulating among family and friends. I was surprised by it because I'd never heard her talk about her war experience. "You see," she later explained to me, "I hadn't ever spoken about it, so people didn't know what happened." As soon as I started reading her memoir I knew I wanted to translate it. What attracted me most about her story was its simple integrity.

Claire was an English teacher at Collège Sévigné, a well-known girls' school in Paris, when she discovered, in October, 1942, that there was an organized underground working against the occupying Germans. She joined this effort—she never heard it called "the Resistance" until after the Liberation—working first for its Paris Air Operations, and later for its Code Service (Service du Chiffre de la Délégation Générale du Gouvernement Provisoire), which she headed in 1944. It was Claire and her team who coded many of the telegrams in *Is Paris Burning?* Claire's memoir evokes the back rooms of the Resistance where this code work was deciphered and transcribed. It is a world we've heard little about until now.

Claire's memoir also gives abundant detail about what daily life was like for the French elite during the German occupation. Claire's father, André Chevrillon (1864–1957), was a man of letters in the early decades of this century—"the first literary critic in France," according to his good friend Edith Wharton. He was the author of more than twenty books, a member of both the French Academy and the American Academy of Arts and Letters, and was particularly noted as an interpreter of English literature and culture, introducing Shelley, Ruskin, Galsworthy, and Kipling to French readers. He was also a travel writer about India, the Middle East, North Africa, and Brittany, where he had a summer home on the north coast in a small town called Port-Blanc. (Port-Blanc figures prominently in this memoir.) His book most cited by scholars today is *Taine: formation de sa pensée* (1932), a study of his maternal uncle, the philosopher and historian Hippolyte Taine, in whose home André grew up after his own father died. In 1934 André wrote a prescient book about the dangers of Nazism, *La Menace allemande*. In the years before the war, André and his wife sheltered anti-Nazi refugees in their large house in Saint-Cloud. "Very interesting people came to our home and told us horrible things," Claire says, "so we were somewhat aware of Hitler's implications—although no one was ever really aware."

Claire's mother, Clarisse Porges Chevrillon (1868–1952), was from a large assimilated Jewish family that suffered greatly during the war. Much of Claire's memoir is taken up with the persecution and deportation of Clarisse's nephews Jacques (1884–1943?) and Charles (1887–1942?) Ferdinand-Dreyfus. Until the Nazi occupation, Jacques, one of the founders and a director of the French Social Security system, worked in the Ministry of Labor. Charles directed the Bel-Air School Farm at Soucy.

Claire had an older brother, Pierre (1903–75), and sister, Antoinette (1905–73). In 1934 Antoinette married Paul Fabre (1911–83), a physicist. Antoinette and Paul are important figures in Claire's memoir, and the nine grandnieces and grandnephews for whom Claire wrote it, and to whom she dedicates it, are their grandchildren.

In the winter of 1944, her work for the underground over, Claire was sent to England by the French Ministry of Foreign Affairs to give talks on the Occupation and the Resistance. To prepare for this trip, she spent a month and a half jotting down notes on her war experience and interviewing other members of the underground. It was during this time, she says, that she learned "all those secrets I'd gone along the edge of, while I was coding, without knowing exactly what they meant." Much of Claire's memoir draws on the information she gathered for this assignment.

After the war, Claire worked for the United Nations Relief and Repatriation Association in Germany, helping refugees find their way back to France, Belgium, and the Netherlands. She then taught again at Collège Sévigné (1946) and at Bristol University (1947) in England. She returned to Paris the following year and for a decade supervised Bristol's contingent of French students enrolled in the Cours de la Civilisation Française at the Sorbonne. In 1957 she was invited by the French cultural attaché in Morocco to set up a cultural center in Fez. Twelve years later she transferred to the French Cultural Library in Tunis, where she remained until her retirement in 1972. She now lives in Paris.

Claire's memoir is remarkably understated. When she writes about her work for the Code Service, she so underplays her role as head of it, she almost obscures the fact that she was the main link in the lines of communication running between the Free French Government in London and de Gaulle's Delegation in France. Claire sees nothing heroic about her efforts: "It was austere, not at all adventurous," she insists. "I stayed in my corner the whole time." Her restraint and evenhanded style (she writes about the deportation of her relatives without bitterness) raise questions of continuing and profound interest: what enables people to forgive? Or for that matter, what enables them to resist? Claire's memoir doesn't provide answers to these questions, except by way of example. Claire wasn't interested in answers or in using her memoir as a vehicle to judge or dramatize; she considers her memoir testimony. "My goal was to set forward the facts," she told me, "and not to analyze myself or my characters. My instinct was to maintain a positive, cheerful outlook on things—which might offend people, because it was really more dramatic than I say it was." The fact that Claire doesn't dramatize or embellish her material is perhaps as revealing and instructive as the information her memoir contains.

Translator's Acknowledgments

Many people contributed to this English version of Claire Chevrillon's memoir, and I am very grateful for their kindness: Claire herself worked closely with me to preserve the original intent of her narrative and, at the same time, adapt it for a wider audience. John Sweets very generously wrote the foreword. Bill Stott frequently lent his seasoned editorial eye; David Shalk provided the enthusiasm and gentle guidance without which the project would never have been completed. Jane Kramer and Vincent Crapanzano broadened my horizons and offered delightful hospitality on trips to Paris; Janice Rossen championed the book from the start and was an invaluable resource. The late Nancy Barker helped me see the important connections, and B. J. Fernea, with patience and good humor, made sure I stayed the course. I want also to extend heartfelt thanks to Rick Bretell, Ina Caro, Jean-Pierre Cauvin, Louisa Cauvin, Richard Cohen, M. R. D. Foot, Elizabeth Hall, Michael Hall, Roger Hall, Patrice Higonnet, Nancy Lewis, R. W. B. Lewis, Helen Morton, Geneviève Noufflard, Marcel Ophuls, Laurel Otte, and Ellen Temple, who all, in one way or another, have had a salutary effect on this undertaking. Any remaining infelicities are my own.

Jane Kielty Stott

Foreword

When I was first asked to read the manuscript of Claire Chevrillon's memoirs, I remember thinking to myself: "Oh, no, not another Resistance memoir." However, as I began to read the text I recognized almost immediately that this was, in fact, not just another Resistance memoir, but an account of the intertwined lives of several remarkable individuals whose experiences were at once fascinating and extraordinarily informative about many aspects of life during the German Occupation of France. Moreover, in common with some of the most impressive of the classic memoirs of the French Resistance, such as Guillain de Bénouville's *Le Sacrifice du matin*,[1] Christian Pineau's *La Simple vérité*,[2] or Alban Vistel's *La Nuit sans ombre*,[3] Chevrillon's account has at times an almost poetic or lyrical quality which conveys vividly the atmosphere of this tragic era of France's modern history.

One of the most striking features of these memoirs is the exceptional way the author's life intersected with a remarkable circle of individuals: her father was a fellow member of the French Academy with the writer Georges Duhamel; the husband of her best friend from childhood was a friend of the Croix de feu leader, Colonel de la Rocque; a cousin was one of the founders of the French Social Security system during the Popular Front era; and a more distant relative by marriage was the General Director of the Bibliothèque Nationale. All of these people, and other prominent personalities, enter the author's story at some point. In her work as a resister, Claire coded and decoded messages for many of the most important representatives of the Gaullist *délégation* in France, including Daniel Cordier (Jean Moulin's close associate), Claude Serreulles, Jacques Bingen, and Alexandre Parodi. She was, in fact, very much at the center of things, even though, because of the clandestine nature of the Resistance's struggle, she was not always aware of the significance of her actions or of the messages she had transcribed.

Even more astounding than the range of her contacts was the fact that the author experienced, personally and directly, so many different aspects of the Occupation era. In the opening weeks of the Battle of

France she was on the road during the Exodus, witnessing the panic and disarray of fleeing civilians and soldiers and arriving in Bordeaux at about the same time as the French government, which stopped over there before moving to Vichy for the duration of the Occupation. Later adventures would include several illegal crossings of the demarcation line established by the German Occupation troops. Because her mother and several other relatives were defined as Jews by the Vichy Regime's anti-Semitic laws, Claire experienced at close second hand the distress imposed by the obligation to wear a yellow star, the agony of arrest and deportation of loved ones, and ultimately the disappearance of family and friends in Hitler's grotesque "final solution." Arrested on suspicion of her Resistance activity (probably after a denunciation by one of her fellow citizens), Claire went through interrogations and spent several months in a flea-infested prison at Fresnes. Later, during the last year of the Occupation, she would be forced to disappear into the "underground," leaving her parents with no knowledge of her whereabouts or of the nature of her activities.

These memoirs have the special merit of recounting the Occupation era from the point of view of a woman. While there have been a surplus of "masculine" Resistance memoirs, quite often featuring exploits of derring-do, from spying adventures to accounts of sabotage attacks or open combat with the Germans, there have been relatively few memoirs written by French women. Despite frequent brief acknowledgments of the often-crucial roles played by women in the Resistance, with a few notable exceptions this same imbalance is reflected in the scholarly literature on the Resistance as well. Thus the perspective offered by Claire Chevrillon is welcome and particularly illuminating. For example, the reader is allowed to glimpse the Occupation through the eyes of Claire's sister, Antoinette, whose husband spent the whole period as a prisoner of war in Germany. Antoinette's travail in caring for the children and trying to keep in touch with her husband by way of an irregular and always censored mail service illustrates the common lot of many French women who spent the war years "waiting and hoping."[4] Claire's reports about trips to Drancy or Fresnes, as she attempted to pass along food packages or messages to imprisoned friends or family members, portrays another task of "everyday life" that regularly put women under stress and often placed them in situations of abuse or danger. And, of course, merely her own actions in serving as a "mailbox," offering safe haven to resisters or those in flight, acting as a courier, and working as a code clerk for the Resistance, underline the vital part played by women in the struggle against Vichy and the German Occupation.

Above all, in these memoirs one senses the author's compassionate humanity. While the political and ethical or moral conviction that led Claire to side with the Resistance will be apparent to the reader, equally striking is the absence of rancor toward those who followed other paths during the Occupation. We find, for example, that an aunt and uncle were fervent Pétainists. While this fact contributed to a certain distancing or strain in family relations, Claire provides a rational and fairminded explanation of her uncle and aunt's position. This understanding and empathy is extended by her even to individuals who, arrested by the German police, sold out their fellow resisters. Overall, Claire's memoirs are a passionate testimony to the complexity and difficulty of making choices in a society under foreign occupation.

This account of life in occupied France is also very accurate; most aspects of the story correspond to the conclusions of the best historians of the era. Even on those rare occasions where the scholar might quibble about the interpretation of an issue—for example, the imagery of Germans "pulling the strings" of their puppets at Vichy, whereas most historians now highlight the initiatives taken independently by the French leaders of the Vichy Regime—Claire's memoirs are an excellent guide to the sentiments shared by many French people of the time, to what was "believed to be true," whether or not this was in fact the case.

Finally, unlike so many highly romanticized thrill-a-minute Resistance tales, this author reminds her readers that many aspects of "life as usual" continued throughout the occupation era. Not only did individuals like Claire's father, who persisted in his work at the Academy on the never-ending task of revising the French dictionary to "protect the French language," attempt to make life as "normal" as possible, despite the presence of the German troops. But we see the period from the perspective of young children who experienced the particularly hard winters of the first occupation years as a wonderful opportunity to sled and play in the snow. Similarly, Claire recalls bombing raids on the Renault factories at Boulogne-Billancourt which, despite their often deadly results, provided spectacular fireworks shows for those who watched from Parisian rooftops at a safe distance. The harsh conditions of the Occupation did not prevent the young Claire from taking pleasure in simple things: discovering unfamiliar sections of Paris as she bicycled on streets relatively devoid of traffic because of gasoline shortages and travel restrictions, or gorging herself on raspberries after working hard to prepare a safe house for a member of the Gaullist délégation. In one picturesque scene the reader is introduced to the lush tones, colors, sounds, and tastes of a fall day in Corrèze—a sweet coating on the bitter pill of reality, perhaps, but one is reminded that for most French people life went on during the Occupation. Claire Chevrillon has given us a portrait of that life in its many dimensions as few witnesses have done before.

John F. Sweets
University of Kansas

Preface

To Matthieu, Benoît, Claire, Béatrice, Samuel, Anne, Adeline, Nicolas, and Alexandre; and to their parents:

Dear children, you have often asked me to write down what it was like for our family to live through the Second World War. I haven't ever done this because I was always too caught up in the flow of life to want to look back. Lately, however, I have changed my mind. Now that I am older, I find my thoughts frequently wandering through the past, and I realize that what stands out as especially vivid and significant is the war. Perhaps this is true for most of us who were adults then.

So, dear ones, here is an account of the war as your family and I lived it. It may not be what you expected because it's not a confessional novel or thriller; it has no romance, and no plot beyond the start and end of the war. It's just a narrative of our daily lives seen against great events: the Fall of France, the Occupation, the Collaboration, the Resistance, and the Liberation.

Our family's experience of the war was limited and local, and therefore my account of it is necessarily subjective. And, of course, you won't find on these pages a great deal of what happened elsewhere in France because we heard nothing about those things. But what I tell here did in fact happen. I have changed only a few names.

You may wonder how I was able to write with accuracy and detail about things that took place more than forty years ago. I couldn't have done so had I not had a great many family letters, including my own, as well as various private and public documents from that time. These records brought facts back to life that would otherwise have been lost, and either confirmed or corrected those things I remembered.

I believe Europe, in the late thirties, was headed toward the most evil, powerful dictatorship the world has ever seen. The war saved us from it, but did it once and for all? Sadly, no. The instinct of one nation or race to dominate another doesn't die. It grows insidiously, feeding on private and public unconcern, until suddenly it's too late to prevent disaster. My hope, dear ones, is that you won't ever slip into this kind of careless, cowardly attitude—and that something in my memoir will help put you on your way.

C.C.
August, 1985

*Code Name
Christiane Clouet*

1 *The Phony War*

In August, 1939, I was in the mountains of the Drome, at Valcroissant, helping my old friend Eliane Frey direct a Cub Scout camp. The camp had about a hundred little boys transplanted for a month away from their customary life in Paris to a wild valley of cliffs and hills covered with boxwood, thyme, and lavender. Eliane and I were completely absorbed in the day-to-day problems of running the camp and by the beauty of the countryside.

Then, at the end of the month, a thunderclap: news reached us of a general mobilization. Eliane left immediately as an army nurse. Most of the other Scout leaders were also called up and left. Families telegraphed to say their children should return to Paris.

In fact, we'd known for several years that France was in danger and that Nazi doctrines had spread across most of Europe—just as we knew about the horrible persecutions to which Jews were being subjected.[1] And now there would be war. I remember thinking, "This is the end of happy life."

We decided to close the camp. All at once the children became angelic and helpful. In twenty-four frantic hours everybody and everything was packed in a train to Paris. At the Gare de Lyon the children were immediately snatched away by their parents.

On the first of September we heard that Germany had invaded Poland. Two days later England and France entered the war.

At that time the scouting spirit meant a great deal to me. I was determined to try to be useful. So I did what another scouting friend, Grace Brandt, a social worker, asked me to do: I escorted women and children out of Paris and helped them settle in the country. The terrifying blitzkrieg in Poland raised fears that Paris would be the next target, and the government and newspapers were urging "useless people" to leave the city.

I wore my Scout uniform to appear more professional and carried the obligatory gas mask. I made several trips from Gare Montparnasse, each time on trains teeming with women, rambunctious children, and sick people.

3

We had been advised to maintain an air of confidence. I knew of course where we were supposed to get off, but nothing of what awaited us once we got to our destination. I remember one particular morning I had fourteen cars on a train for Sainte-Gauburge, in Normandy. On our arrival the astounded station master told me that only three hundred people were expected. What was to be done? We chose three cars at random and asked everyone in them to get out. A half-dozen other cars would be sent back to L'Aigle, the rest would continue on to Argentan . . . in God's hands! Along the tracks in Sainte-Gauburge stood families that had arrived the day before. They were already looking for a way back to Paris, so disgusted were they at having spent the night in a barn with rats. "We prefer the blitz to this!" they told the new arrivals. It was a fine welcome.

I went immediately to find out how Sainte-Gauburge planned to accommodate everyone. The mayor was still in bed, and no preparations of any kind had been made. I'm afraid neither sweet words nor indignation helped very much in this case.

I would return from these expeditions exhausted and unconvinced that our efforts were worthwhile. In fact there was no blitz on Paris, and gradually all the refugees returned home.

But the news reports were bad. In mid-September the Soviet Union invaded Poland with Germany's approval. Hitler and Stalin had secretly agreed to such an invasion in August, and by the end of September Poland had collapsed. The Soviet Union then annexed the Baltic states.

At this time I was a teacher of English in two private schools: the Collège Sévigné and the Ecole La Fayette. The first closed down until January, 1940; the second relocated to Normandy, not far from Dieppe, with quite a number of students, several families, and a few teachers. I joined them. We organized three different schools, each about six miles from the others: at Varengeville, Sainte-Marguerite, and Bourg-Dun.

I was in charge of the school at Bourg-Dun. We set up in an old, low, half-timbered Norman house with a restored interior. The rooms on the first floor served as classrooms and the small rooms in the attic as bedrooms. We were three teachers, a cook, and about twenty students, not counting some from the surrounding area whose schools lacked teachers because of the mobilization.

Opposite the school was a house made of wood and wattle and daub whose windows had blue shutters. Like our schoolhouse, it was a vacation house and for rent. I mentioned it in a letter to my sister, Antoinette, whose husband, Paul, had been mobilized in the air defense of Saint-Nazaire, and she arrived in November with André, age three, and Françoise (whom we called Soisette), one, and our friend Marie-France Geoffroy-Dechaume, twenty-one, who helped with the children.

Our school was practically family. My first cousin Michele Cavelier, who wrote novels, was the literature teacher. Her daughter Odile, eighteen, just graduated from high school, was the math teacher. Her son, René, twelve, and her niece, Cécile Hébrard, fifteen, were students. The hospitable Blue House echoed with the sound of recorders and other vestiges of a small choir we had all taken part in the year before. Marie-France sang the songs her mother used to sing: *l'Amour de moi, Au jardin de mon père, O Renaud réveille-toi!* We rented a piano. War seemed remote.

I was in charge of English in the three schools and also taught some French and history. I spent a lot of time in Theodora, my little Peugeot, going from one school to the other—always, it seems to me, with pleasure. The countryside was an open plateau, cut by a valley or two, thick with trees. Off the main road, beyond the downs, was the sea. At one point the road drew near the chalk cliffs. Going to the edge on foot, one heard the great roar and saw far below the crashing ocean, milky white, and seagulls gliding in circles.

The Phony War dragged on.[2] Every night the radio said the same thing: nothing important was happening at the front. Every night Ferdonnet, a Frenchman in Stuttgart, announced that France was sure to lose, Germany could not be beaten. We listened to him, laughing with exasperation, and cut him off.

Paul got to come home on leave once or twice. The Blue House prepared a celebration with special treats, and I drove to Dieppe to pick him up. Antoinette didn't go because she was again pregnant. She was being cared for by a woman doctor, Mme. L——, the mother of one of our students. The delivery was scheduled for the end of February at a clinic in Dieppe.

Toward the middle of January it became terribly cold. Pipes froze and burst and grew stalactites; electric lines snapped; streets became skating rinks. A large tree near the school turned into a fairy-tale candelabra, and the children broke off icicles and sucked them with relish.

One night I woke to hear gravel thrown against my window. I leapt up and looked out. There was Marie-France, in her Chinese silk bathrobe, in the snow. She held her hands to her mouth and shouted that Antoinette's labor had started. I dressed and ran over to the Blue House, stopping on the way to check Theodora. Two flat tires!

My sister was lying in bed and very anxious. She thought she should leave for Dieppe immediately, but was relieved when I told her travel was out of the question. Mme. L—— would come to her. I ran to the town hall to use its telephone (ours was down). Mme. L—— said, "I wouldn't think of going out on a night like this." She hung up.

I ran back to the house to soothe Antoinette and then out again to wake the butcher and ask him to bring a doctor from the countryside in his truck. Alas, his radiator was frozen! I returned to Antoinette.

"Don't come in!" she cried out to me. Then, two minutes later: "You can come in now."

The baby had come! And not at all ugly or wrinkled, but pink and smooth.

"My scissors are in the sewing kit," Antoinette said, sounding tired. I doused the scissors in eau de cologne, took some thread, made two small, tight knots and—suppressing panic—cut the cord.

I wrapped the baby in a wool bathrobe and put him in front of an electric heater, stammered out a few reassuring words, and then suddenly remembered that there was another doctor, Dr. T——, among the students' parents. I ran back to the town hall and phoned him. "What? What are you telling me? The baby's come?" he said. "What have you done? Put it by an electric heater? But you'll burn it! All right, I'm coming, but I'm still in bed and twenty-five miles from you."

My heart was torn with anguish. Convinced my sister wouldn't survive, convinced I had roasted the baby, I returned to the Blue House and scarcely dared enter Antoinette's room. But there she was, smiling. A farm woman was going into raptures about the beauty of the baby. Marie-France, still in her Chinese bathrobe, had run through the snow to the priest's house on the outskirts of town. It was he who recommended the farm wife—a great expert in birthing calves. She was able to assure us that my sister could, without risk, further postpone the usual procedures after childbirth. She comforted us, asked for some black coffee, and began gossiping.

Despite all that, the wait for the doctor was long: forty minutes.

Then suddenly, brouhaha below. I went down and found Dr. T—— facing a furious woman—another doctor! She had been brought in by the butcher, who had finally gotten his radiator defrosted. The two were in the midst of a heated discussion about just who was legally entitled to attend the patient.

I said timidly, "Could you please come up? My sister has been waiting an hour to be tidied up."

The woman doctor disappeared into the night, and Dr. T—— bounded up the stairs, four at a time.

I can still hear his first words on entering the room: "What a battlefield!" Half an hour later, everything had been put in order. We thanked him effusively. He said: "Don't count on me in the future. I am not licensed to practice in this district."

The next day I sought out the woman doctor whom the butcher had brought from the country and who *was* licensed to practice in Bourg-Dun. The thaw had already started. Theodora rolled slowly, splashing through giant puddles of water. I lost my way on unknown, deserted roads. When I finally found the doctor, she said that one really shouldn't disturb two doctors in one night. Furthermore, she was leaving the district for good the next day.

There was nothing left to do but turn again to formidable Mme. L——. She came by at the end of the long day and said to me, accusingly, "You tried to force my hand last night!" My cousin Michele Cavelier, who was there, was too amazed to say anything. And I burst into tears! Mme. L—— threw me a look of withering pity and went up to care for Antoinette. Coming down she said: "I warn you: this is the last time I'm coming. I have no right to practice here."

Thus Antoinette and her baby, Francis, had to take care of themselves—which they did without any problem.

On April 9 the Germany army invaded Denmark and Norway. Almost as quickly an Anglo-French force landed in Norway, at Narvik. Hope was finally born with this first Allied victory. It would be of short duration.

Marie-France's parents came later that month to see their daughter and the Norman spring. M. Geoffroy-Dechaume was a portrait painter and perhaps the most cheerful man I ever met. He had a wooden leg, an injury from the First World War. This did not deter him from physical exploits, even in his sixties, such as climbing up a cherry tree to pick the cherries!

The Geoffroy-Dechaumes had ten children, five boys and five girls, who were exceptionally gifted in the arts—they all became painters, musicians, or dancers. Mme. Geoffroy had a lovely voice. M. Geoffroy's father had been a sculptor who worked with Viollet-le-Duc repairing the statues in Notre Dame de Paris. Beauty also ran in the family. Marie-France looked a little like a thirteenth-century statue.

But shame and horror! The Geoffroys arrived in the midst of an invasion of a particularly ignominious sort: lice. The curly head of little Soisette had to be shaved. Marie-France, her head wrapped in a turquoise turban, tried to look as if nothing odd was happening. We all watched each other discreetly.

M. Geoffroy swept away our qualms by escorting Antoinette to the drugstore and declaring to the pharmacist in a resonant voice: "Mademoiselle, we all have lice. Please give us your biggest bottle of louse-killer!"

My parents also came for several days, eager to see their new grandson and the Norman orchards, white with blossoms. My father was then seventy-six, my mother, seventy-two. They arrived by car, my father driving. They came in early May, just in time. Events happened very quickly after that.

2   The Invasion

MAY–JUNE, 1940

Every now and then I went up to Paris on school business. On May 13 I was there in a bookstore when I happened on a friend who worked for the government. As he took me aside, I noticed he looked haggard. He spoke in a low voice: "The Germans have broken through the Maginot Line. They are pouring into France. The news hasn't gotten out yet."

I remember the extraordinary feeling I had leaving the store—horror, tinged perhaps by a touch of elation: to be the *one* person in the street who knew about the disaster. As the day went on I started to think I might have dreamed it, but that evening the radio broke the news.

I also remember returning home to the Blue House in Bourg-Dun one evening a little later. I was looking forward to relaxing and playing with the children, but the house was empty. A kind of nausea came over me from the shock. I walked to the school and there learned what had happened. Jean Fabre, Antoinette's brother-in-law, a naval officer in Le Havre, had arrived hurriedly that afternoon to evacuate the household.

He had given Antoinette and Marie-France thirty minutes to pack the necessities: they must cross the Seine before the Germans reached it. The river, he explained, was a natural barrier to the German advance, and this was the family's last chance to avoid falling into enemy hands. Antoinette decided to go to our summer house in Port-Blanc, on the north coast of Brittany.

Later Antoinette told me how her brother-in-law left them at a station south of the river, and how from there, with the three children and baggage in tow, they had slowly traveled from one station to another in overcrowded trains that came after endless waits.

Our three schools had already begun to break up. Michele Cavelier had been called back to Paris by her husband and had taken her two children and niece with her. Other students and their families were leaving. The headmistress called the remaining staff together and announced that she herself was leaving for three days to take a friend with heart trouble to a safe place. She appointed me to run the schools in her absence.

The next morning about nine o'clock we were having English class when the mayor of Bourg-Dun appeared at the door and signaled me to come out. "The Germans are at Abbeville," he said. "That's only forty miles from here. They could be in Bourg-Dun very quickly. I advise you to close the school and send everyone home who doesn't belong in town."

I spent the rest of the day gathering up the school's equipment and visiting with the students' families, most of whom were leaving anyway. There was a last-minute complication: the history teacher refused to go. She was the daughter of an officer and vowed never to flee before the enemy. Finally I just left her and drove off. I took Marguerite, our cook, to the village where she was born. Then I headed for Port-Blanc.

As things turned out, the Germans didn't get to the Bourg-Dun area until later. Instead of continuing their drive southwest, they turned north at Abbeville to cut off British and French troops who, at the request of the Belgian king, were trying to counter the German invasion of the Low Countries. But the king and his army soon surrendered. The Anglo-French contingent, its retreat to the south blocked by the Germans, could only withdraw toward the sea. Most of these men were rescued when navy ships, and hundreds of private boats as well, came from England to pick them up, under heavy air attack, from the beaches at Dunkirk.

At Port-Blanc I relaxed a few days, but it was unthinkable to spend my time swimming and fishing as if on vacation. So I went to Paris, naïvely supposing I could do something useful there. In fact, I discovered tremendous confusion in the capital, with almost everyone trying to leave. After Dunkirk the French army, deprived of all British help, hung on desperately, heroically, along the Somme River, but after a week was outflanked and overrun by the Germans. Paris wasn't going to be defended. The Red Cross, the social services, everything was folding up. The government was moving south, burning most of its records and taking the rest with them.

Needing advice, I phoned my cousin Charles Ferdinand-Dreyfus at his Bel-Air School Farm at Soucy, a village halfway between Paris and Chartres. Charles was an exceptional man—tall, bearded, warm, and authoritative. He had spent four years as a German prisoner of war in the First War. When he returned home, both his parents were dead. He used the land and money they left him to found a school to train boys to be qualified farmers.

His voice on the phone was as clear and energetic as ever. He told me he had bought bicycles for twenty or so of his students and had sent them southward in small groups, with money, maps, and letters of introduction, hoping they would find farm work along the way. He himself was going to stay on at his school, which he had turned into a welcome center for the stream of refugees arriving from the north. It was a twenty-four-hour-a-day job, he said, but people in the area were helping him.

"Can *I* help?" I asked.

"If you really want to be helpful," he said, "please take Mme. Hausser and her children to Niort, where she has family." Mme. Hausser, the school superintendent, was a very nervous woman and couldn't stand the pressure.

As it happened, I already had a reason for going south. Another cousin, Olivier Lombard, had sent his wife, Beatrice, who was eight months pregnant, to Bordeaux. Olivier wanted me to go and be with her. "I could do that," I thought, "and go by way of Niort." It seemed a better idea than staying in Paris fiddling about and getting myself caught in the German net.

Thus I became part of the general flight southward—the Exodus, as it came to be called, an estimated ten million refugees on the roads of France that June. The whole thing may now seem incomprehensible, but in our minds at the time the biggest fear was that the pattern of the First World War would be repeated: the German army would cut northern France off from the rest of the country and subject it to a brutal occupation. Until mid-June of 1940, no one—not even the most pessimistic person—thought that the whole of France would surrender, and so we fled south to avoid the fate of those who had stayed home in the last war.

I drove first to Soucy to pick up the Haussers. Charles furnished me with money and gas, and I left on June 11 for Bordeaux, via Niort. As I was leaving Soucy, I suddenly remembered that my brother, Pierre, who was in the army, had been transferred to someplace near Tours. I cabled Port-Blanc to get his address from my parents, requesting a reply by telegram to General Delivery, Tours. My hopes weren't high, given the chaos everywhere.

What with going back and forth between Paris, Normandy, and Brittany for more than a month, I had already had quite a few glimpses of the Exodus. I had usually driven on the smaller roads to avoid the congestion, but going south there was no choice: I had to take the big roads because the small ones were completely blocked by the army.

It was an unbelievable sight, a long, slow, jostling river of trucks and wagons, sleek cars and jalopies, all piled high with furniture and cherished possessions, from a bird cage to a grandfather clock to a statue of the Virgin Mary. There were stalled cars surrounded by distraught families, cars turned over in ditches. There were soldiers who had thrown away their weapons as they trudged along, gray with fatigue and dust. There was a cyclist with his dog bound to his luggage rack like a parcel. A family of peasants from the North lay on the ground in the shade of their wagon, their horses grazing at the side of the road. I remember their children asleep on the road, with their plump rosy cheeks, their flaxen hair in the dust. The sun beat down. We spent as much time stopped as moving.

We had time to talk to the people near us. They had been in bomb attacks and seen terrible slaughter. German Stukas would dive down, their sirens shrieking, drop their bombs, and disappear. We heard that the Italians had also started bombing refugee columns and defenseless towns. The day before, June 10, when France's defeat was obvious, the Italian government, after many threats and long hesitations, entered the war.

The "fifth column" added greatly to the pandemonium. These were Germans in civilian dress or in French or Belgian military uniforms who mixed with the refugees, spreading rumors and panic. Their tactic was to scare people into fleeing the North of France in order to clutter the roads and prevent the French army from moving its troops.

At Tours, much to my astonishment, there was a reply from my parents. It was a miracle that the post office was working. Pierre was in Reugny, a neighboring village.

What luck—I found him in no time. There he was in a field, all alone, dressed in a Zouave uniform, his sleeves rolled up, his fez lying next to him on the grass. He was sitting under an apple tree, eating paté on a baguette—a suitable pastoral activity for a poet like him!

Softly I did my usual "Whoo, whoo!"

He raised his nose.

"What on earth are you doing here?" we both said at the same time, and burst out laughing.

How marvelous! He was enjoying a favorite pastime, an afternoon in the countryside in beautiful weather—a thousand miles from the disaster of war.

We exchanged news. He told me he had been saved from an avalanche of administrative chores by a young farmer who had taken him under his wing and found him the easy job of kitchen assistant. He now spent his time washing dishes, sweeping the floor, and then sprinkling it with water from a pail with a perforated bottom, the French army's traditional way of keeping down the dust.

Pierre and I enjoyed several hours together.

After that interlude I rejoined the Haussers in Tours and took them to Niort the next day.

In Bordeaux I found Beatrice, my best friend from childhood. She was tired and anxious, but so entirely her old self that it was a great comfort to fall into her arms after my long journey.

We shared a room at the hotel. She usually stayed in while I wandered the streets. The French government had retreated to Bordeaux, and the city swarmed with Parisians: administrators, politicians, journalists, writers, artists. The atmosphere was depressing. There was nothing to do but sit in cafés and comment on the latest disaster—often inaccurately. "The Germans are in Paris marching down the Champs-Elysées." "The French army has broken up and is everywhere put to rout." "Ah, but not in the East. A few regiments are fighting there." "It's all the fault of the British, who refused to send their planes." "No, the real culprit is that coward, the Belgian King." "As for Churchill's proposed union between France and England . . . *impossible,* just as Pétain said." "No, no, he's wrong. What I'd have said is . . ."

On June 17, to everyone's dismay, Marshal Pétain told France he had asked Germany for an armistice. He alone, as Conqueror of Verdun, could suggest such a thing and be listened to. Surely this was why, the day before, he had been appointed prime minister. On the radio in his trembling old voice he said: "I think with solicitude, with tenderness, of those millions of refugees hurrying along our roads. We must stop the massacre, we must halt the fighting. We have asked the enemy his conditions for an armistice . . . between soldiers, with honor." The *Marseillaise* followed, in a speeded-up tempo, even more bellicose than usual. I watched Beatrice seated on a step, disbelief on her face, then horror. Surrender!

The next day, the message was repeated, with a slight change: "We must *try* to stop the fighting"—no doubt intending to give the impression that France wouldn't surrender abjectly. Meanwhile, the war continued. Our soldiers were getting themselves killed or captured for nothing. How could they still fight on, knowing that an armistice was about to be signed? I remember the anguish—it lasted seven days—while the terms of armistice were being worked out. Our one hope was that the delay meant that planes, boats, gasoline, and weapons were being transferred to North Africa or to the Allies.

On June 19 I was surprised to bump into an old friend of my father's, the poet Fernand Gregh, whom I'd known all my life and who could find charm even in the worst circumstances. "Yes, my dear, we spent the night in a henhouse on the way down," he said. "We came out covered with feathers! Plenty of quill pens if I had any paper!"

He was excited about something he had heard on the radio the day before. "What, you didn't hear? Ah, it was magnificent!"

He told me about the broadcast of a certain General de Gaulle in London, calling upon the French to continue the fight—a fight for France from outside France.

"We are leaving for London, Harlette and I," Gregh said. "We're leaving on the *Massilia*."[1]

Beatrice and I clung to the radio, but we never could get London, which was jammed. It wasn't until after the Liberation that I knew the actual words of de Gaulle's famous appeal.

The Franco-German Armistice was signed on June 22.

One morning a little later, while Beatrice and I were playing Twenty Questions, our favorite pastime, I caught sight of green-gray uniforms out the window. "They" had arrived.

Several days later, walking along the Garonne, I had to stop for an immense column of men on horseback slowly crossing a bridge. Their faces were tanned, expressionless, and they looked straight ahead from under their round helmets. The column had no end. Had they ridden like this all the way from Germany? It made me think of the Teutonic invasions in the history books.

On the way back to the hotel I stumbled upon a friend from my scouting days, Julien Lelong. He was bare-headed, in khaki shorts and shirt sleeves. He had "demobilized" himself by throwing away his military cap and tunic, and in this way avoided five years in a prison camp. He wanted to get back to his wife in La Baule. Perfect! I wanted to get back to Port-Blanc, and La Baule could be on the route. What a godsend not to travel alone!

But Beatrice was close to term. How could I leave?

At just this moment Colonel de la Rocque, ex-chief of the Croix de feu,[2] providentially appeared. A friend of Beatrice's husband, he invited us to call upon him at his hotel. We found ourselves in front of a dozen of his followers. With more than a trace of melodrama, the colonel declared that since he was leaving Bordeaux he now entrusted to the care of his devoted followers this, his young friend Beatrice, who was alone, without protection, and "in the state you see." Were they ready to help her no matter the cost? In a single voice they said yes.

We returned to the hotel a little dazed and giggly, delighted at this unexpected support.

I drove off a day or two later with Julien Lelong in my faithful little Theodora. I regretted leaving Beatrice (who in fact gave birth two days later), but I was eager to see my family again, having heard nothing from them since the arrival of the Germans in Brittany, and relieved to get out of the heavy atmosphere of Bordeaux.

From this trip I remember chiefly the nerve-wracking blockades. Outside Périgueux, French gendarmes barred our way: "You must camp here three or four days," they said. "That's an order! All roads are blocked by returning refugees. You must stay here till they clear." We saw many cars, their drivers obviously obeying orders, scattered about in the fields. Throwing caution to the wind, we decided to retrace our steps and take a small side road we'd noticed earlier. A quarter-hour later we found ourselves rolling across deserted countryside toward the west.

We continued for a good while, then "Stop!" Another barrier—German this time, no doubt the start of the forbidden coastal zone. The soldiers who detained us were surprisingly young and seemed to be without a commanding officer. Quietly, in simple French, Julien told them we lived in the area and were only going six miles farther. We passed through without incident.

There was a last barrier, south of the Loire. It was the most congested, and we expected difficulty. But luck smiled on us again. As we were waiting in line, a strolling civilian stopped near our car. Without looking at me—indeed, while looking away, his face in profile—he muttered: "Turn around. First left. Then left again." He ambled away as if he'd never said a word. We took his advice and soon the barrier was well behind us.

The bridge at Nantes was heavily guarded by armed patrols, but because we were there, the guards apparently assumed we had a *right* to be there. We nodded to them, crossed the bridge, and drove majestically on.

And Julien got to La Baule, back to Marthe, who was worn out worrying about a husband she was afraid she'd never see again.

The following morning I crossed Brittany without seeing a soul. The Germans were evidently all on the coast and the local inhabitants hiding inside their homes.

When I got to Port-Blanc, I stopped in the lane near our house, thinking my sudden arrival might be too great a shock for my mother. Just then my cousin Lily Ferdinand-Dreyfus came out of the house and said, "Oh, Claire! How wonderful! Wait—don't go in! Let me prepare Aunt Kisse."[3]

I had started up the steps when I heard Lily say, "I have good news to tell you."

And then my mother's voice: "Claire's arrived!"

3   *Port-Blanc*

JULY–AUGUST, 1940

My parents had bought our summer house in 1912, so it and the miraculous Port-Blanc coast—the rocky beaches and the bay filling and emptying twice a day—have always been part of my life. The house, which we call the Big House, there being next door a Small House we often rented out, stands in a pine woods on a hill overlooking the bay. It's a simple, square house with three stories, green shutters, and creepers growing up the sides.

When I arrived the house was overflowing with relatives and friends who had taken refuge there at the invitation of my parents and Antoinette. Among them were three of my first cousins: Michele Cavelier and her children, Odile and René, who had been at the Bourg-Dun school; Denise Pelletier, Michele's sister, who had walked all the way from Normandy; and Lily Ferdinand-Dreyfus and her four daughters. Lily's husband, Jacques, had gone south with the Ministry of Labor of which he was a member. Their son, Daniel, was in the army, no one knew where.

The rest of the family was scattered across the country, as was typical of most French families after the defeat. We spent a good deal of time talking about those who weren't with us.

First and foremost, about Antoinette's husband, Paul. For three weeks there had been no word from him, and Antoinette had feared the worst. Then, the day before I arrived, she learned he was a prisoner of war. It was almost good news. Along with hundreds of other French officers, he was being held in the Great Seminary of Laval. He had been captured sixty miles south of Nantes, without a fight. He had followed orders and stayed in place with his unit, though I think at the last minute he took it upon himself to dismiss his men so they could avoid capture. He was always angry and ashamed at the stupidity of his own capture. Alas, in the general chaos, his experience was quite common.

My brother, Pierre, had the good fortune not to be an officer and so had been able to retreat, on foot and by bicycle. After many mishaps he was safe in the South and about to be demobilized.

Mme. Fabre, Paul's mother, was still in Paris. Paul had guessed this would happen. He wrote me on June 15, the day after the Germans entered the city: "I'm sure she's stayed home. She would not want to take the place of someone who could be more useful than herself."

Antoine Geoffroy-Dechaume, Marie-France's eldest brother, was one of the 330,000 French and British troops who, at the end of May, were saved from the beaches of Dunkirk. Like many French soldiers he immediately returned from England to fight again. He joined his unit at Le Mans—only to find its members ordered to rally at a certain point in the South. He was lucky enough to get himself a bicycle, and by the time the Armistice was signed he'd reached the Dordogne. Marie-France had received word he was safe. Their brother Jean-Pierre hadn't been so lucky. Captured at Dunkirk, he was a prisoner in Germany.

Of M. Cassel, the last of several German Jewish refugees who had lived with my parents in Saint-Cloud, there was no news at all. He disappeared just before the Germans took over my parents' house. We never learned what became of him.

Just before I arrived, our cousin Michele Cavelier had gotten word that her house had been obliterated by German air power during the systematic bombing of Beauvais. The whole city was destroyed, except for the cathedral. "We are not barbarians," the Germans said. "We don't destroy cathedrals." (Their allusion was to the Reims cathedral, which they had been accused—rightly—of damaging in the First World War.) The Caveliers lost everything. It's hard to imagine what it means to lose everything: clothes, books, furniture, letters, photographs, all the tokens of one's past. A month after the bombing Michele went back to see if anything could be saved. She especially hoped to retrieve a stone statue that meant a lot to her, but there was nothing left. A radiator hung zigzag from the second floor.

My mother, though exhausted and distressed by the country's defeat, nonetheless kept our large household running. My father, also full of grief, kept himself busy by jotting down notes on the war as he listened to the BBC. He told me about Churchill's latest messages. The first message paid tribute to our soldiers and expressed sympathy for "the gallant French people who have fallen into this terrible misfortune." The second, however, was severe: "His Majesty's Government have heard with grief and amazement that the terms dictated by the Germans have been accepted by the French Government at Bordeaux. They cannot feel that such, or similar terms, could have been submitted to by any French Government which possessed freedom, independence, and constitutional authority."

The British, who now defended the free world alone, were greatly concerned about the French fleet, the most powerful after their own. The French government had pledged never to let the fleet fall into German hands, but the armistice agreement specified that it had to be brought back to France and put under German and Italian control. Hitler had said he had no intention of using it, but what was that claim worth? Another clause specified that all war equipment, including planes (which could have flown away so easily!) and all stocks of raw materials were to be handed over to the enemy.

We talked these things over in the living room of the Big House. Like General de Gaulle, we thought the government should have moved to

North Africa. From there it could have continued the war at the side of its British ally, sustained by its overseas territories, its fleet (which was intact), its air force (somewhat reduced), and a large part of its army (which could regroup). Only Michele argued that because we didn't know all the facts we had to put our trust in Marshal Pétain.

As we talked, the Germans moved in next door. They commandeered the Small House, our garage, and the garden. They didn't take over our car and boat, but they forbade us to use them.

The German soldiers were under orders to be polite, and so they were. The local people, frightened at first, soon told anyone who would listen how "decent" they were. My father observed that the Germans kept themselves on a short leash in Brittany. Two months earlier in Poland they had behaved quite differently. In Port-Blanc they did everything they could to curry favor. They avoided going into homes, or when they had to, did it deferentially. They gave candy to the children. In shops or farms they paid a bit more than the going rate for whatever they bought. This was easy for them because the authorities had decreed the mark to be worth twenty francs,[1] so that "Fritz" was rich and could send his family in Germany things now inaccessible to the French. The message the Germans wanted to get across was on posters they'd put up all over town showing a Nazi soldier carrying a toddler. The caption read: "Put your trust in German soldiers."

Hardly had I arrived when, on July 3, there was the tragedy of Mers-el-Kebir, which fit right in with the German propaganda. A large part of the disarmed French fleet was at anchor near Oran in Algeria. The British, determined to keep the fleet out of German hands, issued an ultimatum to Admiral Gensoul: surrender or scuttle your ships. Under orders from Vichy, the fleet refused and the British sank it. One thousand three hundred French sailors died.

We were horrified. French radio and newspapers spoke of nothing else. Throughout France the shock and bitterness were intense, and nowhere more so than in Brittany, because the majority of those unfortunate sailors were Breton. The Germans did everything they could to stir up hatred against England: "treacherous ex-ally," they called it, "hereditary enemy," "perfidious Albion."

We were grateful some days later when the BBC announced that the ultimatum had in fact given Admiral Gensoul two further options: to sail either to a British port or to a distant French one, like Martinique, and stay there until the war ended. A little later when the same problem arose in Alexandria, the French admiral, paying no attention to Vichy, dealt directly with his British counterpart and arranged to keep his ships demobilized in port under his own command.

The Germans built a handsome little observatory on what we called "the terrace," a flat area in the sloping pine wood on a cliff that commanded a vast view of the islands and the sea beyond, from east to west. They made it out of pine trees cut from the pine wood and kept watch there around the clock during the four years of occupation.

They tethered some sixty of their horses to the trunks of our trees along the path that bordered the pine wood. The poor beasts must not have been getting enough to eat because they chewed the bark from the trees, which then not surprisingly, died.

The horses needed water, as did the Germans and our family. Every morning it was a question who would get first pump at the well. (At that time there was no water in the house, and the well was drying up.) French and Germans would meet at 6:00, 5:30, 5:00 in the morning, each day a little earlier, they with wooden casks, we with metal pails. They were always polite: "We zank you."

One morning, great surprise—a machine gun on the lawn. My father asked to see the officer in charge and explained that a machine gun was not acceptable: there were children in the house. By evening it had disappeared.

Another time there was a knock at the door. It was a soldier. He stood to attention in front of me. "Would you allow me to pick some flowers?" he asked.

Was he making fun of me? Apparently not.

"It's for this evening—the captain's birthday."

Hitler was preparing to invade England, and his soldiers in Brittany readied themselves for the undertaking. Their ignorance surprised us. One day a friend was looking through binoculars at the horizon. A German officer came up to her and asked to borrow the glasses—"to see the English coast," he said.

Rowboats from the port were requisitioned for exercises, but the Germans didn't know how to handle them. Under the amused eyes of the local people, they turned round and round, letting the oars drop into the water. The Ile du Chateau was chosen for landing maneuvers, and dummies were set up as targets representing the British. We watched all this through binoculars and enjoyed it enormously.

Fishermen came across drowned German soldiers in the water and thought they had made a find. They towed the bodies to the German headquarters, expecting a nice reward for their effort. Instead they got a bawling out from the officer on duty, who probably felt troop morale would be adversely affected by such discoveries. After that, when corpses were found, the fishermen kept the boots.

The children led their normal lives in the garden and on the beach. For several months twelve-year-old René Cavelier had been taking loving care of a parakeet, first in Beauvais, then in Paris, and now in Port-Blanc. One morning he found it dead. His sorrow was immense. The parakeet was buried with ceremony amid the birch trees in the woods, and the whole family, Uncle André leading, went to its grave.

Denise Pelletier, who had never married, was thrilled to push Francis in his baby carriage. That anyone would trust her with a baby filled her with joy. "Titi," who was becoming rounder and pinker every day, smiled at everyone, including the Germans we passed in the garden. Four-year-old André, on the other hand, from the first moment he saw the Germans, sensed that one shouldn't be friendly to them. He would turn his back and walk away with dignity.

Paul was still a prisoner in Laval. Mail didn't get through, and until Antoinette was able to visit him late in July, he had no news from Port-Blanc. With lots of free time on his hands, he was taking classes in German, which his fellow prisoners had organized. He himself had organized a class in physics. There was a library and a garden. He wrote me July 15: "We suffer more from the idea of being prisoners than from the detention itself."

He was sure he would be quickly released—we all were sure of it. The Germans encouraged this illusion in order to head off attempts at escape. As time passed and Antoinette's inquiries always met with the same "*Ja, Morgen*,"[2] our impatience grew. In August I went to visit Paul. He was worried about Antoinette and asked me to take special care of her during his absence. Was he planning an escape? He wasn't: his comrades would suffer reprisals. Further, I think that on at least one occasion he had received permission to leave the seminary and walk about freely in Laval. For that privilege he had probably given his word never to try to escape.

In September my sister received the letters she had recently been writing to Paul, all in a packet stamped "Undeliverable." A little later the newspapers reported that the prisoners in Laval had been sent to Germany.

We would not see Paul for nearly five years.

As I mentioned, my parents' house in Saint-Cloud had been requisitioned by the Germans. The Luftwaffe used it as a barracks, no doubt because the house was very big.[3] On August 28, Juliette Pellissier, our friend and laundress, wrote: "On Sunday afternoon the weather was beautiful. We walked by your house, and there, up on the roof, were quite a few men, their chests bare, sunbathing. They were singing at the top of their lungs to a loud record. When we passed by again later, these gentlemen were having tea in the dining room, on one of your beautiful tablecloths. I was enraged, but could say or do nothing. The damned Third Air Force!"

We were told the owners of commandeered houses had to express the wish to recover their property or else they might forfeit their rights. Thus in mid-September my parents went to Paris (they stayed with Lily Ferdinand-Dreyfus at her home on Avenue Villiers) to see what was happening and to rescue what they could.

My mother wrote us:

> In a downpour I made all the necessary arrangements to get into our house with Papa and Juliette. My pleading worked. (At the moment you have no right to enter your own house!)
>
> The next day, we entered the house in torrential rain. Poor Papa was very depressed, and Juliette couldn't keep from crying. Eighty men are living in our house. *Everything* is dirty. A water leak on the stairs. The new hot water heater destroyed: "It burst," I was told. All the furniture moved around. Several pieces broken.
>
> In Papa's study, a little more respect; I saw nothing actually ruined. But all the chests and bookcases were topsy-turvy, as were his clothes (the few that are left). Not one of his good suits was there, nor his new overcoat, nor his many pairs of shoes, nor his green embroidered suit.[4] I haven't told him about the shoes and Academy suit.
>
> My six dresses have disappeared along with two winter coats. But perhaps we'll find these clothes in the cellar or on the roof—anything is possible. My reclining chair is on top of the furniture in the garden room.
>
> With a kind-looking soldier patiently keeping watch over us Juliette

and I will begin our search again tomorrow. It will be our fourth session, each of which has lasted three hours.

Mother's letters, written rapidly in her strained handwriting at the end of exhausting days, show the courage and energy she was to demonstrate throughout the war, as well as the way she always tried to spare my father the least distress.

After a few days in Paris my parents returned to Port-Blanc. Then I went to Paris.

4 *Paris*

FALL, 1940

What struck me most about the Paris I returned to was its beauty and strange emptiness. Except for the great boulevards which teemed with military vehicles and tourist buses carrying Germans in uniform, the city seemed to have fallen under a spell. There were no cars about (French people weren't allowed to buy gasoline), the streets were silent, and the shutters on the houses were closed because most Parisians hadn't yet come home.

I remember also the shock I felt every time I went out and saw huge Nazi flags, with black swastikas, proudly flying from our public buildings and monuments.

Where was I going to live? That was my first problem. Paul's mother, Mme. Fabre, with her usual kindness invited me to stay with her, pointing out how close she was to Collège Sévigné. I must say she always intimidated me a little. At the same time I was attracted by her personality. So it was with mixed emotions that I moved in with her, temporarily, while I looked for something permanent.

Mme. Fabre was a remarkable woman. She was delicate and frail with a fine triangular face that, young, must have been lovely. It still possessed an unmistakable beauty, though her cheeks were hollow, and her eyes, behind steel-rimmed glasses, had faded to the palest blue. She spoke lightly, but often with a fierce irony—all the while looking innocent. She was exceptionally well-read, but you had to discover this: she never made a show of it.

She had spent many years taking care of her paralyzed mother, sleeping next to her on a mattress on the floor. Perhaps that explains how she acquired the habit of taking so little account of herself and of living for others. After rationing began, most of her time was spent standing in interminable lines—for friends or neighbors more than for herself, or else for something she could send on to Antoinette to be included in a package for Paul. He was constantly on her mind, I know, though she spoke of many other things. Her hope was to see him again before she died.

Starting in 1941, some prisoners of war were repatriated: veterans, fathers of four children, those whose work was "necessary to France," Bretons who signed a declaration in favor of an autonomous Brittany (very few did), and those with pull. Our efforts for Paul were in vain. Mme. Fabre began eating less and less. The winter was harsh, and she caught cold one day in January—probably standing in line. I watched her strength gradually fail, but she kept her clearness of mind and concern for others to the last. She died May 19, 1941.

Since most of what France produced was sent to Germany, the basics had to be rationed: wheat, meat, milk, butter, cheese, vegetables and fruit, cloth, leather, tobacco, and coal. As for imported luxuries like chocolate, coffee, tea, oranges, and lemons, they vanished as soon as they reached Marseille. French people drew ration tickets each month— and had to stand in line for them. There were eight categories of tickets: infant, youth, adult, elderly, manual laborer, and so forth. Only children to the age of six had milk.

A ration ticket didn't mean there was food to be bought. Often you'd spend a half-hour in line only to hear, "Finished! There's nothing left!" And the line would then break up in silence. Everyone lost weight. By the end of the first year, my father had lost thirty-six pounds; my mother's weight dropped to eighty-four pounds. However, after a few months, most Parisians managed to supplement their rations either through people they knew in the country—we were always helped by Antoinette's parcels from Brittany—or through the black market. Nevertheless, food seemed to be the main topic of conversation in Paris in 1940.

In Port-Blanc, where food was plentiful and the BBC loud and clear, the main topic was the war. As early as October, 1940, Hitler apparently realized that he couldn't invade England by sea. The maritime exercises that had caused us such merriment stopped. Massive aerial bombardment of English cities began, in an attempt to break the morale of the civilian population. To everyone's surprise, Goering's enormous bombers were intercepted by nimble Spitfires, guided by a secret device, microwave radar, that we learned about only later. Unprecedented battles erupted in the sky; cities burned; German losses grew heavier; and Churchill's words expressed the anger and courage of the British people and their fierce pride at being the only country to stand up against Nazism.

In Paris the dear BBC was so jammed that no matter how we fiddled with the knobs and strained our ears we still heard nothing but sputters and gurgling. Radio-Paris was always on, with its Pétainist exhortations to repent our pre-war depravity and endure our just punishment, its invectives against our ex-ally and the "émigrés"[1] in London, and its celebration of the New Order and Greater Europe—both under the German boot, naturally.

As German soldiers advanced south along the coast, our legislature had withdrawn from Bordeaux to Vichy, the spa resort in central France, which became our new political capital largely because its many hotels could provide the uprooted government with beds and offices. The legislature then effectively voted itself out of power. The deputy prime minister, Pierre Laval, a past master at conjuring tricks, got the two parliamentary chambers to surrender their authority to Marshal Pétain and ask him to draft a new constitution. Suddenly we no longer had a president but "a Head of the French State" with, apparently, absolute power. Were we still a republic? The word was now taboo.

In his first radio message after taking power Pétain announced that he was bestowing on France "the gift of my person"—memorable phrase. The Marshal was then eighty-four. Everything about him inspired deference and sympathy: his age; his noble bearing; his handsome impassive face, so like marble; and, above all, his career. The French remembered the way he had strengthened the morale of our soldiers in the First War. Now, in our disarray and shame, his air of rectitude and military simplicity gave the French people a measure of confidence. His tone was firm, he looked virtuous, and half of France, probably more, turned to him with gratitude. After all, what could have moved him to take the job but love of country? No one could reasonably suspect him, at his age, of personal ambition.

And yet my parents and I remembered—uneasily—a pamphlet that had circulated a few years earlier entitled *"C'est Pétain qu'il nous faut"* ("We Need Pétain"). It argued for a new French government along the lines of the successful fascist dictatorships. We were sure Pétain hadn't written it himself, but he had certainly heard of it and, so far as anybody knew, had never disavowed it. My father remembered, too, that Poincaré in his memoirs had criticized Pétain's defeatism at a crucial moment in the First World War.

The France that Pétain envisioned, his New Order, was very much the France envisioned in the pamphlet. "Work, Family, and Country" replaced the republican "Liberty, Equality, Fraternity." According to Pétain, we were suffering because we hadn't sacrificed enough. "Our defeat was a consequence of our lack of discipline," he said in his first message. "The pursuit of pleasure destroyed what the spirit of sacrifice built. . . . I invite you to an intellectual and moral rebirth. Frenchmen, you will accept this challenge, and you will see, I swear it, a new France rise from your fervor." His style was more that of a stern grandfather than of a fascist dictator. "We will make an *organized* France where the discipline of subordinates precisely balances the authority of leaders, with justice for all. . . . Work must be sacred. The international capitalism and international socialism that exploited and degraded France belong to the period before the war. We will no longer suffer their shadowy alliance. We will suppress dissension in our society. We will not tolerate it inside our factories, our farms."

Pétain's themes were exaggerated in the media, especially in the Northern Zone where the Germans exercised the most control. Newspapers wrote of Judeo-Masonic plots; of the English as the butchers of Joan of Arc; of the German virtues of work, discipline, and sacrifice; of the French vices of frivolity and laziness. Frankly, I can't say much more about the French press. Its vileness and toadyism were so nauseating that I did my best not to read it.

But one couldn't avoid seeing the billboards everywhere. They were so heavy handed that it was hard to believe they persuaded anybody. One of them showed a ragged French soldier and a woman clasping a baby, standing among the ruins of a home, with the silhouette of a smirking British officer, arms akimbo, looming over them. The caption: "The English have done this to us!" As if we could forget who had really done it.

The most repulsive billboards were the caricatures of Jews shown as greedy debauchees trailing blood and bags of money and weaving international plots. In the Southern Zone, no doubt the propaganda was a little more subtle.

The armistice had partitioned France into seven zones—not just two, as is commonly thought. These zones were:

1. the "Free Zone" in the south governed by Pétain and his counselors at Vichy. They in turn were governed by the Germans, although there were no German soldiers in this zone until November, 1942, when the Allies invaded North Africa.

2. the Occupied Zone in the North, supposedly governed by Vichy but with Germans holding all the important offices. The demarcation line between zones 1 and 2 ran from Lake Geneva to the Spanish frontier, essentially cutting the country in half.

3. the Italian Occupied Zone, including Savoy, Nice, and Corsica. The Italian occupation was much milder than the German.

4. and 5. the Forbidden Zones: the coast along the English Channel and the Atlantic Ocean, and an area in the Northeast abutting the Occupied Zone. These zones were under German battlefield command and fortified against attack.

6. Alsace and part of Lorraine were immediately annexed by the Reich, which tried to Germanize the population by expelling all those who wouldn't or "couldn't" assimilate. The tens of thousands of people expelled were given the choice of going to live in either Germany or the Free Zone. They chose the Free Zone.

7. the French prisoner of war camps in Germany: 1.8 million men behind barbed wire.

Among the seven zones, all civilian traffic, all telegraph and telephone communication were forbidden. To cross a frontier you had to have a pass card, an *Ausweis*, from the German command. Even mail was forbidden, except on specially prepared postcards.

Supposedly the reasons for partitioning France were military, but they were also political. Thanks to Pétain and his government, the French now had the illusion that their country, unlike the rest of occupied Europe, retained its sovereignty and "honor" (one of the marshal's favorite words). Most people believed that in supporting Pétain they were being good Frenchmen. What they didn't know was that the Germans pulled the strings behind him. Some defended Pétain's giving in to German demands, saying that if he hadn't our prisoners would suffer terrible reprisals. Others believed Pétain was playing a double game and was secretly working with the British. I remember hearing a man who considered himself very wise say, "The Marshal is our shield; de Gaulle, our spear."

But in fact the opposition between Pétainists and Gaullists began immediately (de Gaulle, after all, was condemned to death in absentia by a French military court on August 2, 1940) and only grew more bitter until after the war. In the eyes of the Gaullists, everything Vichy did was tainted with cowardice, pro-German zeal, and treason. In the eyes of the Pétainists, rebels like the Gaullists brought nothing but chaos to France, their efforts prolonging our useless sacrifices. Because French opinion was divided in this way, concerted reaction against the occupying forces was impossible.

5   Paris

FALL, 1940—CONTINUED

After a fortnight at Mme. Fabre's, I moved in with some old friends, the Léon Rigals, who lived at 86 rue de Grenelle in a vast three-story apartment with a grand eighteenth-century stone staircase. Léon was a professor at a scientific college that was resettling in Lyons, and he, his wife, Véronique, and their six children would be leaving in January. I was given a small upstairs room that was quiet and bright. Another spare room was given to Marie-France Geoffroy-Dechaume, who had come to Paris looking for work.

After a busy day it was very agreeable to join this animated family. The whole household would gather in the living room, the walls of which were filled with Léon's paintings of somber landscapes and industrial suburbs and with a large Chinese embroidery of animals romping about. Léon would clown and tell jokes and play the flute with me at the piano—a sonata of Handel or Bach. We weren't good but that didn't diminish our pleasure. Soon after I arrived, he bought a silver flute and sold me his old one. I started taking lessons with his former teacher, M. Blanquart. Marie-France sang (I can still hear her voice filling the room with the "Et exultavit" from Bach's *Magnificat*), and friends came to hear her and to play themselves.

After supper and homework I would hear a low buzzing in the children's room that puzzled me for a long time. Then one night I found the family saying evening prayers together. After prayers we made more music or gathered around the record player. Léon liked to turn the volume up as high as it would go, which recharged our spirits if by some misfortune they were low. I remember particularly a recording of Bach's Preludes, sumptuously orchestrated by an American composer whose name I wish I could recall. It was while living with the Rigals that I learned what vitality and poise Bach's music can communicate.

My life that fall revolved around teaching at Collège Sévigné,[1] friends and music, visits to the Saint-Denis barracks (about which I will tell you in a moment), and trying to liberate Paul from Germany and to recover possessions from our house in Saint-Cloud.

At Sévigné, I had a class of forty-three students: a little large for an English class, but current events made the subject a popular one. The general atmosphere at the school was one of trust and friendliness, which enabled me to speak freely of England, the English, and English literature without ever alluding to the war. Despite my caution, I couldn't help catching sight of the occasional smile of complicity on a student's face.

All British civilians in France were interned by the Germans at the start of the Occupation, and that October I became the liaison between my students and an internee in a large barracks at Saint-Denis, just outside Paris. His name was Walter McDowell, but there was nothing of the Scotsman about him. He was West Indian and had been amazed when the Germans arrested him because he had never considered himself British. Four months an internee, he had received neither visits nor packages. He didn't even have a change of shirt. The German Relief Committee ignored him, preferring his white prisonmates "for whom," he wrote me, "internment is like a picnic of unlimited time." Every week my students brought a little something for him. When the donations were pooled, the result was rather substantial: if each student brought one or two pieces of sugar, that made a pound.

Then something unexpected happened: the current reversed itself. The slow but generous British Red Cross discovered Walter, and now it was he who passed me tea, coffee, chocolate, and soap. This was accomplished under, or more often *on*, the long table in the visiting room, the prisoners on one side, the visitors on the other. The table was so wide you couldn't pass things under it easily. Instead, you had to push or roll your gift across the table, like a billiard ball, when the guards turned their backs. While doing this, you spoke loudly enough to cover the sound. When eight or ten people did this at the same time, you can imagine the hullabaloo.

Thanks to Walter, I was able to correspond with my friends in England. The system took months because all letters had to pass both the German and British censors. It allowed only family news, but that at least was something.

Another prisoner at Saint-Denis was an Englishman whose son, Bob Hicks, had been one of my Wolf Cub Scouts in Saint-Cloud. Later on, in the fall of 1942, there was a ring at my door. I opened it, and Bob burst in, slamming the door behind him. He was sweating and disheveled. "He's a fugitive!" I thought before he had time to say a word. He was fifteen or sixteen and had only recently been interned in Saint-Denis. And he had escaped! The Germans would be after him.

I offered him a bath and tea, and soon he was almost together again. He said he couldn't bear the idea of being confined twenty-four hours a day with hundreds of other men until the end of the war. He had to get to England and join the army. He told me about his escape in a laundry truck; he was thrilled with the adventure. He had now decided to go to Tours, he said, to an address he'd heard about some weeks earlier where there was someone who could smuggle him across the Demarcation Line. That seemed a little iffy to me, and I told him about my friend Eliane Frey, with whom I'd run the Scout camp in Valcroissant. All youth movements were now forbidden, but many continued to function unofficially. Eliane, who was head of one of the three Boy Scout divisions in the Occupied Zone, was in constant touch with Scout leaders in the South and an expert at crossing the line.

We were in luck: I phoned and she was in Paris. I visited her the next morning. She was a big, strong Alsatian woman, very believing, very Protestant. She told me she would be crossing into the Free Zone in six days and would accept responsibility for leading Bob. But six days! It was unwise to keep Bob at my place because the German authorities at Saint-Denis knew I had visited his father. Eliane suggested I ask her sister in Neuilly to take him in.

When I returned from Neuilly, I found a note from Bob on my table. He had gone, he said, because he didn't want to waste any more time.

A little later I learned from Bob's father that the address in Tours hadn't worked. (For security reasons, underground groups frequently changed their locales.) Bob was so nonplussed at being turned away that he could think of nothing better to do than to go home to Saint-Cloud.

Scarcely had he embraced his mother when the Germans, who'd been waiting, pounced upon him and led him back to Saint-Denis. He remained there until the end of the war.

Much to our surprise, in October, 1940, the Luftwaffe decided to abandon my parents' house in Saint-Cloud. They gave no reason for the decision; they never gave reasons. I had bicycled out to the house several times in September and October to show that we wanted to have it back and on those occasions had taken away what I could in a trailer behind my bike.

From a letter to my mother, October 5:

> The Germans are going to leave the house in several days. I was only supposed to collect some books, but I was also able to take the Japanese kakemono and Ménard's *Mont Blanc*—and a woolen blanket! After having said no to me at first, the N C O who took me around the house must have repented. We did well to get what we did: the Hunzikers [our neighbors] weren't even allowed to go back into their house.

To my sister, October 26:

> We were at Saint-Cloud yesterday and there was no one there anymore. I had some good surprises—saw almost all the furniture. But there was a big flood that has soiled the wall on the stairs, many locks are broken, and chairs have been smashed and then burned in the garden. The portrait of Mother is there, but without its frame. There is a knife slash in the portrait of Aunt Marie, and bullet holes in the little Lucien Simon and in Léon's painting. The other paintings are intact. I found two British and American flags spread out on my bed—a thoughtful and unexpected farewell!

I found what I had really been looking for in a corner of the garden, all jumbled together in an enormous pile: my father's papers—letters, manuscripts, and notebooks—damaged but not illegible.

After the Germans left the house, my father felt too disheartened to move back into it. For years my mother had wanted to sell it: it was too huge, too much to care for, too expensive. She had struggled in vain against my father's inertia. "How can I leave?" he would say sweetly, with the air of a victim. "It would be like tearing a barnacle out of its shell." There had never been any reply to that.

Thus, for Mother, the German despoiling of the house was almost providential. She and Father decided to spend the winter in Brittany with my sister and her children, and then rent an apartment in Paris.

The house in Saint-Cloud thereafter underwent a series of quick transformations. The municipality put it back in shape and used it as a school for apprentices. A year or so later it became the Museum of Saint-Cloud. Finally, in 1946, an association for the physically handicapped bought it and turned it into a hospital, which it remains today.

6 Two Incidents Concerning My Parents

PORT-BLANC, FALL, 1940

At Port-Blanc relations with the Germans had deteriorated. They were no longer called "Fritz" or "Fridolin," but "Doryphore"—potato bug, a pest the Bretons know only too well, devastator of entire fields and fortunes. Farmers saw their wealth stolen from their hands: butter, eggs, lard, ham, vegetables, flour—all requisitioned by the Vichy regime, under the terms of the armistice, to feed the Germans. It took cunning and nerve for farmers to keep more than they needed to feed themselves— enough, say, for friends and maybe the black market.

The Germans had thought the Bretons would be friendly because they were told Bretons were anti-French and wanted independence. They thought fraternizing would be easy because in Breton *yes* is *ja,* as in German, which led them to conclude, "The Breton language is Germanic." Well, they were mistaken: the Bretons talked to them in an incomprehensible patois. The Germans couldn't miss the mocking looks and fits of hilarity the Bretons made no attempt to disguise.

The German's "lightning victory" over Britain wasn't happening, and the Bretons knew it. They could listen every night to the forbidden *Les Français parlent aux Français* ("The French Speak to the French") broadcast from London; it was the voice of hope. Even German officers listened to it, trusting it more than Goebbels's broadcasts. But soon all radios throughout the country were confiscated and my parents had theirs taken away. The experience hurt and angered them. I wrote Mother on October 6: "I am worried now that little Diora has gone. Her absence will change your life. What a blow, and now what emptiness for you!" My choice of words was cryptic because of the censor.

My parents quickly got another radio, and someone must have noticed it because one day, not much later, there was a commotion of boots and voices at the front door. My father went to see what it was all about. He stood in the hallway near the staircase, barring passage to several soldiers, protesting this unwarranted intrusion. An officer put his hand on Father's chest, pushed him aside, and barged into the living room, followed by the other soldiers. The officer demanded the radio. My father, very upset, said he no longer had it. He went upstairs to get the receipt to show he'd turned the radio in—and quickly hid the new radio. The Germans were annoyed and threatening, but they didn't insist on searching the house. My father was deeply shaken by this incident.

A second, more serious incident happened soon after that.

My parents were suddenly, and without explanation, summoned to the local Kommandantur (German administrative headquarters). My sister watched them leave, sick at heart. Two or three hours later they returned, seeming to have aged twenty years, she told me.

I cannot describe what happened in detail because my parents never said much about it, but it all stemmed from the fact that my mother was Jewish. The Germans made her listen to a diatribe against the Jews, the source of everything evil in the world, notably the current war. They told her she was forbidden to travel, own a telephone, correspond with anyone not a relative, and other things I no longer remember. They stamped her identity card diagonally with the large word "Jew."

I imagine that my father tried to answer the lies the Germans spewed forth and that my mother, in contrast, didn't move or utter a word. I know this incident was engraved in her heart. Now that she had been officially recognized as a Jew, we had to fear the worst for her. Until the Liberation, she had to take precautions each time there was the threat of a roundup.

How had the Germans learned of my mother's Jewish origin? We were astonished by this. It had never come up as a question in Port-Blanc because no one there cared about such things. We later found out that the informer was a local bistro owner who, knowing that the Ferdinand-Dreyfuses[1] were our cousins, told the Germans. No doubt he hoped to ingratiate himself.

7 *The Persecution of Jews*

FALL, 1940–JUNE, 1942

For us, the first sign of the persecution of Jews was what I've just described. I wish I could say the Germans alone were responsible for it, but unfortunately this was not so.

The Vichy regime persecuted Jews in stages, no doubt hoping to avoid a public outcry. The first stage began October 3, 1940, when the government issued a statute affecting all Jews of French nationality. The statute defined a Jew as any person with three Jewish grandparents or two Jewish grandparents and a Jewish spouse: thus, for example, though my mother was Jewish, my sister and brother and I were not. Jews were forbidden to hold or run for elective office, or to work in the civil service, the judiciary, or as officers in the army. They were not permitted to teach school or have anything to do with publishing, radio, films, or theater.

The consequences of these rules were felt everywhere. I will give you a few instances we knew of firsthand:

- Our friend Robert Siohan, the choirmaster at the Paris Opera, was asked by the government to submit a list of his Jewish singers. He replied that the only kind of list he could make was one that told who sang well and who didn't.
- I was a member of the Philharmonic Choir of Paris at the time, and each of us was told to sign a declaration swearing that he did not have three Jewish grandparents. (I obviously didn't sign the declaration because I still have the form.)
- Mme. Salomon, headmistress of Collège Sévigné since January, 1940, and assistant headmistress since 1913, was forced to resign, much to the dismay of the whole school. She lived hidden on the fifth floor of the building until the Liberation.
- My first cousin Jacques Ferdinand-Dreyfus, one of the founders of the Social Security system, was forced to retire from his directorship at the Ministry of Labor in the fall of 1940. I will describe later what became of him.
- Julien Cain, Jacques's brother-in-law, was fired as general director of the Bibliothèque Nationale in July, 1940. He was later deported to Buchenwald—less because he was Jewish than because he was

known to be anti-Nazi. He was luckier than most because, though not a Communist himself, he was protected by a well-organized Communist group. After the war he resumed his post at the library.

The proclamation of the Jewish statute was accompanied by the solemn promise that no harm would come to any Jews or to their property.

Six months later, on June 2, 1941, the definition of a Jew was expanded. Henceforth, it would include any person who had a Jewish parent or two Jewish grandparents and who was neither Catholic nor Protestant. Thus, if our parents hadn't brought us up Protestant, we would have been Jews.

In addition, every Jew now had to declare himself to be a Jew at his police station or suffer grave consequences.

On June 21 the number of Jews permitted access to lycées and universities was limited to 3 percent of the total enrollment. (My cousin Françoise Ferdinand-Dreyfus, Jacques and Lily's daughter, was among the 3 percent admitted to the Sorbonne in 1941.)

On July 22 a law was promulgated to "eliminate all Jewish influence in the national economy." From that time forward any Jewish business owner could be replaced by a "provisional administrator" appointed by the General Commission on Jewish Affairs, an office founded by Vichy.

On August 11 the number of Jewish doctors permitted to practice in any district of France was limited to 2 percent of the total number of doctors there.

I have dryly recounted these hateful measures, which excluded tens of thousands of French people from the life of their own country, and leave you to imagine the terrible distress they caused.[1] Many of these anti-Jewish measures were passed without our noticing them because we were absorbed in our own problems and responsibilities, and because, as I've noted, we didn't read the papers.

I can give no direct testimony about the foreign Jews who had come from all over Nazi-occupied Europe in hopes of finding security in France. Most of them were anti-Nazi German refugees who'd fled Hitler. From October, 1940, on, the Vichy government tracked them down, arrested them, and held them in camps with deplorable living conditions, and when the Nazis demanded, handed them over in contingents of one hundred, five hundred, one thousand to be sent east to concentration camps that proved to be death camps. This was more criminal than anything else Vichy did.

It must be added that a good number of these refugees were helped, hidden, and saved by French people.

In the Occupied Zone the Germans added their own laws to those of Vichy, and they were even more humiliating than the French ones. Among the most important, Jews

- had to carry an identity card marked "Jew" and could not buy food without a special food card, also marked "Jew" (obtaining this card involved endless harassment);
- were forbidden to practice any profession that put them in contact with Aryans;
- were not allowed in cafés, restaurants, theaters, movie houses, public gardens, parks, or on the main boulevards; were not allowed to sit on public benches or use public telephones;
- had to observe an 8 P.M. curfew;
- could not make purchases except at specified hours, which most often occurred between 11 A.M. and noon—by which time, so far as food went, there was nothing left;
- were forbidden to ride the Métro except in the last car;
- were forbidden to have either a radio or telephone;
- could withdraw only a certain amount of money from the bank each month; and finally,
- if over the age of six, had to wear a yellow star on their clothes. From the Ordinance of June 6, 1942: "The Jewish star is made of yellow material and says 'Jew' in black letters. It must be worn, plainly visible, on the left side of the chest and must be sewn on securely."

All this was trivial compared with what was to follow because the wearing of the Yellow Star was the beginning of the selection for death. We did not know this at the time.[2] Though we had presentiments, we didn't really know what was going on in the concentration camps in Germany and Poland until after the war.

Of course a number of Jews refused to submit to these rules, but they then ran the daily risk of being denounced and arrested. Some tried to go into hiding in the Free Zone. Their escape had to be clandestine since they were forbidden to travel and the Demarcation Line was closely watched. Our Jewish relatives didn't try to go south. Neither did most foreign Jews and those recently naturalized, who had too few resources and connections to relocate.

8 *Paris*

FALL, 1940–42

At the end of October we were appalled to hear that Marshal Pétain had gone to Montoire, a village not far from Tours, to meet with Hitler. The newspapers and radio were full of this historic event. They gloated over the way Hitler received Pétain with the honors due a noble enemy. Pétain said over the radio: "I accepted the Führer's invitation of my own free will. . . . We discussed collaboration between our two countries. I agreed to it in principle. . . . It is with honor and in order to preserve the unity of France—a unity that goes back ten centuries—that I embark today upon the path of collaboration to build the New European Order."

How could we explain this? Even though we didn't share the general veneration of Pétain, we could hardly believe it. Did he think that, once the English were beaten, France could play a significant role in Europe? Or did he hope to outwit Hitler and gain some advantage, like the return of our prisoners? He was dealing with someone much stronger than he, someone who certainly knew how to play on his old age, vanity, and blindness.

The comedy continued into December as we learned that Hitler, in his magnanimity, wanted to return the ashes of Napoleon's son from Vienna to Paris—a chivalric gesture meant to delight the press. The marshal sent Admiral Darlan, one of his advisors, to receive the ashes at Les Invalides. Several hundred people came to applaud. It was rumored that one of them called out, "We'd rather have coal than ashes!"

In the meantime, the first public rebellion broke out. On November 11, in defiance of a German ban, high school and university students carried flowers to the Arc de Triomphe to commemorate the Allied victory in the First World War. They marched in a procession led by two students, each carrying a fishing pole: hence, two poles—in French, *deux gaules,* a pun on de Gaulle's name. They were greeted by machine guns. Blood was shed, and several students were arrested. But their courage shook up the general despondency.

For people *were* depressed: there was always hunger, fatigue, lines, turnips, beets, blackout at night, subways packed with Germans (free fare for them), infrequent buses (using charcoal for gas), opulent restaurants reserved for German officers and their courtesans, censorship of the mails, yellow posters everywhere saying "*Interdit aux Juifs*" ("No Jews Allowed"), and anxiety over those who were absent. Nothing was easy. You couldn't find books in English or by authors such as Freud, Mann, Maurois, Bergson, Heine (I hadn't known he was Jewish), Trotsky, or any music by Mendelssohn or Darius Milhaud. There was nothing to look forward to, no plausible hope. The English were standing up under the bombings (less intense now than before), but how and when, we wondered, were we going to escape our plight? The French people were either gagged or collaborating.

A singer in a night club act expressed it all. He raised his arm in the Nazi salute and shouted: "Up to here! Up to here! We are up to here in shit!"

Personally I had little to complain about. There were quite a few good things about my daily life. I was young and healthy; food was no real problem, and losing a little weight no subject for despair. Besides, our school provided us with as many vitamin-fortified cookies as we liked. I don't remember ever standing in line for food during the war. Marie-France and I had a theory about the lines: people complained about them but didn't really dislike them because standing in them was useful and easy and offered an opportunity for self-congratulation and self-pity. However, I now recall benefiting from the kindness of a friend who lived next door. She stood in line for her family and often got things for us as well.

I didn't have to line up for transport either: I had my bicycle. It gave me a surge of freedom to speed along the empty streets. From a bicyclist's viewpoint, Paris was never so pleasant as during the Occupation!

Another sort of pleasure came from our friends who frequently dropped by. For all of us Vichy was beneath contempt, Paris a Slough of Despond, and London the Good Place. Each time we met it was a comfort to feel these opinions shared.

Last but not least, my life was centered around my two main interests: my ardent young students and my music. I even found a way of combining the two: I had the students learn English songs and rounds, old and new, and perform them, much to their surprise and delight, in harmony. After some weeks the most enthusiastic students started coming regularly to my house, and our repertoire grew. But of course we didn't just sing: each of us told of our adventures during the Exodus, and we exchanged and commented on the news. We avoided speaking of politics, though, because I had banned the subject. Gradually a tie began to bind us together, a tie that two years later would be put to the test.

There is an old saying that wartime winters are colder than others, and the first three years of this war certainly followed the rule. We all had chilblains—lack of butter, they said. I can still see myself before dawn (we were on German war time: two hours earlier than normal) biking to Sévigné on slippery dark streets, or else correcting homework in my room at 86 rue de Grenelle, wrapped in a blanket with a hot water bottle on my knees.

In summer, by contrast, the heat in my little room was sometimes unendurable. I would then take my mattress up on the roof and sleep under the stars. Even with my eyes closed I could sense the beauty of the sky and enjoy—why not say it?—floating above all those thousands of Parisians shut up in their dim little boxes below while I was free to the night. Once a friend and I witnessed a heavy bombardment not far off, toward the west. I confess it was a magnificent spectacle, equal to the most splendid fireworks. The following day we learned the British had bombed the Renault factory in suburban Boulogne.

Blackouts, though, are nothing to romanticize about. My cousin Cécile Hébrard was the victim of one. She was sixteen or seventeen at the time, tall and beautiful, and was walking fast to get to choir practice at the home of the writer Georges Duhamel. In the dark she ran into the railing of the Métro stairway and fell over into the void. She fell six to ten feet and crushed her face on the lower steps of the staircase. Fortunately her cries were heard by Marie-France and her sister Sylvie, who were on their way to the same choir practice. Horrified at the sight of their friend covered with blood, one of them ran to get the Duhamels.

I was called from the hospital. Jean Duhamel, then a medical student, said: "Cécile has had an accident, but it is not serious. Tell her parents."

I got out my bicycle. I found her mother, Irène, already in bed. She hurried as fast as she could. After several long waits for Métros, there we were, in front of poor Cécile, who was absolutely unrecognizable.

We had to leave almost immediately because of the curfew. We missed the last Métro and came back all the way on foot. I shall always remember that long walk in the night, arm in arm with Irène across the deserted city—our haste, our silence, our anguish. We had only one question on our minds: was Cécile's life ruined?

No. After many months, thanks to surgery, her beauty was restored.

9 Paul's Captivity

In January, 1941, we finally had news of Paul. It came from two of his fellow prisoners who visited Paris—by what privilege, I never knew—on "captivity leave."[1]

Paul was in Oflag 13A, a camp of 7,000 prisoners. (An *Oflag* was an officers' camp; a *Stalag*, a camp for enlisted soldiers and noncommissioned officers.) The camp had been built before the war to house the 1937 Nuremberg Congress put on by the Hitler Youth. In consequence, it was one of the best oflags: the barracks were made of double thicknesses of wood and were heated by coal stoves. There were 110 men in a barracks and sixteen barracks in a "block." The blocks were separated by two fences of barbed wire; nonetheless, prisoners could get a written message from one end of the camp to the other in ten minutes.

The camp was in a vast field surrounded by fir trees, less than five miles from Nuremberg. The church towers of the city were visible on a good day. Within the camp itself there was not a tree, and Paul found this particularly depressing.

In the barracks the beds were triple-decker, with mattresses of straw or wood shavings. Each bed was for three people sleeping side by side. The latrines were covered and (after Hitler and Pétain's meeting in Montoire) heated. The camp had a chapel, a theater, libraries, and a canteen selling German and Italian newspapers, beer, etc.

On his return Paul told us that what he'd suffered from most in captivity was always, always, day and night, being with other people. He wrote me in January, 1943:

> I'm fine really, in good physical shape, but I often feel depressed and helpless. This is due to the pressures of communal living. A recent reorganization of the barrack has given me a top-level bed with a headboard. I can spend most of my time there reading; the light is good by day, and fairly good in the evening. It's a relief to be above all the brouhaha and gossip.

About the food, he wrote that it was "healthy and sufficient for the little work we do"—which in Paul's terms meant it was pitiful. A frequent dish was pellets of flour and bits of potato. Once a week there were slices of bread soaked in whale blubber. The prisoners would scrape off the blubber and fry the bread like a fritter—quite delicious, they said. They also stewed nettles and other herbs for soup, and grilled potato skins.

From November, 1940, prisoners began to receive packages and could thus enrich their menu. The packages were not tampered with. They were opened and searched in front of the recipient, and perforations were made in the cans (glass jars were forbidden) to keep food from being stockpiled for an escape.

Paul had five or six friends with whom he shared everything. One of them had an aunt who sold poultry; her five-kilogram packages arrived every two months—always an event! Paul and his friends stayed together till the end of their captivity.

In September, 1941, the Oflag 13 campsite became a transit center for French volunteers on their way to work in Germany. (These were authentic volunteers. In February, 1943, Vichy began drafting French workmen to work in German factories.) The prisoners of war were dispersed to other Oflags, and Paul and his friends wound up in Oflag 4D, northeast of Dresden. The writer Bernard Auffray, who was a prisoner there, remembers that

> the camp was surrounded by two high rows of barbed wire; between them stood a number of lookout towers with sentinels on top armed with machine-guns, ready to prevent any escape attempt. Guards with police dogs patrolled inside and around the camp. The Silesian plains stretched to infinity, barren, desolate. There was neither spring nor fall. We passed in a few days from 0 Fahrenheit in winter to over 90 in summer. Nothing stopped the wind—icy in winter, torrid in summer.[2]

What most depressed Auffray was the dreariness of the landscape. But sometimes the end of the day would bring splendid sunsets that gradually set the sky on fire. I remember Paul told us that during his imprisonment the sky at twilight had been the one beautiful thing he'd experienced.

Moving to the new camp changed practically nothing in Paul's life. Twice a day, at 9 A.M. and 4 P.M., the prisoners, mustered by blocks, were counted and recounted in lines of five, standing at attention in whatever weather. The rest of the time they were free to do what they liked.

What relations did they have with the Germans? Almost none. There were delegates who spoke to the authorities when complaints had to be made (this seldom happened) or if something was needed for a special occasion.

The prisoners, all officers, were well-educated; many were teachers. They organized lectures and courses on a wide range of subjects, as well as theatrical and musical performances that were often quite elaborate. Each oflag was like a little university in exile.

Paul at first took many courses and himself gave one in physics. But he soon became involved with Scouting at the suggestion of another prisoner of war, his friend Eugene Arnaud, former National Commissioner of the Boy Scouts of France. M. Arnaud recently wrote me that in 1942–43 there were some four hundred officers in the camp who joined the Scouts. "Paul took responsibility for one of the groups made up chiefly of primary school teachers."[3] He organized discussions on subjects like morals and pedagogy and once wrote us that there had been a "speech to the clan on the failures and mistakes of Scouting—by me naturally!" He put new teaching ideas into practice with experimental games and physical exercises.

After Paul's death, one of the school teachers who was in Oflag 4D wrote me his memory of him:

> At first Poil d'Her[4] was a bit intimidating—his black beard gave him a rather austere and academic air. He had a lot of prestige, thanks to his university degree and the fact that he had worked at Maurice de Broglie's Center for Physics Research. He was "somebody" and my admiration was great.
>
> I found that no matter who Paul was talking to he was always polite, straightforward, gentle, and attentive. From the start he wove the bonds of confidence. His smile reassured you.
>
> I am grateful to him for his counsel when I was chief of the clan and had to deal with some rather difficult people.[5]

Did the study groups discuss politics? I suspect not: Paul always looked for grounds for understanding rather than confrontation. Moreover, Scouting was apolitical in principle. But in Oflag 4, as in all French prisoner of war camps, Pétainist propaganda was energetically dispensed. A copy of *Trait d'Union*, a government newspaper, went to every prisoner. Vichy also sent around an "Inspector-Ambassador" named Scapini to boost morale. He was blind (perfect for an inspector!), having been badly wounded in the First War. He tried to obtain some advantages for the prisoners—in particular, freedom for veterans—but what he did mainly was give sermons. "You must bear your cross with patience," he would say. "For more than twenty-five years have I not been a prisoner behind the bars of my blindness?"

He pleaded for Vichy's policy of collaboration. "Whether you like it or not you must consider two facts," he said. "First, the Germans are our neighbors. Second, they have crushed us. Let us overcome our bitterness and loyally shake the hand they hold out to us."

De Gaulle and what he stood for were somewhat known factors, thanks to several clandestine radios and the BBC. At first these broadcasts were received with the same skepticism as the Pétainist propaganda. With most officers, discipline counted: they had confidence in the marshal, who was chief of state and called for military virtues like obedience and self-sacrifice. From the beginning, though, there wasn't much disagreement between the Anglophiles and the Anglophobes. The Anglophiles said, "May the British win!" The Anglophobes said, "May those British swine win!"

Real antagonism between Vichyites and Gaullists started when the defeat of England grew less likely and the spirit of resistance won ground. Paul leaned towards Gaullism, but his scientific temperament inspired him to wait till he was out from behind barbed wire and could have better knowledge of the question. When he rejoined Antoinette in June, 1945, they weren't quite on the same wave length. It took him and other prisoners a while to realize that we civilians had also been through a bitter struggle, that Vichy's great fault lay in ignoring or hiding the Nazis' real objectives, and that the marshal's prestige had kept millions of Frenchmen who might otherwise have done so from taking part in the fight against the Germans.

Paul and Antoinette hoped the mail, for which they waited avidly, would keep them together in their thinking. But the mail was brief, censored, and sometimes interrupted by long waits, as it was after Paul's moves in September, 1940, and September, 1941, and after the Normandy landings. Though tricks of vocabulary could say more than was apparent, there couldn't be real communication between people whose lives had grown so different.

Granted, Paul and his fellow officers were not brutalized, but to be kept in the dark for five years, out of touch with the changing and strenuous life of his dear ones and the world at large, who can say how deeply this must have scarred him?

The school at Bourg-Dun, Winter, 1940.

Paul on leave, with Marie-France Geoffroy-
Dechaume, André and Françoise.

Antoinette and her children, André, Françoise, and
Francis, Spring, 1940.

German officers and soldiers mix with French patrons
at the Café de la Paix, Place de l'Opera, June, 1940.
Photo: B. H. Estampes, Collection Safara.

Above: André and Clarisse Chevrillon in Port-Blanc, 1938.
Below: André Chevrillon braiding his granddaughter's hair.

Antoinette and her children in the garden at Port-Blanc, with René and Marie-France.

Mme. Fabre.

Private cars were outlawed in Paris, except for
pedicabs—this one called "Why Not?"
Photo: B. H. Estompes.

Paul in Oflag 4D.

10 *The Spirit of Resistance Grows*

SUMMER, 1940–JUNE, 1942

At first the French people's hostility toward the Germans who had taken over our country showed itself in very modest ways. Certain writers and artists withdrew into silence. Posters were torn down or changed so they said the opposite of what was intended. The cross of Lorraine—de Gaulle's symbol—was chalked on walls in haste. There were guffaws during the newsreels in the movie theaters. When a German soldier tried to start a conversation or wanted directions, he'd be met by blank stares. In a food line someone innocently hummed the chorus of a Free French tune often heard on the BBC:

> *Radio-Paris ment, Radio-Paris ment,*
> *Radio-Paris est allemand!*
>
> (Radio-Paris lies, Radio-Paris lies,
> Radio-Paris is German!)

and everyone smiled. And when by chance a British leaflet dropped from the skies, it was snatched up, copied, and passed on.

As early as summer, 1940, a few underground papers started appearing, but they were rare and most of us only heard of them later. I do remember, however, an important underground report—thirty pages, closely typeset—describing in detail the brutal German takeover of Alsace-Lorraine and the province's forced integration into the Reich. This was something most people knew nothing about, and I kept the report for others to read.[1] Thus, from the first months of the Occupation, we ordinary French citizens who opposed Pétain's regime were aware of signs of rebellion and knew there were sources of information that contradicted the Vichy line. But that clandestine networks were being organized in both the Occupied and Free zones—of this my family, friends, and I knew nothing, at least until the fall of 1941. Incidentally, I don't remember hearing the term "the Resistance" until after the Liberation.

In the summer of that year new notices started cropping up on the walls of Paris attracting small, silent crowds. These signs were usually printed on red paper, bordered in black, with the text in both German and French:

NOTICE	*Shot for terrorist acts against German troops . . . (There followed a list of three to ten names each preceded by "the Jew" or "the Communist" or "the person named.")*
NOTICE	*Shot for sabotage . . .*
NOTICE	*Shot for spying . . .*
NOTICE	*Shot for participation in an anti-German demonstration . . .*
NOTICE	*Three Communists have been guillotined . . .*
NOTICE	*Reward of a million francs to whoever denounces the perpetrator of the following deed . . .*
NOTICE	*Henceforth, all French people arrested will be considered hostages. When a hostile act occurs, a number of hostages commensurate with the seriousness of the act will be shot.*

The spiral of attack and repression had begun. At the end of October, forty-eight hostages were executed at Châteaubriant for the murder of the German field commander in Nantes. The next day, fifty more hostages were executed at Bordeaux for the murder of a German officer. These reprisals made us feel even more powerless.

The increase in violence was partly because the Communists had joined the anti-Nazi fight after Hitler attacked the Soviet Union in June, 1941. Some of the Communists had fought with the International Brigades in Spain. They were accustomed to underground activity and the discipline and self-sacrifice it required. Communists organized and led groups of paramilitary snipers, the Francs-Tireurs-Partisans (FTP). One of their methods was to kill as many German officers as possible, believing that this kind of harassment demoralized the Germans and embittered relations between occupier and occupied.

But, as I say, at first most of us knew nothing about any form of collective action against the Germans. Those who resisted did so on their own. I'm going to tell you about a close friend and about a relative who resisted, insofar as they could, without belonging to any organized network.

The friend was Charles Geoffroy-Dechaume, who had sung out for louse killer in the Bourg-Dun pharmacy. In July, 1940, while visiting in the Free Zone, Geoffroy, as we called him, wrote a personal letter to Marshal Pétain protesting the Armistice with Hitler. He wrote as a veteran who had lost a leg in the First War and earned the Médaille militaire and the Légion d'honneur. He received an answer from Pétain's secretary, Dr. Bernard Ménétrel, inviting him to elaborate on his point of view, which Geoffroy did in a letter that said:

> Defeat is not dishonorable; to collaborate with an unprincipled enemy is dishonorable. . . . I implore the Marshal not to give in to traitors, no matter what material benefits are offered. There are things more important than eating well and living comfortably. We are ready to die, if we must. But spare us the shame of collaboration.[2]

Pétain sent several people to see Geoffroy and test his loyalty. Geoffroy refused to be intimidated. He reminded them of the British sacrifices during the Great War and loudly predicted Britain's eventual victory in this one.

Some two years later Geoffroy wrote the words for a song for the Maquisards, the rebels in the hills who refused to do forced labor in Germany. It was an excellent song—his son Antoine wrote the music for it—and could just as well have been adopted as the famous "Chant des Partisans" composed in London by Joseph Kessel and Maurice Druon. The Geoffroys didn't have a way of making their song known, and it fell into oblivion.[3]

Whenever I could I visited M. and Mme. Geoffroy in their big old house at Valmondois, a suburb north of Paris. Each time I came back enormously revived. They were disgusted not only with the press but with everybody's griping about lack of food and the little miseries of the Occupation. One day Geoffroy found among his many books Harold Nicolson's *Why Britain Is at War*, which had appeared in 1939. It was a book the French people needed to read, he said, and he suggested I translate it.

The book began by describing a triple murder that had filled the British papers a short time before. A man lovingly courted and then married a rich woman. Each made a will in the other's favor. One day he told her she looked ill, gave her a pill, and coaxed her into taking a bath. When she dozed, it was easy to drown her and thus inherit her fortune. The next year he remarried—again a rich beauty. Several months later, oh horror! he found his new wife drowned in *her* bath. Again, an inheritance to pocket sorrowfully. When the same thing happened a third time, the police caught on and he was hanged.

For Nicolson, the murderous husband was of course Hitler, and the successive wives, Austria, Czechoslovakia, and Poland. Quoting *Mein Kampf* at length, Nicolson showed what would happen in Europe if the Allies didn't rise against the Nazis. He made clear the real reasons for the war—reasons Geoffroy thought the French were forgetting. I set about translating the book. The task wasn't easy, but provided a good exercise for two of my best students whom I asked to help me. I will mention later what became of this undertaking.

As the war continued, Geoffroy got involved in organized underground work. His daughter Sylvie was surprised when, in July, 1943, he wrote about a huge indoor plant his daughter Marie-France had brought him. "And then," he continued, "she entirely spoiled us by bringing four more! We now have them on a trolley in the reception room. They are covered with beautiful blooms that would make anyone's mouth water. We see them often. It's been a joy for us these last days."

Indoor plants? Sylvie wondered. Though her father had a big garden and many odd enthusiasms, this was a new one. It took her several days to realize that the plants must be British airmen.

The second person I want to tell you about is my cousin Charles Ferdinand-Dreyfus. I had seen him, you remember, at his Bel-Air School Farm in early June, 1940, coping with the flow of refugees pouring into the South of France.

That October my mother and I went to visit him. I remember we had lunch with perhaps forty apprentices and farm workers. Charles had grown thin, almost gaunt behind his beard, but otherwise he was fine, a commanding presence and kind toward everyone. He told us about the arrival of the first German troops a few days after my visit. They had bombarded the farmhouse with artillery shells and machine gun fire. Charles made all the refugee women and children go down to the cellar and forbade anyone to leave the house. The Germans came to the front door where he met them, presenting himself as a veteran and as the Director of the School Farm. He asked to speak to the officer in charge. He told the officer that the unnecessary bombardment had killed a French woman and two German soldiers.

He set up a mortuary room for the woman in the farm lodge. The two soldiers were buried in the garden. When he returned to the house to change his bloodstained shirt, he found soldiers rifling through his closet. They took eight or ten thousand francs' worth of clothes. A few hours later all the soldiers left.

He spent nine days serving food to the flood of exhausted refugees. He was helped by only two women farmworkers and a few of the refugees themselves. He did not go to bed during this time.

Then more Germans arrived in the area, 150 of whom he had to shelter at the farm. They slept everywhere, in the sheds, in the stables, in the open air—but not in the school dormitory. Keeping them out of it, Charles told us, was the crowning achievement of his life!

All of that happened during the first weeks in June. Afterwards things got a little bit easier.

July 14, 1940, letter from Charles to my mother:
> Thanks to the Germans, the Farm is overcrowded—except for the main house—170 horses in the stables, in the shed, in the chicken yard. Everything is going well. Everyone blesses the "Herr Direktor" whose forge comes in so handy and who condescends to give endless explanations to peaceful Prussian cultivators. But who isn't joking in the many *Verbotens* he has chalked on doors and blackboards around the farm. "How well you learned German to write so many prohibitions—which you're quite right to enforce!" someone said to me yesterday.

July 31:
> My health is perfect. I survived nine nights in June without undressing. What I cannot stand, however (I wake at three in the morning tormented by it), is the spinelessness, the sloppiness, the stupidity, the laziness, and the selfishness of a people[4] who, up to June 15, I believed morally superior to those who led them.

August 18:
> The Farm is crowded. We are now fifty at table. Tomorrow I will confront the "bureaucracy" and tell them what I have done, what I am doing, and what I want to do next. I will ask for substantial credits, without which my plan for the fall will collapse.

Charles's plan was, typically, a combination of idealism and practicality. He proposed "making apprentices of a few children, and trainee-farmers of the greatest possible number of adults, particularly the unemployed." Of course he didn't get the money he needed. But the School Farm stayed open for two more years, and he continued to devote himself entirely to it. Actually, there was an interlude in March and April, 1941, during which he was absent from the farm. He had neglected to tell the bureaucracy of the existence of a certain mule and was arrested by the French police. He spent four weeks in Fresnes prison, about five miles south of Paris.

April 17, 1941, letter to my mother:

> Returned yesterday morning after four weeks of rest, relaxation, reading history and philosophy (at least 4,000 pages), and overfeeding, thanks to some splendid packages. . . . I was never cold. I flooded the cell with sun until noon by opening a large window. . . . The only thing that pained me were a number of boys from 16 to 19 who didn't have money for the canteen and who received no packages. The ration of turnips was scandalously thin (fishy goings-on in the prison kitchen). The prison staff were all French, most of them decent fellows, if cowardly. They were obviously upset by the overcrowded cells and their own increased responsibilities.[5]

As soon as Charles got out of Fresnes, he resumed his work at Bel-Air. Sometimes he had to come to Paris on farm business, and he would spend an hour or so with my parents, arriving with his arms full of fruits and vegetables. There had always been a special closeness between him and my mother. He knew what interested her, he knew her little ailments, and he would go into the details with kindness.

Despite his notoriously Jewish name, he continued at the School Farm right up to his arrest on August 24, 1942. Given the political awareness he showed over the years and the anti-Semitic measures that multiplied around us, Charles must have known what could happen. Why, you may wonder, didn't he get away?

Probably there were several reasons. The most important may have been that running away was contrary to his character. He would never have repudiated his Jewish ancestry, even though he'd always felt he was French first and foremost. He didn't want to avoid sharing the fate of other Jews, including his brother, Jacques, who had just been arrested, and several of his close friends. Perhaps he also felt that, were he to run away, his life without the School Farm would have little of the meaning he wished it to have. I think too that because he was so emotionally and physically exhausted by all the efforts he'd made since June, 1940 (which had come on top of a bad car accident he'd suffered two years earlier), he may have lost the strength, even the desire, to fight for his life.

11 *Interlude: The Children at Orgeval*

Toward the end of summer, 1941, Paul wrote from his far-off oflag to say that one of his fellow prisoners wondered whether Antoinette and the children would like to spend the winter at his house in the country, near Orgeval, twenty-five miles from Paris. The house was on a large old farm, which could provide some food; in the village there would be a school for André. Best of all, the visit would break the long isolation of winter in Port-Blanc, which would be even more isolated that year because my parents were taking an apartment in Paris.

So that November Antoinette arrived in Orgeval with her brood and Sylvie Geoffroy-Dechaume who came to help with the children as her sister, Marie-France, had the year before at Bourg-Dun. The house was on a rise with a wide view of the plain. In front there were fruit trees, which were glorious in springtime. On a clear day one could see the Eiffel Tower to the east and, toward the northwest, the brilliant loops of the Seine and its confluence with the Oise.

Sylvie was seventeen, and the children responded immediately to her sweetness and, perhaps without realizing it, to her beauty. For me, it was of course wonderful to be able to come out from the city whenever I could and spend the afternoon on Antoinette's small island of intimacy, laughing and singing. Sylvie was very musical, like the rest of her family.

Sylvie has recently given me several of the letters she wrote her parents from Orgeval, which give a good idea of life there.

Snow has been falling for two days and nights. Today, Antoinette and I were able to admire the sun rising on the horizon like a big red orange with a white tablecloth of sparkling snow beneath it, stretching off into the distance as far as we could see.

Just now, it is −2 degrees. We are always falling in the snow, me most of all, which makes the children laugh a lot. I often walk with them to a garden where there are big yew trees, clipped round, covered with snow. They look like giant sugar loaves, and we play hide-and-seek among them. If you saw me on a toboggan flat on my belly or sitting with the little one on my knees, you would really laugh.

André has no fear at all and throws himself headlong on the toboggan like a mad Indian. He will be six next month and works hard at school: he has an hour a day there, followed by work at home. I am astonished at what he is asked to do and how easily he does it. Françoise, if you want her to do something or if you want to help her, may be charming or else say "NO!" with a big frown. Then there is nothing to be done, except indirectly, because if you try to insist, she howls. But sometimes—when Antoinette isn't here—we get on quite well.

Francis is lying in his bed while I write, and he throws smiles at me when I look at him. The 31st I must make a nice cake for his second birthday. Antoinette is counting on me, and there will be visitors! It appears that those with J3 cards have the right to nuts. I will try to find some! We have three eggs a week for the children. No fruit. And we are running short of bread.

Antoinette is very busy and makes butter every three days with the skin from boiled milk, beaten with a fork (very good). I made some biscuits from milk skin and took some to M. and Mme. Chevrillon, as well as to Claire and Denis.[1]

Denis is very cold in Paris. It's almost colder in the studio, he says, than outside, and he's hungry! I sometimes sleep at the studio and at Claire's. M. and Mme. Chevrillon, always charming, are there also, because their new apartment is being repaired.

Very beautiful moonlights—especially last night when we had a front seat.[2]

[Then two months later, March 19, 1942:] The weather is very changeable, but the sun rarely goes under. The children are happy and spend their days out of doors leaping about. With my tickets I just got some scented soap!

12   The Persecution of Jews, Second Phase

JULY–OCTOBER, 1942

At the beginning of June, 1942, the question arose whether my mother should go to a Paris police station and claim her Yellow Star, the wearing of which was now obligatory. By doing this, she would irrevocably identify herself as Jewish and expose herself to all the aggravations of the anti-Semitic laws. In addition, every time she left the house she would expose herself to harassment by any anti-Semitic lunatic on the street.

If, on the other hand, she didn't get her star and wear it, she risked being arrested for an infraction of the law and suffering what were termed "severe sanctions." Part of the problem for us was our ignorance of what the Paris authorities knew. Mother's identity card had been marked "Jew" in Port-Blanc. Was she classified as a Jew in Paris? Perhaps not.

My father and I were of the opinion that she should not get her star, though I remember thinking that in her place I would probably do so. Mother didn't hesitate. She went and stood in an interminable line and bought—yes, one had to pay—three stars. (A Jew was allowed to have three pieces of outer clothing in which to appear in public.)

First my mother wore the star. Then she took it off. Then she put it on again. She oscillated this way for several months—certainly the worst thing to do—and finally stopped wearing it altogether. Later through the underground I got her a false identity card with the name of Mme. Charpentier, which at least allowed her to avoid being caught in a street roundup.

When summer holidays came, I joined Antoinette and the children at Port-Blanc. Things were in a lively state of disorder because they were settling into the Big House for good. They wouldn't be staying in Orgeval the next winter because we feared the Germans would take over the Big House if it were left empty.[1] I helped with the children and was soon immersed in their lives.

I believe this is why I don't personally remember the great roundup at Vél d'Hiv, as it has come to be called. On July 16 and 17, 1942, between three and four in the morning, French police burst into the homes of 7,000 foreign Jewish families living in Paris, mostly poor people in the east end of the city. The police rounded up 12,844 people, of whom 4,051 were children, gave them scarcely time to put anything in a suitcase, and bundled them off in buses to the Vélodrome d'Hiver, an indoor bicycle track. There the Jews stayed for six days in terrible conditions, without bedding or sanitary facilities, almost without food and water, before being transferred to Pithiviers and Beaune-la-Rolande, two internment camps for Jews in the Loiret, and then finally deported east to Auschwitz-Birkenau.

After this awful event my mother could no longer risk travel, and my parents spent the next several months staying with Mother's nephew Jacques Ferdinand-Dreyfus and his wife, Lily, at Montfort-l'Amaury, a small village twenty-five miles west of Paris.

At Montfort windows opened onto a radiant summer, with fruits and flowers in profusion. Evenings were long enough for everything the family loved: reading aloud, Jacques's quips and puns, poetry-recitation contests between my father and Lily—who could recite whole plays of Racine—and talk of the old days. There was even time for Father to give English lessons to pretty nine-year-old Claudine. But underneath there was constant anxiety and a sadness no one could shake off. Jacques was a Socialist and believed deeply in his work for the Ministry of Labor and in the Social Security system he had helped create. When the Vichy regime took his job away from him because he was a Jew, a large part of his reason for living went too.

Jacques and Lily's daughter Renée, fourteen, kept a diary at the time. She has kindly allowed me to cite the following passages:

August 1:

There was a terrible persecution of foreign Jews two weeks ago. Men, women, children, sick people, people with tuberculosis, were all arrested and interned at the Vélodrome d'Hiver. The Red Cross, the Salvation Army, and a third welfare service did what they could. Now all those people are in Poland.

Yesterday, a French gendarme came to tell Daddy that he must report to the gendarmerie at two o'clock today. The other Jew living in Montfort was also summoned. Let's hope it's nothing serious! A few days ago, each ring of the telephone scared us. But now that they have cut off the phone, it's each ring of the doorbell!

This morning, leaving with my Yellow Star, I thought of Jean Valjean[2] and his yellow passport. But he had committed a crime, even if it was tiny, while I am completely innocent!

My uncle and aunt Chevrillon, who are staying with us for the time being, told Mummy they found Daddy nervous.

About the arrest of foreign Jews, they say in Paris that the Germans first demanded the arrest of all Jews in the Occupied Zone. Laval refused to hand over French Jews but, in return, had to give up the foreigners living in the Free Zone. They even came to Montfort to look for the doctor's maid, an Aryan Pole with a baby. It is sheer terror!

Later the same day:

Daddy went to the gendarmerie. They told him to be very careful to wear the Yellow Star.

Still later the same day:

At about 7, I was sewing with Geneviève.[3] I stepped into the garden and saw two gendarmes. I asked them what they wanted and they said,

"Mr. Dreyfus knows what it's about." That made me terribly anxious, and I went running upstairs where I found my aunt Chevrillon looking so anguished (I will never forget the look in her eyes) that I understood. In our room, Alice and Claudine were crying. "You know," Alice told me, "they're taking Daddy." His suitcase was packed and he left with the gendarmes. He will leave at dawn tomorrow for Drancy.[4] We all went to the gendarmerie to say good-bye to him.

August 4:
Mummy left for Paris yesterday. She is marvelously brave. She went to an office which takes care of prisoners and keeps in contact with their families, the UGIF (the General Union of French Jews), and people there were sympathetic. She also went to the Ministry of Labor. (It must have been painful to go and plead for Daddy in the very place where he was the Director three years ago.) She saw two of Daddy's former secretaries. One said that she was going to think about what to do; the other promised to speak to the prison chaplain.

August 8:
Mummy went back to Paris yesterday to try new approaches. Her brother just left for the Free Zone so hastily he didn't say good-bye to her. It appears that Drancy has been improved. Daddy wrote us the following card: "Health perfect. I can write a card every two weeks. Send me packages. Some friends of ours are here. I am happy to have this experience. Much love."

The evening before last, the doorbell rang. It was some Alsatian Jews who, fearing a roundup, wanted to take shelter with us. They asked us if they could spend the night, having left their children at the convent next door. We couldn't turn them away. They left unobtrusively yesterday morning.

August 31:
We are very anxious about Uncle Charles, Daddy's brother, who directs the Bel-Air School Farm. Saturday at 2:30 Mummy got a telegram from the farm's superintendent: "Without news of your brother-in-law."

Mummy immediately sent her a telegram telling her to phone a certain number at seven o'clock (since they had cut off our phone), which she did and here is what she told Mummy: Uncle Charles left Thursday morning for Paris and lunched with a friend. He should have returned to the farm the following morning, but they have not seen him. Nobody knows what his plans were. We worried all day. My aunt Chevrillon feared Charles had fallen ill, but another possibility, much more probable and awful, proved to be the correct one. A letter from M. Paulian, a friend of his, told us that Uncle Charles had been summoned to the Kommandantur at Maisons-Laffitte and that he, Mr. Paulian, had later heard a faltering, bewildered voice on the phone, saying Uncle Charles "had gone to join his brother."

September 3:

Mummy has a heartbreaking letter from Uncle Charles: they put him through an interrogation and insisted that he was not reading Marshal Pétain's speeches aloud to his students, following which they declared him arrested. We think that he and Daddy have been transferred to Pithiviers, which is supposed to be better than Drancy.

September 10:

Today a card from Daddy: "I'm in good spirits. Stay in contact with Bel-Air and with the UGIF. You can send me a package of unlimited weight (that's *not* what they told Mummy in Paris) but no rationed items (that will not be easy since everything is rationed!). Food of good quality. I don't miss Drancy in the least."

September 12:

Letter from Daddy. He gives us information about life in camp. Mornings, he makes his bed, helps with the peeling of vegetables (happily this is the only chore required of him), reads the newspaper *l'Oeuvre,* walks, then has lunch: soup, and a choice of tomato salad, pear, or cheese. After a short rest, dominoes and crossword puzzles. Evenings, he has soup and a vegetable. Uncle Charles is troubled by frequent insomnia. He tries to keep the young people busy in camp. There are quite a few nice people with them: lawyers, a brother of Léon Blum, etc.

They summoned Mummy to town hall and ordered her to choose between her two houses, here or in Paris. She asked for several days to think about it, which was granted.

I am preparing, without great hope, for an exam to enter my first year at Lycée Racine. If we can no longer live on avenue Villiers, I will have to be a boarder at school, which I would prefer to going to school here, even though it will be very painful to be separated from my family. At this moment, Daniel's absence is particularly hard. What a support he would be for mummy! At least for him it's better to be in the south. When will we see him again?

September 17:
Mummy came back from Paris with a letter from Uncle Charles. He and Daddy are living in bad conditions: they sleep on wooden boards, and when they sit on their beds at night they knock their heads on the bunk above. They are covered with flea bites (at Drancy there were bedbugs) and are terribly hungry. Uncle Charles says that he isn't fed half of what he needs and that he doesn't sleep at all—but that his spirits are perfect. The courage and energy of the women there, he says, is stunning.

September 21:
Yesterday we were forbidden to go out from three to midnight because of a bomb scare (probably in the movie theater). And there were 116 executions, and deportations in great numbers—among them, it seems, some from Pithiviers. Letter from Daddy thinking of everyone and very courageous.

Later the same day:
This afternoon Mummy took the bus to Paris to get news. We are terribly worried because a 100 franc money order she'd sent Daddy in Pithiviers was returned to her.

September 22:
Telegram from Claire,[5] who went to Pithiviers: "Jacques here, Charles left yesterday for Drancy." A terrible anxiety weighs on us all.

September 23:
Letter from Claire. At the UGIF little hope: 1,000 to 1,400 of those at Pithiviers have been deported—men older than 70 or those married to Aryans are not deportable. Those from Drancy left this morning (Uncle Charles?). The Germans give as a pretext that not enough foreigners have been delivered to them from the Free Zone. A friend of Claire's saw the Loiret police chief who said he was completely powerless. He didn't even know about the last deportations.

September 24:
Claire's call somewhat reassuring: she saw Daddy at Pithiviers on Tuesday. He looked pale but was not sick. Wednesday she went to

Drancy. Happily, Uncle Charles has not been sent to Germany; they transferred him to Beaune-la-Rolande near Pithiviers. We thus have hope for both of them.

September 25:

Françoise and Alice were in Paris yesterday and brought back only vague information. Daddy is still at Pithiviers and Uncle Charles probably at Drancy. Mummy is very courageous, but she looks awful. Jews no longer have the right to travel, so we must go to Paris as little as possible.

This morning Claire called (through a neighbor) and was very worried about Uncle Charles. Yesterday she was at Drancy but could learn nothing. There were some departures Wednesday and Thursday. Here is the cause of these deportations: the Americans protested to Vichy about the arrest of Jewish foreigners in the Free Zone, and Vichy, intimidated, did not deliver the promised contingent. To take revenge, the Nazis deported those French from Pithiviers who, they had said, were "not deportable." Our cousin Claude Dreyfus has been liberated thanks to a large sum of money.

September 27:

Claire came last night. She finally had definite word about Uncle Charles, and our horrible fear has been confirmed: he was deported. A doctor from Drancy has promised to take good care of Daddy. In addition, we take hope from the fact that Daddy has the Legion of Honor.

September 30:

Mummy came home last night from Paris, very pale and worn out. Friday, we received a heartbreaking farewell card from Uncle Charles. He left believing that Daddy was already in Silesia. His card finished this way: "My spirit is with you and Clarisse and the young ones and Bel-Air—to all, my last thoughts of France. I love you, I clasp you in my arms. France will live."

A letter full of courage Saturday from Daddy in which he says he hopes to be with us for New Year's Eve. He has returned to Drancy. A student of Uncle Charles's saw Daddy at a distance at Pithiviers, and Daddy made him a sign that he was hungry.

My aunt Lucienne Cain has been burgled by someone who passed himself off as an escapee from the camp where her husband[6] is interned.

October 1:

A secret letter from Daddy to Alice: he worries much about Uncle Charles. The Chevrillons left last night. Good news from Daniel.

October 3:

Nothing official about Daddy for ten days. What does that mean? We are once more very anxious. Let's hope there have been no new deportations!

Paris, October 4:

Yesterday, a long and painful trip with Mummy to Paris. It took three hours! The only news about Daddy: a certificate that he was alive on September 29 and word from Mlle. Monod,[7] who found him Tuesday "very courageous and in good health."

This morning I had to run some errands with the Yellow Star, which was very painful for me. To get used to wearing it (and also because I didn't have any money) I came back on foot from the boulevard Saint-Germain.

Paris, October 8:

I've just had dinner alone because Mummy has gone back to Montfort. I passed my exam. I am very happy because it was for Daddy that I worked so hard. I start classes tomorrow.

Paris, October 23:

Air raid! There was one yesterday, but Mummy was here, while I am alone today. I was working, and the light must have filtered through the shutters, because after the sirens stopped someone knocked at the door (a policeman, I suppose). I went to the door, but there was no one there. I hear big explosions, but I am not afraid, I am continuing to work.

Renée has said everything that needs to be said, I think. I bitterly regret I didn't go to Pithiviers as soon as I heard Charles was there. I went almost three weeks later and arrived the very morning he left—probably for Drancy—with a group of internees.

The guards at the entrance to the camp—they were all French—wouldn't give me any news about Charles or accept the package I'd brought him. It was of course impossible for me to enter the vast camp, which was surrounded with a double row of barbed wire. I walked along the wire and stopped at the point farthest from the front gate. There were prisoners wandering alone or in bunches. I succeeded in attracting the attention of one of them. He approached and I called to him to get Jacques and Charles Ferdinand-Dreyfus. I waited a long time. Then Jacques arrived, thin, bewildered. And Charles? He made a sign that he had gone. I tried to speak to Jacques, shouting because we were so far apart. He responded hesitantly, mostly in signs. He put his hands to his mouth, meaning he was hungry. That was the last time I saw him.

I was determined not to go home with my package. I hid it under a bush and returned to the guard room. A guard who seemed to be a decent fellow was standing a bit to one side. We chatted a minute, and then I offered him some money (which he took) and asked him to look for the package after his watch and give it to Jacques the next day. "So what if he keeps it for himself!" I thought. Two weeks later I learned that Jacques had received it.

The next day, having returned to Paris, I bicycled to the dreaded Drancy. It was in a northern suburb, a large, ugly, dilapidated building.[8] At the front gate there were many gendarmes. They had only vague information. They said Charles had probably been transferred along with some others to Beaune-la-Rolande.

I returned the next day and the day after and finally learned that a large convoy of prisoners, Charles almost certainly among them, had left or was leaving from the Drancy-le-Bourget railroad station. I immediately went there. A train was in the station. It was impossible to get close to it because it was guarded every few yards by armed soldiers some of whom were holding police dogs on leashes. They had their backs turned to the train and were making threatening gestures toward the few people, like me, who loitered about. I was panicked, I confess, and completely demoralized. I went home.

Thus Charles left France, and life, without a sign from us. During his internment he had written six letters, two of which were very long and gave detailed advice for the running of the Bel-Air School Farm, and two for his family and friends on the eve of his departure. These last letters are printed in the Appendix to this book.

Jacques remained interned in France another ten months. Lily spent all her time doing what she could for him. He was transferred back and forth between Drancy and Beaune-la-Rolande, and each time we feared the worst.

The worst happened on July 31, 1943.

13 *My Journey to the Free Zone*

OCTOBER–NOVEMBER, 1942

One day in December, 1941, I was astonished on opening the door to find my friend Anne-Marie Bauer standing on the threshold. Anne-Marie, who was a few years younger than I, had also trained as an English teacher. When the war began, she joined the ambulance corps. I'd not seen her since the Exodus because the Bauers, who were Jewish, had wisely chosen to stay in the Free Zone.

Anne-Marie had come up from Lyons to Paris for just a few days. She told me her family's apartment had been cleverly defended by the concierge and thus was still theirs. The rule was that if a Jewish family hadn't returned to their home by September 1, 1940, the Nazis took possession of it and its contents. Sometimes the home was then offered to a favored French collaborator.

As we talked, I must have bemoaned the passivity that gripped us all, because she said, "No. Not everyone is passive." She passed on to another topic.

Scarcely had she left when her words came back to me. The more I thought about them, the more I was sure she was working against the Germans—and the more I regretted not having questioned her. But she was gone; it was too late.

From that moment I longed to go to Lyons and find out what she meant. But I had to find a credible reason for going that I could tell my family, Collège Sévigné, and my friends. And of course I needed a way to cross the line legally, since my trip could not be a secret. No possibility occurred during the sad summer of 1942.

But in October circumstances suddenly became favorable. We learned that my brother, Pierre, now a professor at the French Institute in Barcelona, was going to re-enter France with his wife, Andrée, for a brief visit with Andrée's parents in Lyons. Since June, 1940, when I saw him under the apple trees in Touraine, we had had only indirect news of him.

It was perfect: all my relatives encouraged me to go to Lyons. I was even able to get an *Ausweis* into the Free Zone. Anne Gondinet, a young war widow who was living with me at the Rigals' on rue de Grenelle, had just been given one, thanks to some property she owned in the South. Would she lend it to me—as well as the deed to the property?

She readily agreed, laughing at the idea of playing a trick on the Germans. The only other thing I needed was a leave of absence from my school. Without asking any questions, the headmistress said she was confident that once I returned my class would catch up posthaste. Kindness and tact were the general rule at the school.

What a relief to get away from the oppressive atmosphere of Paris! I intended to make the most of my unexpected vacation and mapped out an ambitious itinerary: to see Pierre and Andrée and Anne-Marie in Lyons, friends from Port-Blanc in Clermont-Ferrand, the Antoine Geoffroy-Dechaumes in Corrèze, the Louis Chevrillons in Toulouse, Daniel Ferdinand-Dreyfus in Avignon, and return to Lyons again before going back to Paris.

I set off happily with the identity card, property deed, and *Ausweis* of Anne Gondinet, widow. The photo and description were not perfect—she had blue eyes—but in the darkness of the night train to Lyons, the German who held my papers saw only a young woman in black, half-asleep, about whom there was nothing suspicious.

In Lyons I was welcomed by Andrée's parents. Pierre, who was coming by way of Vichy, had not yet arrived. "Andrée, thank God, is with us," I wrote my sister. "Her father and aunt don't share the same views, which makes our conversations quite electric."

The next day it was I who picked up Pierre at the station, much to his astonishment. We strolled around the suburbs of Lyons. Politically he was with me on every point. Personally he was locked with his director in a merciless academic war, the twists and turns of which he described with his usual ebullience. It took me a while to respond to this drama.

I saw Anne-Marie Bauer the following day. She spoke only vaguely about her work, and I didn't dare question her much. She said she would talk to her boss about me. Soon thereafter I learned I had an appointment a few days later in a public garden in Clermont-Ferrand with a friend of hers named Robert Gautier.[1]

In Clermont-Ferrand I stayed with Port-Blanc friends, the Foëxes, now refugees from Strasbourg. M. Foëx was a professor at the University of Strasbourg which, because of its proximity to the frontier, had been moved to Clermont-Ferrand at the outbreak of the war. I had last seen the Foëxes during the summer of 1939. How many sad things had happened since then. Still, it was a comfort to be able to discuss and share them.

In a card to my sister I mentioned that the Foëxes' daughter Françoise was unfortunately suffering from eye trouble. I have just learned from Françoise herself—today, July 11, 1984, as I write this—that her eye trouble was only a pretext so that she could go to Lyons and work for the Resistance. We were even more on the same wave length than we knew!

The interview with Robert Gautier—a pleasant-looking man in his twenties—was brief. He told me he had organized the reception of parachute drops from London in the Free Zone and now was going to do the same thing in the Occupied Zone. Could I find him a place to live in Paris? Would I be his "mailbox"? He would arrive in two or three weeks. I was overcome with surprise and joy and gave him my address, and then asked if by any chance he needed more help with the parachutes in the Free Zone. I could speak about it, I said, with a friend in Corrèze, whom I was just going to see.

"Yes, certainly," he said. "Talk to Anne-Marie about that.... See you soon."

We had exchanged only a few words. I admit I'd expected more, but I felt as though something unspoken had passed between us, as if we'd known each other a long time. Perhaps this was even better than words.

Simplicity, alertness, an astonishingly quick trust in me with, underneath, something buoyant and warm: those were my first impressions of a man who was going to introduce me to an aspect of the war about which I had been entirely ignorant.

I next went to Corrèze to visit Antoine Geoffroy and his family. Antoine was an old friend of mine and a musician: organist, harpsichordist, and, when he had time, composer.[2] I'd studied music with him for several years before the war and had joined a small choir he conducted in which his sisters, Marie-France and Sylvie, also sang. You may remember Antoine had been at Dunkirk in June, 1940, and later had come south on a bicycle only to be demobilized at the time of the Armistice. His wife and children had followed in the Exodus, joining him in Corrèze, where they all fell in love with the splendor of the countryside. There was little to attract them back to occupied Paris, and Antoine, in the right place at the right time, had been appointed district food supervisor—a piece of luck for a musician short of cash!

Antoine met me in Tulle, the capital of Corrèze, and drove me some forty miles to his house in the village of Saint-Pardoux-la-Croisille. We had not seen each other since the collapse of France. Nearly three years. ... As we drove to Saint-Pardoux through the gorges of the Dordogne,

I thought back to the time of fighting in the North and how I'd wondered if I'd ever see him again.

When I asked him whether he'd help with the parachute drops, he didn't hesitate an instant. His quiet "yes" would have consequences we didn't imagine. It would lead him to Buchenwald, and to the bottom of a salt mine converted into a German war factory.

But for now we'd come to his old thatched cottage covered with climbing roses, isolated and primitive. For me these were days of total relaxation; I could be oblivious to the rest of the world. All around were great sloping moors, a forest of autumn colors, streams running through gorges, springs and moss, ferns and mushrooms. If you wanted delicious chestnuts, you had only to pick them up from the ground and put them in the embers of the fireplace. A few minutes before mealtime someone would gather a basket of flap mushrooms for an omelette tasting of the woods around us. There must have been music. Antoine had his eighteenth-century ivory flute, and we our voices.

In Toulouse, my cousin Monique, Louis Chevrillon's twenty-two-year-old daughter, met me at the station with her new husband, Marc J———, a captain in the reserves. The details of my time in Toulouse have been erased from my memory by the shock of hearing on the radio at breakfast on November 8 that the Allies, under American command, had landed in North Africa. Marc disappeared at once to join the Armistice Army.[3]

Fearing troop movements and travel obstructions, I abandoned the rest of my trip and took the first train to Paris.

14 Events in North Africa Seen from Home

NOVEMBER–DECEMBER, 1942

My parents had moved to an apartment at 197 boulevard Saint-Germain, only five minutes from me, and I went to see them as soon as I got back to Paris. They were trying to listen to the BBC, thrilled because de Gaulle was going to speak (as yet we had not heard him). But the jamming was so loud we caught only a few words.[1]

Over the next several weeks I had supper with my parents every night, and we did the best we could to keep up with events. The Allied landing filled us with joy. At one point I remember having a flash of hope that Pétain would fly to Algiers and join the Allies. It would have been a fine opportunity to show who the real enemy was and to bring the French people together.

"No, he won't go," my father said. "He's too old. The old are sedentary." He told us what he had heard a woman admirer say of Pétain: "Ah, what a splendid man! So handsome! And he walks all by himself!"

On November 11 the Germans marched into the Free Zone. Pétain solemnly protested this (predictable) violation of the Armistice. His voice was lost amid the sound of boots.

Then suddenly we learned that Admiral Darlan, Pétain's number-one man while Laval was in disgrace (December, 1940-April, 1942), and now commander-in-chief of the armed forces, was in Algiers. Could Pétain have sent him to deal with the Allies? We lost ourselves in speculation. (In fact, his presence in Algiers at that moment was by chance. He had come several days before the Allied landing because his son was in a hospital there, stricken with polio, his life in danger.) Immediately Darlan took command in the name of Vichy—but, alas, only to order his troops to push the Allies back into the sea. For two days the French army, navy, and air force fought the invader; the upshot was three thousand men killed and wounded on each side. The outcry provoked by this absurdity caused Darlan to order a cease-fire, again in the name of Marshal Pétain, who responded by calling him a traitor.

And then we heard that Darlan was being supported by the Americans! He who for us embodied Vichy became High Commissioner of North Africa on November 15. That didn't last long because he was assassinated on December 24, which should have simplified the situation except it wasn't clear which side killed him. Darlan's successor, General Giraud, was also chosen by Roosevelt. Captured in 1940, he'd escaped in April, 1942, from a fortress in eastern Germany and made it back to France. Once here, he'd courted Vichy and the Americans, ignoring de Gaulle and the Resistance.

"But what is de Gaulle doing?" we wondered. It was he who embodied the fight of the French at the side of the Allies. Had he fallen into a trap? We had no idea of the endless difficulties he had to struggle against: French intrigues and, more important, Roosevelt's hostility. About the Byzantine twists of this incredible situation I am not going to say any more.[2] I will only say how we saw things from Paris.

We were indignant when Vichy told the Armistice Army to hand over its weapons to the Germans, who had ordered its demobilization because of alleged complicity with the Allied invasion. We were appalled when we heard over the radio that the Toulon fleet had been sunk "to save its honor."[3]

My parents were very distressed by these events. My mother reacted with apparent calm and took solace in toiling even harder than before, always without complaint. She'd gone to a great deal of trouble to find an apartment while my father, it seemed to me, did nothing but give his opinion about which one to rent—expressing bitter regret as soon as the decision was made! Undaunted, my mother had taken it upon herself to rescue and move the Saint-Cloud furniture. And she was immersed in other tasks such as gathering food, welcoming friends, putting together parcels of clothing, books, and games for my sister and her children, and preparing lessons and amusements for a little Jewish girl whose mother had been deported.

My father, physically, was no more than a shadow of himself. He became a recluse in his study. He read a great deal and wrote, but published nothing. Every Thursday he went round to the Academy. He enjoyed walking from the boulevard Saint-Germain to the Institut de France through small streets crowded with beautiful old shops and empty of uniforms. He liked to meet his colleagues there and discuss recent events. He reported to us any political gossip that surprised or amused him. The collaborationist members (there were two or three) had withdrawn—provisionally, they thought. The others were sure they would be definitively replaced, but elections were postponed until a more serene time.

My father was a member of the dictionary commission. Refining the sense of words and making them more precise did not bore him. It was a welcome distraction from the distress of the day.

15 Our Team

DECEMBER, 1942–MARCH, 1943

I didn't breathe a word to anyone about what kept going through my mind: the conversation I'd had in a public garden in Clermont-Ferrand. "Would you be my mailbox?" I had accepted, but what had I accepted? I didn't know. All I knew was that I wanted to be a *good* mailbox!

Several weeks, a month, went by without a sign from Gautier. Had the project changed? Had he found a better mailbox? Had he been arrested? Or had I dreamed our brief encounter?

Then one evening just before Christmas, there he was at my door on the rue de Grenelle. It is curious how waiting intensely for something to happen (I have often experienced this) may increase the shock when it finally does.

Soon we were at dinner, sitting across the table from each other. I'd brought out everything I could from the cupboard, and Gautier was merry. He announced he was a sales representative for ham-slicing machines. I didn't know what to say, and he burst out laughing. In fact, he said, he was an ex-navy ensign who had escaped to England in June, 1940, responding to de Gaulle's appeal, and was now an officer of the FFL on a secret mission in France.[1]

(He spoke of the FFL, Forces Françaises Libres, the Free French Forces under de Gaulle. But only later did I learn the specific organization to which he belonged—BCRA, Bureau Central de Renseignement et d'Action, the FFL's Intelligence Service—and his specific assignment, which was to help run BOA, Bureau des Opérations Aeriennes, BCRA's Air Operations in France.)

In bits and pieces he told me his story. He had parachuted into France in July, 1942, somewhere near Montluçon in the center of the country. His fall was bad: he'd hurt his head and had to be looked after for several weeks by a fellow BCRA agent because going to a hospital was out of the question.[2] Before that, while in Britain, he and other handpicked FFL volunteers had received months of training in undercover warfare. He had learned to handle weapons, disarm and frisk enemies, throw policemen off track, shadow a suspect, code messages, work a radio transmitter, disguise his appearance and behavior, and if necessary, vanish. He had been offered a suicide pill for use if torture were imminent, but had refused. Others had accepted.

I was dumbfounded by all this. He was delighted to be able to talk so freely.

"How are the English doing?" I asked.

"A stupendous morale," he replied, and gave examples I have forgotten. "Everyone works, one way or another, for the war," he said. "It is a real brotherhood. No one complains or grumbles."

He spoke less about his work in France, and I felt I shouldn't pry. In the course of time I learned that he was working directly under General de Gaulle's personal representative in France, Jean Moulin.[3] Moulin had assigned him the job of finding landing fields for air operations around

Paris. Gautier was to recruit teams which, by the light of the moon, would receive parachuted arms, explosives, radios, money, and, last but not least, BCRA agents like himself, trained to sabotage the German occupation of France. The teams would need to improvise landing fields big enough to accommodate Lysander planes so that people who couldn't parachute could be landed and so that political figures rallying to de Gaulle, Allied airmen, and agents hunted by the Gestapo could be picked up.

"And I?" I said. "What can I do?"

"Very simple," he said. "You will be my cover."

"What?" I said. "I thought I was going to be your mailbox."

He burst out laughing. "It's the same thing! You'll be my smoke screen, if you prefer." He explained that all I would have to do was receive his mail, his phone calls, packages, and messages, and give them to him. This wouldn't take much time and wouldn't interfere with my professional or family life.

That sounded fine. Was he going to live in hiding with me here at the Rigals' on the rue de Grenelle?

He laughed. "No, but you're going to have to invent some good story to explain my hanging around a while."

Well, the story was easily found. I would say that I had known him before, in Scouting, and had just met him on the street, that his ship had been scuttled two weeks earlier at Toulon, and he'd been put ashore in the South. Without lodging, without work, without much money, he had come up to Paris, and while he was getting organized, I had offered him lodging.

Gautier said the story was fine and told me to tell it to everyone: the concierge, my parents, Antoinette, the Rigals, any of my friends who saw him, and later, if necessary, the French police and Gestapo. It was essential to make sure that all witnesses agreed.

I showed him his room and the secrets of the Rigals' vast apartment. We climbed up on the roof and crossed to neighboring roofs. It was a pity the front door was the only exit.

My life continued without apparent change. But everything had changed. I now possessed a secret joy that was constant and intense. No matter what was going on, I could return to it in my thoughts. At last I was part of a great network, unknown but long suspected, of those who fought the Enemy.

Gautier needed time to get his bearings and make contacts slowly and discreetly. Meanwhile I went off to Port-Blanc. I arrived on Christmas Eve. What happiness next morning when the children woke up and heard that the night before I'd found Santa Claus by the fireplace, unpacking their presents, and that he'd hurried away the moment he saw me! They were enchanted with this idea.

Antoinette had a special talent with children. Before the war she'd had a nursery school and had been even more devoted to Scouting than I. This Christmas she invited in the children of the neighborhood with their mothers, and presided over the festivities. Her three little ones mimed the old carol "From Whence Come You, Shepherdess?," with André, six, playing the shepherdess in a big straw hat, and Françoise, three, and Francis, two, playing angels in white nightshirts. If I remember correctly, their effort at piety moved them to huge outbursts of silliness just a few minutes later.

The days were beautiful, as they often are in Port-Blanc in winter. The air was clean and motionless, the sea like a white mirror under the sun. The furze had started to bloom, and violets and primroses hid in the ditches. Time passed too quickly.

On my return to Paris I found Gautier very busy. In addition to organizing BOA operations in the Occupied Zone, he was the liaison between one of the resistance groups, Libération Zone Nord, and London. The apartment on the rue de Grenelle was full of people: Gautier; Marie-France and Sylvie Geoffroy-Dechaume and, sometimes, their brother Denis; Anne Gondinet, who had lent me her *Ausweis* to the Free Zone; Jacqueline d'Alincourt, a young war widow whom Anne had taken in three months before; and often one or more of the Rigals themselves.

I should add that the Rigals knew nothing of our gang and our political views. In fact, Léon Rigal often showed his distrust of the British and disapproval of the Gaullists, who he felt only increased France's suffering. Since we were the Rigals' guests, we were obviously abusing their friendship—which was very great indeed.

So many people about made Gautier nervous. He told me he wanted to live in a less public place. A large room was empty on the ground floor at the far end of the building's courtyard, and my parents knew its owner. Renting it was easily arranged. Thus Gautier had elbow room for his activities, but he and I could still communicate every evening without going out on the street.

He was impatiently waiting for Charles Baron, a radio operator in the Free Zone who was going to work with him in Paris.[4] Charles had been a novitiate with the White Fathers when he heard de Gaulle's appeal in June, 1940. With his younger brother he left his native Brittany and sailed to England, where after much waiting and difficulty, he was selected for the Secret Service. He volunteered to serve in France and took the difficult training course Gautier had described to me. The two of them parachuted into France together and were great friends.

The day Charles was scheduled to arrive, January 7, 1943, came and went without him. He didn't appear the next day or the next. The only sign of him was notification that his suitcase could be picked up at the Gare de Lyon.

Gautier got more and more nervous. He finally asked me to go and get the bag. I went, filled with apprehension. It was the first dangerous act I had undertaken. I was sure they would open the suitcase packed with radio equipment right under my nose. I tried to think of a plausible explanation—in vain. I remember the fear I felt; it was almost a physical sensation.

The suitcase was delivered to me without incident.

I was so relieved I got a bit reckless. At the bottom of a Métro stairway I asked a German woman auxiliary in the Wehrmacht, one of the so-called Gray Mice because of the gray uniforms they wore, to help me get the suitcase up to the street. She was delighted to lend a hand.

Later Gautier told me how angry he had been with himself for asking me to get the bag while he stayed safe at home. But we agreed that he had been right because he was mission chief: my arrest would obviously be less important than his.

Several days later we were relieved to learn that Charles had been arrested at the Demarcation Line. There was some irregularity in his papers, and he had to spend eight weeks in prison.[5]

I just mentioned Jacqueline d'Alincourt, who entered our lives that winter. She was twenty-two, her full title was Comtesse de Lorne d'Alincourt, and she radiated youth, vitality, and beauty. The oldest of nine children, she had lost her father when she was twelve, married at nineteen, and been widowed at twenty-one when her husband died in a German prisoner of war camp. The only member of her family in Paris at the time, she was teaching little girls in a convent near us. Her personal grief had not broken her inner strength, which was sustained, I understood later, by a deep-rooted religious faith.

She seemed to be on our side, and I wanted to get her involved in Gautier's work, but the law of silence was such that I hesitated. Perhaps I was influenced by one of my mother's admonitions: never trust charming people! One day, though, when Jacqueline asked if she could hide English pilots in the Rigals' apartment, further hesitation seemed ludicrous. Soon Gautier had taught us both how to code his messages for London.

At about this time, in January, my mother was startled on opening the door to find her grandnephew Daniel Ferdinand-Dreyfus, twenty-three, Jacques and Lily's son. We hadn't seen him since before the war. The last news from him was a letter to his mother from Avignon, just after the Allied landing in North Africa. She had thought he was going to Algiers to join the army.

Now he was standing in my parents' front hall, exhausted, feverish, and boyishly awkward as ever. His clothes were filthy and torn. In fact he'd been through quite an odyssey. He'd set off to cross the Pyrenees with a group of men who also wanted to escape France and fight the enemy. They were betrayed by their guide and turned over to the frontier guards. Daniel was taken to Bordeaux, imprisoned in Fort du Ha, and then moved to Compiègne, a transit camp for those being deported.

Several days later he was crammed in a sealed freight car on the way to Germany. A fellow prisoner, working desperately, managed to pull apart the iron wires of the seal and open the door. He jumped from the moving train. Daniel held back. He wasn't athletic and he knew it. But he also knew that once across the frontier, it would be too late. So he jumped. He fell on the crushed rock of the track bed and rolled into a ditch where he lay for a long while, gathering his strength and hugging his bruised arm. Then he started to walk. How he had managed to reach a station and get on a train to Paris without a sou, I no longer remember. You can imagine the welcome my parents gave him, and how they hastened to get in touch with his mother and sisters.

But there was a problem. Daniel had no identity card, no ration card, and no job. (Before the war he had been a law student.) He didn't want to stay with my parents and possibly compromise them. Nor did he want to stay with his mother and sisters at Montfort lest he be arrested like his father.

Did he want to be put in contact with an underground network? He was thrilled! That was what he wanted most. Gautier was happy to have a recruit who had already shown so much courage. He would furnish him with the false papers he needed, and Daniel would be paid by BCRA. Gautier in fact had large sums of money at his disposal. I remember being flabbergasted one day when I saw him unpack an enormous wad of bills that had been parachuted in from London.

Daniel chose the name Marc and became a radio transporter. You couldn't broadcast from the same area for more than ten minutes because "gonios"—cars with electromagnetic-detecting radiogoniometers—prowled around. Daniel's job was to travel about on a bicycle fitted up with a valise marked with a big red cross. Inside the valise was a radio or spare parts. He carried the credentials of a first-aid assistant and a pass allowing him to be out after curfew. As for his housing, I got him a room at the Protestant Students' Hall through Eliane Frey, the friend with whom I'd run the Scout camp in 1939. Eliane had recently married Jean Bichon, the hall's director.

Everything seemed fine. Daniel came to see me often, because being undercover, he couldn't resume contact with his old friends. Affectionate, brimming over with jokes and puns, capable of reciting hundreds, perhaps thousands, of lines of verse, he was wonderful company and always welcome.

One day he arrived looking troubled. He had waited at his rendezvous in vain. This happened several times, and then he lost contact with the agent supervising him. He came to see me, worried and depressed.

I spoke to Gautier.

"Yes," he said, "it's a problem. The others don't want to work with him. They're afraid to. He makes himself conspicuous by taking too many precautions. He isn't natural. It's not his fault—he's like that. I can't explain it to him because he wouldn't understand. Tell him whatever you like. He'll be disappointed, but I can't keep him on."

How did I tell him his work was over? I don't remember. I probably said something about changes in the service. Since our work was so compartmentalized, there was little chance he would find out I had lied. He continued to come and see me often. Then things happened which made me lose sight of him for several months.

16 *Arrests in Our Team*

On February 27 Charles Baron was freed. He telegraphed to say he would arrive that evening. Gautier went to meet him at the Gare de Lyon and got him settled in his room, where everything had been prepared with happy anticipation.[1]

Jacqueline and I found Charles to be a tranquil, straightforward man, attentive to others. We all quickly became friends. Gautier recruited a young assistant for Charles to help prepare transmission sites and keep watch during the transmissions. Gilbert—as Gautier codenamed him— came to us through Médéric, one of the leaders of Ceux de la Libération, an underground group in the North of France. I was asked to find Gilbert a room, which I did; he would stay with an old woman who lived around the corner.

At last—was the work of our team going to begin?

No, more complications set in. In spite of Charles's endless patience and ingenuity, he was unable to contact London. The equipment was bad. The only thing he could do was return to Lyons and get another radio. I couldn't tell whether Charles was seething with impatience. He certainly didn't show it. I don't think he was, because his serenity was so deep. It was contagious and touched all of us, perhaps even Gautier.

When I was around Gautier I could sense that important things were happening—what, I couldn't tell, and asked no questions. I was a small cog in a big machine and that was knowledge enough. The strict compartmentalization of the underground was respected by all, and the limited knowledge each of us had of the others protected all of us. Gautier told me that he often saw "a man" who knew me and asked after me, but he wouldn't tell me who the man was and enjoyed teasing me about it. (Much later I learned the man was the well-known journalist Pierre Brossolette, who taught history at Collège Sévigné. Brossolette had come to France with Colonel Passy, BCRA's chief of intelligence, to take stock of the different resistance movements, coordinate them, and begin planning the future administrative structure of France.[2] After weeks of meetings and discussion, they helped Jean Moulin unify all underground organizations in the National Council of the Resistance, the CNR, with Moulin as its head.[3])

Suddenly Collège Sévigné had an unexpected vacation. "The public health inspector," I wrote my sister on March 2, "found that the general state of health among students and teachers is so poor that everyone needs a week of rest." It was certainly true that malnutrition was rampant, despite the vitamin-fortified cookies distributed at the school.

I did as I always did when I had the time: I traveled to Port-Blanc for some rest and because I was concerned about my sister's solitary life, so different from my own. I arrived by train in Guingamp, some twenty-two miles from our house, but I didn't then take the bus, fearing that it would be checked by German military police. The entire coast was a forbidden zone, and now that I was a member of what the press called "a band of terrorists" I needed to be extra careful. I walked to Port-Blanc. Fortunately I was wearing rope-soled shoes. All ordinary shoes had wooden soles—leather, as I have mentioned, had been requisitioned—and were impossible on a long walk.

On the trip back to Paris my train passed through Rennes the night after a bomb attack. "As there was moonlight," I wrote my sister on March 16,

> I could see the chaos in the streets leading out of Rennes. . . . According to people on the train with me, flying fortresses in broad daylight were set upon by fighters and jettisoned their bombs anywhere, trying to get away. One bomb fell in front of the railroad station as travelers were coming out, another on a fair in the Champs de Mars, another in the cemetery (horrible), another on a public laundry where women were washing, etc. The talk is of 250 to 300 dead.

Charles Baron returned from Lyons with new equipment, and finally, two months later than expected, the radio link with London was established. Celebration! My letter to Antoinette mentions that Jacqueline, Anne Gondinet, Gautier, Charles, and I enjoyed a "small Belshazzar" of "marvelous duck" and Breton crepes, embellished with records, songs, and cigarettes.

We were waiting for another BCRA officer from Lyons, whom Jean Moulin was sending to help Gautier organize air operations. This man, Dominique,[4] had parachuted into France in May, 1942. Two months later, with his squad, he had received Gautier and Charles on the ground when they parachuted in. Dominique then sheltered Gautier and nursed him for several weeks while he was recovering from his head injury. This kind of thing creates a bond.

Dominique arrived accompanied by a beautiful, smiling woman: Françoise Foëx. What a surprise! They had just married, but it was a secret. Their marriage had been blessed privately by a minister in Clermont. After my trip to Clermont in November, Françoise had been appointed Dominique's assistant, and the rest had followed.

Our small team was now complete. Things looked propitious.

On April 4 and 5 we wondered where Charles Baron was. We hadn't seen him since the third. The sixth, in the afternoon, Gautier and Dominique were leaving our house on the rue de Grenelle when they ran into Gilbert, Charles's young assistant. Gautier said hello and asked where Charles was.[5]

"What? You don't know what happened?"

"No."

"We were arrested at Garches on Saturday as we were transmitting.[6] They surrounded the house. Charles started to fight, and they handcuffed him. Then they took us in a car to avenue Foch and separated us.[7] Charles told them everything. I didn't say a word. Then Monday night they released me. I guess they thought I was too unimportant."

"Did they beat you?"

"No, just slapped my face."

Gautier and Dominique took him to a friend's apartment ten minutes away. Gautier felt sure that Gilbert was lying and had turned traitor. Why else would the Gestapo have released him so quickly? He questioned Gilbert for more than an hour and at one point was on the verge of killing him—had his hand on the pistol in his pocket. Later Gautier reproached himself bitterly for not having done it, he told me. But to kill a man you know, who is seated in front of you and is speaking to you . . . the British Secret Service had prepared him for many things, but not for that.

Finally he ordered Gilbert to have no further contact with anyone from our team or Ceux de la Libération. He gave him some money and told him to get out of Paris, into the country, and not to budge.

Gilbert walked away.

The next days were very tense. We warned everyone who had been in contact with Charles and Gilbert about their arrest. We moved Gautier into a new place. We wiped out all traces that could compromise those who had lodged Charles, not because we feared that he would talk—his friends trusted him completely—but because we feared Gilbert.[8]

Those days are very confused in my memory. I remember going to warn a radio operator and the family lodging him near the Porte de Saint-Cloud. He wasn't there, and I remember the family's anxiety on learning that he had to move and their surprise when I opened the grand piano, took out a revolver, and stuffed it in my satchel.[9] I then was forced to spend the night in their flat because of the curfew.

Another night Jacqueline and I crept out of our rooms at three in the morning with a suitcase, a key, and an unlit flashlight. I think I will always remember our coming down the grand stone staircase of the Rigals' house. I tried to behave as if we were on a lark, but I was actually filled with anguish and doubt. I never confessed this to Jacqueline, the fearless one. The whole idea was hers, and she was enjoying it! Was our game worth the risk? Certainly not, but there could be no question of retreating. The game was to go to the far end of the courtyard and get into Gautier's studio, which had been searched and sealed by the Gestapo that morning, and look for things that Gautier, in his haste, had neglected to take with him: radio crystals, clothing, cigarettes. The risk, of course, was arrest and all that would follow.

Crossing the courtyard I thought: "One or two men are going to spring out at us—I'm sure of it!" What a marvelous relief to find the door still sealed: it meant no one was inside. The seals themselves were not wax, as I had thought, but two small pieces of paper displaying the German eagle, and they were merely pasted to the door jambs! The game now was to peel them half off without tearing them, and open the door with our key—which we did without much trouble. We went through the room, taking our time, finding everything we were looking for, and cramming our suitcase. We locked the door and restuck the seals on it. Once again across the courtyard and then up the staircase, this time full of jubilation.

A week passed. Underground workers I didn't know were arrested. No possible doubt: Gilbert was betraying us. The team was now dispersed except for Jacqueline and me, who were not undercover. Ordinary life continued. I did my classes, visited my parents, worked on the flute.

Then one day the doorbell rang. In the half-light of the entrance I saw . . . yes, it was Gilbert! (I recoiled inwardly.) I welcomed him and led him into the living room. He looked awful, with rings under his eyes, utterly worn out. We chatted for twenty minutes.

"How lucky you were to be freed!" I said. "Were you treated badly?"

"Not at all. They're not what people say. They're well behaved."

After a moment he said, "I need to see Gautier. Could you give me his address?"

"Unfortunately, I don't have it."

"It's very important for him," Gilbert said. "It's absolutely necessary that I contact him."

"I have no doubt. But, as I say, I've lost touch with him."

We talked about other things. Poor little Gilbert—only seventeen or eighteen and hounded by both the Gestapo and the Resistance. He wasn't going to escape. It may seem surprising, but my sympathy was not fake when I said good-bye.

I immediately got word to Gautier about this visit. He asked to see me right away and I suggested we meet at Collège Sévigné. I waited for him there the following evening in the teachers' lounge after everyone else had gone.

He arrived with Dominique. Both of them were very worried about my safety. Arrests had multiplied over the last ten days.

At one moment Gautier exclaimed, "To think that I had him in front of me, my gun loaded, and I let him get away!"

They told me there had been an attempt to poison Gilbert in a café near Saint-Lazare. Cyanide had been put in his glass of beer when he went to take a phone call. A nice try, but it had failed because Gilbert left without drinking the beer.

They told me I had been wrong to let Gilbert know that I was aware of his arrest and that I knew Gautier. I would certainly be arrested now. "Destroy every trace of evidence as quickly as you can," they said. "Prepare your defense very carefully, and above all, when they interrogate you, deny everything."

I didn't completely agree with their advice. First of all, I was not convinced that Gilbert was going to betray me. Second, to me it seemed impossible that I could plausibly deny I knew both Gautier and Gilbert.

But they told me one thing that proved very useful: always seem to act with good will toward the Gestapo. Never refuse to answer anything, or you will be lost. "And don't forget," they added, "the Gestapo will have only Gilbert's testimony against you, and it's meagre, after all. Perhaps it will count less than yours. They may not even detain you."

We said good-bye to each other, and I returned home alone. For them, I was now contaminated. I felt my solitude deeply, but I also felt sustained by their friendship.

I never saw Gautier again.

The following day I went through all my papers and made sure they contained nothing of interest. Then after class I called over Ginette Janin, one of the two students who was working with me on the translation of Harold Nicolson's book. I told her not to worry if I disappeared from view for a while. If I did, would she take charge of the translation and finish it?

She caught her breath but said, "Of course."

I gave her the address of Father Riquet, the Jesuit priest who had agreed to publish the book in *Témoignage Chrétien,* an underground series.

17 *My Arrest*

APRIL, 1943

A few days later Easter vacation began. I left Paris on April 18 or 19 and went to Port-Blanc. It was now more than two weeks since Gilbert had been arrested and I thought I could begin to relax. How lovely to be in Port-Blanc again!

On the morning of the twenty-first I was still in bed when I heard a commotion downstairs in the hall—men's voices. It was the police, come to arrest me. Antoinette, horrified, came into my room to tell me. They gave me time to dress, and as I was doing so, I noticed a certain piece of paper on the table, put it in my pocket, and went downstairs. There were six French policemen in plain clothes waiting for me.

I hugged little André, whose eyes were shining, and slipped the paper into his hand, whispering that he should throw it in the toilet, which he immediately did. What was on the piece of paper? I no longer remember.

Antoinette and I spoke loudly to each other, saying that a mistake had obviously been made.

The men were polite but in a hurry. They went up to search my room, taking all the papers from my table, and then we left in two cars. I felt torn, leaving my sister in such anxiety. She had no idea why I was being arrested. On the way to the station I asked the policemen what charges were being brought against me. They knew nothing about it, they said; they were merely taking orders from Paris. Then one of them said he believed it was related to the murder of some young man. It was just as I thought.

All seven of us had lunch in a restaurant in Guingamp. (Rumor went back to Port-Blanc that the Chevrillon girl had been on a spree with some men in Guingamp.) In the train I had time to polish what I was going to say. Suddenly I remembered a letter I'd received the day before that they would have taken from the table along with the others. It didn't relate to our network, of course, but it was written stupidly, in obscure terms that could only arouse curiosity. The letter was about getting false papers for Daniel Ferdinand-Dreyfus, and it mentioned Grace Brandt, the social worker friend who got me involved escorting women and children from Paris in the fall of 1939. Grace was now giving clandestine help to Jews. How was I going to explain the letter? I started obsessing on the problem.

We got off the train at Rennes, where I was taken to police headquarters and briefly questioned. I then spent the night in a chair, trying to force myself to recall exactly what was in the letter and to invent a harmless explanation for it, but without success. I was pessimistic the next morning when the Rennes police escorted me to a train. The trip to Paris was interminable because there had again been bombings on the line.

We arrived at Paris police headquarters, rue Bassano, April 23, at two in the morning. It had taken forty-two hours from Port-Blanc, ordinarily a six-hour trip. I was led into a room that had some twenty prisoners in it. Rather than huddle with them on the floor, I stretched out on a table and spent the rest of the night there.

In the morning they came to get me for the interrogation. We climbed to an office on the top floor, and I found myself in front of a burly man behind a desk. He had the cold look of authority: Police Commissioner Guichard. He told me to sit down. It was the Germans who were arresting me, he said. On behalf of the French police, he was simply taking advantage of my being en route to the Germans to ask some questions about a matter he was investigating.

"Do you know Marcel Goron?" Marcel Goron was Gilbert's real name.

"Goron? Yes, I've met him. Why?"

"He's been murdered. He was found dead in the Meudon woods."

"What!" I feigned amazement.

"What do you know about him? How did you meet him?"

"A friend asked me if I could find him a room, and I did. I don't know anything about his private life. In fact, I only saw him twice."

There were several questions about the friend. I told him the story I had prepared long ago: Robert Gautier was someone I'd known back in my Scouting days whom I'd recently run into on the street, etc.

Commissioner Guichard examined the papers the police had taken from my room. He pored over the letter that was tormenting me and asked me to explain it. I don't recall now whether I told him that I was very sorry but couldn't explain it or whether I embarked on the story I'd painfully thought out during the long train trip—a story I knew didn't hold up. The letter had become, as I feared it would, the obstacle I couldn't get past.

Guichard stared at me. "It's in your interest to tell me all the truth," he said. "The Germans will be coming to get you tomorrow morning."

I was taken downstairs again to the room where the other prisoners were waiting.

That afternoon I was taken up to the commissioner's office again.

What a surprise to find my father there! He was the last person I expected to see. We embraced, but without any pleasure on my part. I had always been especially careful to keep my parents from any illegality.

A painful scene followed.

"But really, Claire, why don't you explain this letter to the commissioner? Can't you see how kind he is? He only wants to help you."

My father kept insisting. I thought it would last forever. I was mute as a mule. My father went away vexed and unhappy. I went downstairs again, very much perturbed. Was I wrong to mistrust this policeman? I was so exhausted I couldn't decide what was best to do.

The third interrogation came later that day. This time the officer who questioned me, Assistant Commissioner Terrier, was talkative and more cordial than Guichard. He immediately placed a photo on the table.

"Do you recognize this man?"

Gilbert's body showed underneath some bushes.

"Yes. . . ."

Little by little, the questioning took on the tone of a conversation, which put me more at ease. He concluded by saying with warmth that the Germans would be interested in me only as a witness and would surely not detain me.

I took a risk: "Monsieur, if you want to help me, would you please destroy a letter that's a great nuisance to me? I can't explain the letter, and it's obviously going to keep me from being freed. It's a letter about false food tickets and of no importance."

He raised his arms towards the ceiling. "A typical woman's request! How could you think such a thing possible? That letter is number one on the list of your papers—they have a copy of the list in Rennes! There is no question of changing it. Nothing can be done. So that's that. But good-bye and good luck anyway!"

Toward eleven that night, I was ready for sleep when they came to get me for a fourth time.

"Well," said my neighbors, "you're lucky. At least they're paying attention."

I found myself in front of both of my interrogators, Guichard and Terrier. They closed the door behind me with a key. There was a long silence. Then Guichard announced:

"I, too, am French. And I never hound Gaullists—only Communists. Tomorrow you will be in the hands of the Gestapo. I've decided to help you. We are going to destroy that letter."

He lit a candle and, in a twinkling of an eye, the letter mentioning Grace Brandt was gone.

"Now," he said, "we must put another letter in its place, with the same date."

He gave me pen and paper.

"No, wait a minute! You wouldn't know how to disguise your own handwriting."

He took the paper and wrote at my dictation: "Mademoiselle, will you please excuse my daughter from class today," etc.

Staggered by this, I took a chance and said, "While we're at it, would you please show me all the letters on the list?" Some of them named other friends, and it was silly to let them run the risk of being visited by the Gestapo.

They gave me a pair of scissors and an eraser—the names disappeared.

I went back to the basement with a light heart.

When the Gestapo came for me early the next morning, I felt calm, even euphoric—undoubtedly a reaction to the events of the last three days. I already imagined myself skipping down the boulevard Saint-Germain and surprising my parents.

They took me to rue des Saussaies, where the Gestapo was installed in the Ministry of Interior. (For us, avenue Foch and rue des Saussaies were synonymous with Gestapo.) The interrogation began without delay. There were two officials, one who asked questions and one who typed the answers—identity, address, profession, etc. The tone was polite. Gilbert was of no interest to them; they didn't even mention him. Gautier was at the center of all their questions: How did he live? How did he spend his time? What could I tell them about his contacts? his trips? It was easy to answer in the vaguest way.

"But you were sleeping together?"

"No, we weren't."

"Don't kid me. That's pretty unlikely."

"Unlikely, perhaps, but true."

The interrogation lasted for hours.

At the end of the morning a third official entered the room. He was obviously superior in rank to the others and spoke German in a rapid, hard voice. Glancing over the notes in front of him, he shrugged and then turned toward me with a furious look. A battery of questions: Gautier's friends? their names? appearance? behavior? meetings? I made a great effort to remember.

"Yes, I must have seen one or two of them. Gautier didn't introduce them, so they didn't make much of an impression on me. Ah yes, there was a big fellow with brown hair, named Michel, I think."

"When did Michel come?"

"I really don't remember now. I saw another friend named Marguerite." Mentioning only first names had a way of exasperating them.

Finally he said: "Your memory will come back to you. You may be assured of that! We are going to give you time to think. Take her away." He stormed out of the room.

They locked me up in a cubicle without a window. I was in complete darkness, and soon my situation seemed desperate. I was very hungry. I was there an hour, perhaps two. . . .

Suddenly the door opened. The man who'd questioned me first stood there and said, in a pleasant tone of voice, "Well, Mlle. Chevrillon, have you thought things over?"

I asked for something to eat.

"What? They haven't given you anything to eat?"

He went out to get me a sandwich, which I devoured in front of him.

"You know, I can stay here twenty-four, forty-eight hours," I said. "But I can't say what I simply don't know. You must understand that. Of course I can invent. Does your colleague want me to invent? Try to explain that to him, please."

After they had photographed me from all angles, the cross-examination resumed. I remember nothing about it except that we went over the same ground again and again, but the tone was no longer menacing. Finally we got up. It was over. I was not unhappy with myself. I thought I had given an impression of truthfulness. They led me down to the courtyard. I was going to be freed.

They took me to a paddy wagon. "What? Where are you taking me? Can't I spend Easter with my parents?"

"You are going to Fresnes like everybody else," replied a guard. The word Fresnes, so often heard and so charged with anguish, gave me a shock.

The paddy wagon was crowded. Faces were haggard, unshaven; clothes wrinkled and soiled. There were no ties, belts, or laces on shoes. I exchanged a few words with the person next to me, but guards barked at us to be quiet. Someone handed me several pieces of sugar—very welcome. I understood that I was lucky not to have been tortured, not even bullied.

But would that continue? Let's not linger over the question. Each hour brings its own pain.

18 *Fresnes*

APRIL–JUNE, 1943

What I remember about arriving at Fresnes are the dark, subterranean, endless corridors through which I walked followed by a guard, as if in a nightmare.

Another prisoner was beside me. "Did they beat you?"

"No. And you?"

"Yes." He asked me for the latest world news. He'd had none for four months. "Has Smolensk been retaken?"

I gave him what news I could until the guard behind us told us to shut up.

We reached an iron door, which the guard opened, pushed me through, and then closed behind me.

The cell was gray and ill-lit. The iron bed had an old straw mattress on it. I wrapped myself in my large cape, lay down, and closed my eyes. Rest at last.

But I couldn't sleep. Soon I was looking around my cell. A table was fixed to the wall and folded upright against it. A stool was chained to the ground. In a corner was something that served as both toilet and sink with a faucet above. Nothing of the outside could be seen through the airhole near the ceiling. The walls were dirty and peeling. Then as I stared at them in the dim light, I began to see quantities of graffiti, some of which I could read: "I am dying at 19." "I am dying at 45." "I am going to die tomorrow. Courage." Names, dates. . . . "Victory soon. Adieu." "Long live France, long live liberty." Was the cell for those condemned to death? I could not believe that would be my fate.

There was a rattling noise. A tin cup with liquid the color of coffee passed through a peephole in the door. Night fell. I needed sleep and got undressed. I still had the suitcase I'd brought with me from Port-Blanc—witness to another world. I closed my eyes.

My mind rejected my surroundings and what was happening. I began singing Marie-France's ancient songs to myself and repeating Psalms I knew. Sleep came.

Suddenly an intense light made me jump. It sought out my eyes, completely dazzling me. It was a flashlight aimed from the peephole in the door. Then it disappeared. Footsteps went away. That happened three times during the night, and each time it gave me a nervous shock. Was this some form of torture? No. I later learned it was done to make sure a new prisoner didn't commit suicide during his or her first night. Still it seemed somewhat sadistic.

Early in the morning voices seemed to rise up from underneath the floor and surround me. They were confused, disquieting. I listened intently and made out, "Good morning, Peter!" "Greetings!" "Yes, it is Easter! The next one will be better!" These exchanges lasted a good five minutes. Then silence. I learned later that the prisoners could greet one another while the day guards replaced the night guards.

At seven there was much rattling at the door and a large woman burst in, raised her arms toward the ceiling, and started bawling me out in German. I gathered that I should not be lying down. I was to leave. I dressed quickly. "Schnell, schnell!" She made a sign that I took to mean I should bring my suitcase. "Raus, raus!"[1]

I followed her through corridors and stairs until we arrived at a small cubicle where she locked me up in complete darkness. I stood in it for about two hours (there was no room to sit down). Happily I could communicate with someone in the next cubicle, on the other side of a partition. We joked and encouraged each other. It is curious how cowardly one is alone, and jaunty when someone else is nearby.

Next I was frisked by a brusque and poking Gray Mouse. I must "schnell, schnell" get undressed. She kept my watch, belt, lipstick, eau de cologne, aspirin, book, pen, and papers. They would be returned to me, she said, when I was liberated.

I then had to turn in my money to a special office. There were about fifteen of us there, and among our number an unexpected sight: a British pilot in uniform. He towered head and shoulders above everyone else and had the pink face of a child. He looked bewildered, his eyes blinking in disbelief. Perhaps just twenty-four hours earlier he had been flying above the clouds. Like a bird fallen from the sky, he was now ensnared in this hostile corner of the world.

A waiting line formed. He got in front of me, his hands behind his back. I wanted to squeeze them but didn't dare, fearing I might startle him and create an incident. A pity: I soon learned that the smallest sign of fellowship in distress can make all the difference.

About 11 A.M. the formalities were over. Another "guardian angel," as we called our guards, took charge of me, and I followed him with my lightened little suitcase. He seemed good-natured, and we exchanged a few words. He took me to the building for women, which was constructed around a long covered cement rectangle. Galleries on each floor overlooked the rectangle; along the inside of the galleries ran the numbered cells. We climbed to the fifth floor. He opened door number 429, and I stepped into a white and, it seemed to me, luminous cell.

I was immediately welcomed by my cellmates. What a relief! They surrounded me with attention, bringing out their supplies, asking me a thousand questions, helping me get settled in.

The cell was small—roughly seven by ten feet—and made for one person; we were three. It had one bed, two sacks of straw on the floor, a stool, a small table fixed to the wall that was kept for food, and a toilet-sink in the corner near the door—in short, just what I'd had in my dungeon the night before, but I was a long time realizing this because the atmosphere was so different. Though we could see nothing through the frosted window, the sky behind it made it glow with light.

"Happy Easter!" said Mme. Roudier, smiling at me.

Mme. Roudier, the doyenne of the cell in age and seniority, was a large, robust woman, fine-featured, with graying hair and a dignified bearing. She had been in prison for several months and made it her business to welcome newcomers. For her the first days at Fresnes had been a horror. To put me at my ease she told her story.

She had been arrested in the fabric shop where she'd worked for years. She'd been led "in an apron and without a hat" to Fresnes and locked in a basement cell for ten days. There she had "lived like a dog," having to eat from a dish without fork or spoon (this seemed to revolt her the most), without nightgown or change of clothing, without comb or soap, and without any sign from the outer world except for an occasional tapping on the wall from a neighboring cell. The tapping, meant to communicate with her, only terrified her. She thought she was going mad. As she told me this, her eyes started out of her head.

"But," she added humbly, "I am not a resistant. I am a thief—perhaps I deserve to be punished. I didn't think it was stealing because it was from the Germans." The Germans had appropriated the shop, and while working for them she appropriated some pieces of fabric. Her husband was so ashamed that even though he was allowed to visit her he never did.

It was Mme. Roudier who initiated me into the customs of the house, some of which were strange, to say the least. Fresnes had been built at the beginning of the century according to the latest hygienic principles, with running water and good ventilation in all cells—a model prison. Nevertheless, forty years later new arrivals invariably retched when they learned they had to wash their faces and do their laundry and dishes in the toilet bowl. As for cleaning the wooden floor, this we did by brushing out each groove with a clothes brush (brooms weren't allowed) and polishing the wood with the back of a teaspoon! Was this a Fresnes tradition or a Germanic invention? I never knew. But out of respect for Mme. Roudier we always did this with care, because a bawling out from the German matron who inspected the cell every morning upset her.

In spite of our efforts, though, we were infested with fleas. Who could kill the most, quickest became a major sport. Each of us had her own particular method and was persuaded it was best. After several weeks, I began asking the matron for insecticide. The response was "Ja, ja, Morgen."

Happily, we had the pleasure of having a shower once—later twice—a week, and of a "walk" every Thursday (I wasn't allowed to walk until I'd been in prison three weeks). We were let out one at a time, for a quarter of an hour, into a small enclosure surrounded by high walls. It was delicious to feel the wind and sun on your face, to see the clouds and swallows and the grass and, perhaps, with a little luck, a flower or two, because it was May, after all.

Not everyone could look on the bright side of prison. I happened to be able to—at least most of the time. It's hard to explain, but generally speaking I wasn't unhappy in Fresnes. I would even say, quite the contrary. What I chiefly remember is lightness—the white cell, the frosted window—and peace of mind—no responsibilities, no more struggle to keep up appearances, no more running all over the place. I had to let go. I was relieved of everything that encumbers life outside prison.

And I felt a very deep bond with those who understood why I was there: Jacqueline and Charles Baron (himself at Fresnes), who were, I knew, connected to me in prayer; and Gautier, Françoise Foëx and Dominique, Antoine, M. Geoffroy, Marie-France and Sylvie, Daniel, my student Ginette Janin, Anne-Marie Bauer, and people I haven't mentioned. The long hours of the night were best for thinking of such things. Then I could appreciate more clearly the suffering and strength of will of the thousands of individuals within the prison and try to entrust them to God as I did myself.[2]

One thought, however, disquieted me, especially at night. It was the anxiety I knew my parents were suffering on my account—and that my sister was suffering, perhaps even more intensely. I was painfully aware of her great fear for me. What would I not have given to be able to communicate with the three of them? I wrote my sister on June 23: "My first great joy came at the end of May when a package showed me that you had finally heard from me. I remember I didn't read anything that day, so absorbed was I in that happiness."

Of course from my imprisonment I recall the times when things were happening, not the empty times. There were many empty times, but my fatigue helped me through them. In the beginning I slept half the day, and since the atmosphere in our cell was one of mutual respect, chatting stopped whenever I lay down to sleep. Then after eight or ten days when at last I understood that it was foolish to wait to be set free, time took on a rhythm of its own and more or less filled itself up.

The day began about 5:30 with hellos shouted out the windows. We couldn't participate because our window was stuck fast, but we listened because Allied victories were often announced, repeated, and made the most of. Each one brought the end of the war nearer. Between 6:00 and 6:30 a rolling wagon delivered the so-called coffee, which I drank in bed, and the day's ration of bread. Then came gymnastics (which I did morning and night so as not to become a mollusk), tidying up, polishing with the teaspoon, and reading. A tin container of lunch arrived about 10:30, the one with dinner (generally bean or cabbage soup) about 3:00. My cellmates shared what they received from the Red Cross or from their families, and I shamelessly accepted their kindness and so was never hungry. I wasn't allowed to receive packages until the end of May, but from then on I was able to contribute.

Antoinette learned that a young girl from Tréguier was at Fresnes and that every other week her mother brought a package to the prison all the way from Brittany. My mother and her mother thereafter took turns bringing our packages and standing in the long line at the prison door. My mother's package was heavy and full of good Breton things or if not, of whatever she had been able to find. I remember small raw string beans that I loved, and raw carrots that my cellmates loved. And of course books, photos, clothes. I sent my mother my dirty clothes and slipped messages into the hems. At least one of them got through. In principle I was allowed to receive letters, but none ever reached me.

Mme. Roudier gave me some cotton yarn and knitting needles and taught me how to make slippers. She was originally from la Creuse in central France and had worked for years at the famous Aubusson tapestry factory. It was fine work, she said, and she spoke of it with nostalgia. The most difficult part of tapestry making is blending one color into another. At this Mme. Roudier was expert.

We spent days talking together. She loved to laugh, and called me the Rare Bird because I was the only woman she'd ever known to arrive at Fresnes without crying and without pouring out her "life" (i.e., her romantic and sexual activities) or her "story" (i.e., the events of her arrest).

I didn't use the needles just for knitting. The window frame was old, and I worked away at it with one of the needles, trying to bore two holes in the wood at eye level. My cellmates looked upon this insect work with skeptical tolerance. I began my endeavor after five in the afternoon when most of the guards had gone off duty and there was less chance of an unexpected visit or of spying through our peephole. With a shoe for a hammer, I made the final triumphant blow: we now could see a piece of the outside world and know the color of the season. Our cell, near the corner of the building, overlooked a seldom-used path bordered with trees. Opposite us was the men's building, and now we could see the prisoners at their open windows and hear better what they shouted.

One morning we were reading or chasing fleas when five women guards burst in. We knew the Germans couldn't say anything without yelling, or get us to do anything without rushing us, but that morning took the cake. "Schnell, schnell," we must strip naked—they were practically tearing the clothes off our backs. Flabbergasted, we stood in a corner while the guards inspected each article of clothing, one by one, holding it in their fingertips against the light. Then "schnell, raus, raus!" we must get dressed again and get out in the corridor. God knew what was going to happen in the cell! Each of us worried about her forbidden treasures. . . . Soon we were locked up in the cell again. A tornado had struck: suitcases opened and overturned, clothing and provisions strewn on the floor. The air was filled with dust because the old mattresses, thrown in a corner, had spewed out much of their contents.

Our only recourse was to clean up, which we did, outraged and mortified. Happily, we could joke about it. Unhappily, each of us had lost something. I'd lost both a precious pencil, which a fellow prisoner had hastily given me one day on our way to the showers, and my treasured copy of Pascal, which my mother had sent me—a real mine of consolation, especially useful for keeping some perspective on myself and my surroundings. I'd also lost the piece of paper on which I'd written a detailed outline of my relations with Gautier since Scouting so as to be sure not to change my story during the next interrogation. This worried me: just adding it to my dossier would be enough to make them suspect I'd lied.

I learned from Mme. Roudier that the devastating ceremony I've just described was known as the Search, and was a regular tradition of the place.

The other prisoner in our cell at the time of my arrival was a young Belgian, nineteen, who looked like a little Madonna. She told us in detail about her many lovers and crooked deals. She was from a world I knew nothing of. She'd been arrested at the Belgian frontier while smuggling gold. The gold came from her lover, a volunteer in the French Anti-Bolshevik Legion who had impersonated a policeman and held up the owner and customers of a Chinese restaurant to get enough money to desert. It was great fun listening to her, but unfortunately she didn't stay long.

Our cell drew the less serious cases. During my brief time I saw nearly a dozen people come and go. As I wrote my sister on June 20 (just after my release),

It was fascinating to have this succession of people in our cell and to get to know them so quickly and well. They arrived at what was probably the most dramatic moment in their lives, and they couldn't help pouring it all out and telling us immediately the most intimate and revealing things about themselves.

The last person I met was a young beauty who looked like a Scandinavian goddess with golden tresses, fair complexion, and athletic body. She was a Jew, and the most anti-Semitic person I've ever met. She was a strong collaborationist but had been arrested for destroying the dossier on her boyfriend, who was about to be sent to work in Germany.

I remember this young woman, Gisèle Aillet, very well: she would not stop singing the praises of her handsome Alexander. Unexpectedly we found our childhoods had points in common. We knew the same English nursery rhymes, for example, and sang "Little Jack Horner," "Humpty Dumpty," and "Three Blind Mice" together. When I was released, she asked me to phone Alexander and give him her news. He came to see me but was nonchalant and evasive—which shocked me because after all she was in prison for him.

Two other cellmates stand out in my mind. The first was the headmistress of a lycée who refused to give an address the Germans wanted. Thrown into our cell, she at first remained completely silent, horrified to her very bones at where she found herself and especially, I think, by the public use of the toilet. I did what I could to put her at ease. We shared an interest in several subjects, and conversation followed. She left at the end of a day or two (without of course having revealed the address) and went immediately to see my parents and reassure them about me.

By far the most remarkable cellmate was a young Alsatian just come from Germany, where she had been in prison after prison. Because she spoke German like a native, lived near the frontier, and knew all the paths in the forest, she had been able to help a number of French prisoners of war escape. Encouraged by her success, she plotted how to free her brother, a prisoner of war in northern Germany. The operation succeeded, but at the end of it she somehow stupidly let herself get caught. How? I can't remember. After thirteen months of prisons and court appearances in Germany, they told her she was going to be escorted to the frontier and set free. Imagine her joy. It didn't happen, though. Her guards stayed with her all the way to Paris, where, to her horror, they led her to Fresnes for what they called "the last formalities." She was especially shocked because another of her brothers had been executed in Fresnes in 1941. Was *she* going to be executed? We told her we didn't think so because she had ended up in our cell.

She stayed only two or three days, but she left a deep impression on me. Here is what I wrote about her seven months later in a letter to my student Ginette Janin: "She was genuinely open with other people, keeping nothing of herself back. Happiness flowed from her. But there were things besides mere self-possession and courage that made her seem at peace. You know what I mean—a sense of being in the hands of God." She showed us the last letter her brother had written before his death; it was marvelous in its faith and strength. Through all her tribulations she had somehow kept the letter with her, folded very small. It had become scarcely readable.

I think I remember she was released a little before I was. I lost sight of her and have always regretted it.

Mme. Roudier watched and listened to her successive cellmates with interest, as I did. She always sat on her bed, her back straight, immutable, in gray clothes, with knitting in her hand (her sister kept her supplied with materials). She often didn't take part in the conversation, but her mere presence gave a quality of sanity and good will to our group.

One morning the door opened and a voice cried, "Matame Routier!"

My heart froze. Like an automaton, she got up.

"Alles zusammen!" (Get your things together.)

That formula barked out, accompanied by a circular gesture, was always the same. But it could mean either deportation or liberation.

I asked, "Für Deutschland?"

"Ja, natürlich!"

Mme. Roudier had already understood. She was putting her things together in silence. Then she embraced us. I had just enough time to put my cloak around her shoulders and say it was a loan—to show her I was confident she would come back.

The door shut after her, in my face.

I felt a kind of collapse. The cell, it seemed to me, had lost its keystone.

There is one more person I want to tell you about at Fresnes, though I never saw her there.

One day, feeling restless, I was seized with a desire to look at the air hole near the ceiling. To do this I piled our blankets on the table, put the stool on top of the pile, and climbed up. There wasn't much to see— a dark hole. "Whoo, whoo!" I called into it. To my amazement a voice responded from far away.

Thus began a new friendship which grew daily until my release. Shortly after five each afternoon I would climb up on my perch and chat with a young woman on the second floor (we were on the fifth) who had been in solitary confinement for three months. She told me her name was Denise, and I called myself Antoinette.[3] Her case was serious; in all probability she was going to be deported. Because she couldn't speak to anyone, and because she was a lawyer, Denise naturally became a torrent of words with me. Her husband was a prisoner of war. Her two children were being taken care of by their grandfather, and this worried her terribly because she didn't think her father would educate them properly. Believing I would get out before she did, she gave me her father's address, with many instructions.

We spoke of everything—the war, of course; politics (she was a Communist); literature. She had great intellectual energy and such a lively spirit that our exchanges became a pleasure I would have found it difficult to do without. Eventually we were making *bouts-rimés*.

I started writing messages to her that I'd ball up and throw down the hole. Soon I was throwing food down the hole, and then a book. Intoxicated by this success, I did a stupid thing: I threw my poetry anthology. I had drawn a great deal of satisfaction from this treasure, and naturally I thought Denise would enjoy it. Well, the anthology was too big and got stuck in the pipe, probably in a curve. In one fell swoop not only was the cherished book lost, but nothing more could be passed— except our voices, thank God!

One day the door opened and there was a harsh bark: "Chefrillon interrokazion!" I jumped to my feet. At the start of my prison stay I'd expected this moment day after day, but since it hadn't come and weeks had gone by, I felt sure I'd been forgotten. I was completely taken aback.

I left the cell with apprehension. The Search had taken place a week earlier, and my paper could easily have been transferred to rue des Saussaies and analyzed by the appropriate department. (I didn't know at the time that German departments rarely cooperated.)

A black Citroën was waiting for me at the prison door. And there I was, on a fine June day, in a private car crossing a familiar blooming Paris suburb. Other fears gnawed at me: Had Gautier been caught? Was I going to be confronted with him? With someone else? I steeled myself, as I had been taught, to give absolutely no sign of recognition.

A new interrogator received me at the rue des Saussaies. He was a large man with a rather friendly air. Right at the start he suggested we speak English. He spoke French badly, he said, but had lived for ten years in the States. "So, since you teach English . . ."

I said, "Okay," and my fright vanished. As everyone knows, most fear is irrational.

He begged me to tell him everything I knew about Gautier, and I spoke at length with the feeling of doing rather well at an oral exam. (When he looked away for a moment, I pinched a pencil from the table, a future treasure for the cell. I mention this as a sign of my relaxation.) He lectured me on the stupidity of terrorist acts that only led to useless deaths on all sides, and on the Bolshevik danger, against which the Wehrmacht was defending the West, etc.

Toward the end of this long soliloquy, he said, "If you were to be released any time soon, you would of course have to promise to tell us if you hear about anti-German activities by your friends."

I frowned, having decided to promise anything they wanted, but still needing to be credible.

"I don't think I'd hear anything," I said. "In any case I would have to think over your proposal."

"Well, think it over. Don't you see . . . ?"

More indoctrination.

Rather quickly I did indeed see his point of view and said so.

I doubt he was fooled. Each of us was playing out a charade for the other.

"You haven't been mistreated, have you?" he said. "If you're released, you'll please say the rumors about us are false."

"I will certainly tell people about my experience," I said.

Late that evening I returned to Fresnes in a paddy wagon. I was filled with a hope I scarcely dared admit to myself. Good things happen only if you aren't expecting them—that has always been my one superstition.

In fact my liberation came about more quickly than I could have wished.

At the crack of dawn, Friday, June 18: "Chefrillon! Alles zusammen!"

Already? My heart was torn. I couldn't say goodbye to Denise. And

Gisèle Aillet, the blond Jew—I still had many things to tell her. Ties had developed between us; she was beginning to see the world differently. I had the impression I was abandoning everyone—fleeing.

But I couldn't wait a minute. They led me to the office where I recovered my money and personal belongings. Everything was scrupulously handed back to me, even the Pascal seized in the Search. Surprise and disappointment, though—I immediately noticed that they had taken the trouble of erasing all my annotations! These Germans would never cease to amaze us: what patience, what conscientious work! Erasure crumbs were everywhere.

They told me I could pick up my identity card and address book at rue des Saussaies. To avoid being arrested for not having the card, I decided to take advantage of a last paddy wagon ride and pay a visit to the Gestapo then and there. As a going-away present I was given several letters from my family. Better late than never!

19 *Return from Fresnes*

JUNE, 1943

When I arrived at my parents' apartment, my mother was in bed. She had been sick for five days with a liver ailment. She was extremely weak, and her face seemed to me to have shrunk. Now that I was safe, though, she said she would quickly get better.

She told me about everything that had happened in my absence. Antoinette had visited in mid-May, still in a state of shock over my arrest. Her isolated life in Port-Blanc fed her anxiety and feelings of helplessness, and it did her a world of good to see our parents leading their normal lives, to enjoy our Paris friends in a relaxed way, and to be free of the children and of making endless packages. After several days she went back to Port-Blanc much refreshed.

My parents had received support from many people while I was in prison. Family and friends came to see them and contributed to packages for me—and not only for me but for friends of mine whom they didn't even know. Thus Mother and Antoinette got together food for Charles Baron, then in Compiègne and about to go to Germany, and for Walter McDowell, the West Indian interned in Saint-Denis.[1]

At the end of my first day home I joined my father for a late afternoon walk in the Tuileries—something we'd often done in happier days but that I'd recently thought might never happen again. We strolled along the balustrade that overhangs the road beside the river, not saying much. The water sparkled behind the plane trees, and the sweet air was ruffled by flights of birds. I thought how strange it is that so much beauty remains unnoticed when one is used to it. As we returned home at sunset and crossed the river reflecting the glow of the sky, I said to myself, "I want to remember this moment to the end of my life."

I was impatient to see Jacqueline again and to resume contact with my BCRA friends, so the next day I went to 86 rue de Grenelle. Alas, she told me I couldn't see them: I had been "burned." I was too hot for the underground; the Gestapo was almost certain to keep watch on me. In my naïveté this idea had never crossed my mind. It came as a shock.

As for Gautier, he had been arrested on April 28, one week after my arrest. His capture had taken place at the apartment of the man who under Gautier's direction ran air operations south of Paris. The police frisked Gautier but in their haste didn't notice two of his pockets that contained compromising papers and microfilm. With a good deal of effort Gautier swallowed the papers and microfilm—behind their backs.

Unfortunately the search of the apartment turned up damaging evidence. Gautier and his friend were taken to the Hotel Cayré on boulevard Raspail, which had become a Gestapo headquarters. They were put in a small room with only one door—the one they'd entered—and a window. Four prisoners were already there, sitting on chairs. The six prisoners were guarded by three armed sentries. There was a two-hour wait during which Gautier was filled with the most awful fear of torture. He concocted desperate plans to ... commit suicide? ... escape? He decided that an escape attempt was a better way to commit suicide than to try to open a vein in his wrist with the pin he happened to be wearing.

About seven o'clock he nodded to one of the prisoners to go to the bathroom, knowing that a sentry would accompany him. A second guard was then called to the telephone. Here was his chance. Gautier leapt on the third guard, tore his gun from him, and knocked him down, then threw himself at the guard who was running back from the phone, pushed aside the rifle leveled at him, and shoved the guard to the floor. He raced through the revolving door at the hotel entrance with such force that several Germans coming in were violently thrust inside. In the general confusion four of the five other prisoners escaped through the window onto the rue du Bac.

Once outside, Gautier ran like a maniac, turned the corner of the boulevard, threaded his way up the rue du Bac, bullets cracking around him, turned right again and out of the line of fire. He darted into the first entryway he came to, at 80 rue de Grenelle, lifted up a woman standing in his way, set her down to one side, crossed the courtyard in a bound, and climbed seven floors of the service staircase. A door opened and a woman stood there looking at him, astounded. He ran past her, caught sight of a trapdoor in the ceiling, and hoisted himself up to the loft. (The woman, suspicious and frightened, went down to consult the concierge about calling the police. He persuaded her not to.) Gautier hoped to get out on the roofs he knew so well from having explored them with me. But no, he was cornered: the loft had no exit.

He had a minute to catch his breath. He was relieved to see that he wasn't wounded (he thought he'd been shot in the arm). A thick coat of debris and dust lay everywhere. He covered himself with it, lay in a corner behind a basket, and didn't move. He heard the shouts of his pursuers, dogs barking, then steps, cries. The trapdoor opened for an instant, and closed.

Later, in the middle of the night, the trapdoor opened again. This time he heard French voices. It was the concierge and his wife.

Gautier was so relieved to find they were on his side that he "let it all out," as he says in a private journal he wrote about his war experiences. "I needed to talk to someone, to be among friends."

At five in the morning he went downstairs to the concierge's apartment to clean up. While washing, he discovered that his shirt and jacket sleeves had four neat bullet holes in them. He drank a big bowl of coffee and milk and ate a lot of bread and butter. Then he put on a raincoat his rescuer gave him and strolled out to the Métro to go to friends in Passy.

He stayed hidden there for a month and a half, resting completely. Dominique, who replaced him as director of air operations for BCRA, came from time to time with Françoise Foëx to give him news and cigarettes. Jean Moulin also came to congratulate him and at the same time to order him back to London because now he too had been burned. On June 15 a plane picked him up at a landing field near Gournay. As soon as Gautier arrived in England, he announced his whereabouts very clearly over Radio Londres so that everyone, including the Gestapo, would hear. I think this was probably the reason the Germans released me a few days later.

"And Gilbert?" I asked Jacqueline. "What exactly happened to him?" She said he'd continued to betray us: six people besides Charles Baron and me had been arrested.[2] This had to stop.

Gilbert was executed by Médéric, who no doubt felt partially responsible for the betrayals since he had recommended Gilbert to Gautier.[3] The situation was rendered still more poignant by the fact that Médéric was a friend of Gilbert's father.

The evening of April 18 Médéric arrived at Gilbert's parents' house in a car stolen from the Gestapo and invited Gilbert to join him for a ride. Here is what Gautier wrote in his unpublished journal:

> Gilbert's parents suspected something was wrong but said nothing. Gilbert was pale. The car drove toward the Meudon woods. Médéric and Gilbert were in the backseat. Two shots were fired and Gilbert crumpled over, hit in the head and heart. Médéric and the driver carried Gilbert's body to the edge of the woods, where it was discovered the next day.

Jacqueline, Gautier, everyone was positive Gilbert had betrayed me. I was never sure. First, as I've said, his visit had given me a sort of intuitive conviction that he wouldn't harm me. Second, I had been arrested three days after his death and a full week after his visit. In general the Gestapo was quicker than that. Finally, if Gilbert had betrayed me, the Gestapo would not have released me; I would have been deported. What seemed to me more likely was that Gilbert's murder prompted the Gestapo to question his landlady and that she, knowing nothing and being frightened, told the truth: she had met Gilbert through Mlle. Chevrillon, 86 rue de Grenelle. I never took the trouble to seek out the woman in question.

There were so many things for Jacqueline and me to tell each other! She said that when Antoinette came to Paris she looked so troubled and despairing that she, Jacqueline, took it upon herself to tell her about our underground work. What a relief this was to Antoinette! What a relief it was for me.

Jacqueline came to my room late that night on tiptoe, and we talked until 2 A.M. I myself was worn out. As I wrote to my sister on June 23, "I don't have Jacqueline's marvelous energy and resilience. She has some kind of taut inner life-spring that keeps her going forever. She never seems to tire—and she looks about 15 years old, with her open, smooth, radiant face."

You cannot imagine the delight I experienced being back on the rue de Grenelle! I wrote my sister early one morning after my return: "I'm in bed writing you and my room is drenched in sunlight. It's marvelous to have all this light and colors and roses all around me, and to be lying between two white sheets."

My first days back I was besieged on all sides. My buoyant cousin Vivou Chevrillon, twenty, marched me to a hairdresser on rue Royale. The procedure took hours, and Vivou stayed the whole time laughing and talking nonsense, lest I run away. The result was surprising, even admirable—but it didn't last long! That same evening Anne Gondinet, who had loaned me her *Ausweis* to travel south, gave a dinner party she'd taken two days preparing: impossible for me, as guest of honor, not to be there.

The day after my return the headmistress of Collège Sévigné appeared, carrying four roses. I could resume my classes immediately, she said. My replacement was about to expire of old age and exhaustion.

So I returned to teaching. After the first burst of welcome—I had become a kind of heroine—my students fell into an apathy I couldn't overcome. They were completely run down: they suffered not only the depressing effect of malnutrition but panic over the approaching baccalauréat exam.

The exception was Ginette Janin, who, having already taken the philosophy exam, was not at all depressed. She told me with undisguised pride that she had finished translating the Harold Nicolson book and that Father Riquet would indeed publish it. I hoped there weren't too many mistakes![4]

Several days later, to dispel the shadows of the "bac" and Fresnes, my students and I went for a picnic in the forest at Marly, where beneath the fine old beeches and oaks we unwound with laughter and song. This was to be my last memory of Collège Sévigné during the war, but of course I didn't know this at the time—any more than I knew about the underground work that involved many of my fellow teachers. I later learned that at least nine of them were arrested for subversive activities. One was the journalist Pierre Brossolette, whom I mentioned earlier and will mention again. Another, Louis François, agrégé in history and a member of the Confrérie Notre-Dame,[5] was deported. A third, Hélène Wuilleumier, a geography professor at whose house I had often played music, was mortally wounded during a Maquis battle in the Jura in July, 1944.

Many other teachers, students, and parents—who knows how many?—either worked in the underground or helped Jewish families, often by taking in their children. I learned this from chance conversations after the war. What surprised me were not these acts of courage (Pascal's "Learn to think aright" was the Collège motto), but to have known nothing whatever about them.

As you might expect, one of the first things I did after returning from Fresnes was to seek out Denise's children and give them her news. I went to her father's house. M. Depuis turned out to be a curious gentleman, a buffoon both affable and surly, married to a woman one-third his age but not at all shy about making advances on other young women. Though full of generous socialist ideas, he was indifferent and dry of heart when speaking of his daughter and grandchildren. He told me the children were in the country, at Triel, with their paternal grandmother. I revisited Denise's father and stepmother several times, invited to sumptuous meals to which I was no longer accustomed. Their apartment was filled with knickknacks, its walls covered in caricatures, anticlerical for the most part. M. Depuis was the life of the party and wrote poetry he found quite enchanting: sentimental verse to celebrate his young wife's pregnancy and very coarse poems to lampoon Pétain.

I went to Triel for an afternoon. Jeannette, nine, was tall, very pale, and not especially communicative. "She seemed to understand many things, even though she hasn't been told where her mother is," I wrote my sister on June 25. "I'm sure she senses a mystery, which must be terrible for her (I didn't dare reveal the truth, coming for the first time). Michel, five, is completely unaware—a bundle of laughter." Their grandmother, a simple, good-hearted woman, was chiefly occupied with taking care of their physical well-being, which she did superbly.

I was sure Denise would love to know that her children were out of her father's hands and well tended, so two days later I took the train to Croix-de-Berny, not far from Fresnes. I prowled around inspecting the prison layout, trying to spot my old building. When I did, it was easy to find the path bordered with trees that we saw from our window, but direct communication with Denise proved impossible: the enclosure wall was too high. The wall posed no problem in speaking to Gisèle Aillet whose cell was on the fifth floor. And I had a message for her from her dear Alexander.

(Here I need a parenthesis. Just before I left Fresnes, a German soldier had been in our cell for plumbing repairs, and we'd asked him,
casually, to unlock and open the window, which he did. There was no
reaction from the Gray Mice, and the window stayed open about eight
inches from the top.)

I recognized our window at once. It was about 5:30. No one was
around.

At the top of my lungs I yelled, "Gi-sèle! Gi-sèle!"

Nothing. I began gathering my strength again. There was a small
movement behind the window. The top of Gisèle's blond head appeared.
I quickly shouted everything I had to say: about Alexander and about
Denise's children. I made Gisèle repeat Denise's message to be sure she
got it right. I added that they shouldn't expect me for a month because
I was going to Brittany, but that I would be back.

Two hours later I was dining with my parents on the boulevard
Saint-Germain.

I returned to Fresnes on July 30 and then every other week for two
months. Conversations over the wall became long and even relaxed. I
also went back to Triel several times. As I suspected, Jeannette had
guessed that her mother was in prison and imagined the most terrible
things. She was relieved to be able to speak freely about her mother and
to exchange messages with her through me.

At the end of September my visits to Fresnes came to an abrupt halt.

20   An Eventful Summer

JUNE–JULY, 1943

Meanwhile, at the beginning of July Antoinette and I had swapped
places. I went to Port-Blanc and she went to Paris, leaving the children
with me. We had wanted to do this for a long time, but it hadn't been
possible earlier.

For us at Port-Blanc the fine summer days glided by uneventfully.
Bare-chested German soldiers in short pants fished from the rocks,
sunned themselves, or listlessly watched the local men build the Atlantic
Wall. The idea of making an eight-foot-high, five-foot-thick concrete
wall along our coast was curious indeed. The shore was strewn with
natural dangers—obviously an impractical place to land a fleet. But
there was no doubt Fritz preferred supervising the construction of the

wall, fishing in our waters, and lying in the sun to getting killed in Russia. That we understood!

During my stay I got to know Marie Lelay, the grocer at Penvénan. I still clearly recall her young face, the earnest look in her blue eyes, and her lustrous hair already graying. She suffered from tuberculosis of the kidneys, which at the time was a fatal disease. Antoinette had told me a great deal about her. They had gotten to know each other over the packages Antoinette put together for Paul and other relatives. They reacted the same way to events, whether international or local, and shared a fervent hope for an Allied victory. Antoinette was moved by Marie's gentleness, her courage, her self-sacrifice in the acceptance of her illness, and by the faith that was the source of her strength. When later I went underground, it was through Marie that I wrote Antoinette, whose mail risked being watched.

I confess I was apprehensive about being responsible for Antoinette's precious and delicate young ones. André was extremely sensitive and very much attached to his mother—would I be up to that challenge? Soisette, four, was subject to inner storms, which, when she kept them bottled up, were frightening, and, when she didn't, were even more so! Titi, as I recall, had no problems.

The good weather made things easier than I had expected. "Soisette has just brought me a horseshoe," I wrote my sister from the Saliou Woods, where we'd gone on a picnic to get away from the heat. "'I finded the horseshoe!' she says, sticking out her chest, her eyes bright with pride, while her eyebrows frown to make sure she isn't looking too happy with herself. André pays lots of attention to Titi and whispers advice in his ear—which is quite unnecessary, as Titi is angelic!" André by this time had acquired a strong sense of responsibility. He was only seven, but Antoinette often shared her worries with him, and he often anticipated her wishes. Now he did the same for me.

I found it hard returning to Paris at the end of July. Terrible things were happening. There had been a new roundup of Jews. I remember being told what an old man said to his wife when they were arrested: "My darling, we've been living so long in fear. Now we're going to live in hope."

From his internment camp, my cousin Jacques Ferdinand-Dreyfus had sent a message in invisible ink to his gardener at Montfort begging him to warn his family that they "must leave immediately for their health." The four daughters were scattered among friends, my parents taking in Françoise. Daniel had to leave the Protestant hostel where he was living.

My mother, alerted by our friend Evelyne Garnier,[1] went into hiding herself for three days with our cousins Irene and Raymond Hébrard, whose daughter Cécile took the terrible fall down the Métro stairs. Ever since "Jew" had been stamped on her identity card, my mother kept a little suitcase packed so that at a moment's notice she could disappear into the home of friends or relations who had said, "If you're in danger, come to us."

Throughout Jacques's internment we had been assured that he was "protected." Was he not a wounded veteran of the First War? Had he not been the former Director of Social Security in the Ministry of Labor? Had he not been awarded the Légion d'honneur? Did he not have powerful friends?

We alternated between hope and despondency, with Lily, Jacques's wife, doing everything she could—seeing, or trying to see, everyone who could speak on his behalf. Already thin, she ate less and less. My mother couldn't sleep. At the beginning of August Lily and her daughters returned to Montfort. Young Renée wrote in her diary on August 10:

> The threat of sudden arrest is still there, and each ring of the doorbell frightens us. A friend says we should go to the Free Zone, but Mummy explained to her we couldn't leave Daddy, and that we had to stay as near his camp as possible. Besides, we couldn't afford to set up a new life elsewhere.

But in fact by that time Jacques was no longer in France. He had been deported on July 31. On September 20 Renée wrote:

> I haven't written in this diary for a long time because I have been so upset by the horrible news. Daddy has probably been deported. We know it because of a note one of his colleagues received at the Ministry: "Jacques F. of Montfort is on his way to Germany. He is in excellent physical and mental condition."

Renée's use of the word "probably" shows how difficult it was for her to give up hope.

In the Resistance one disaster followed another. On June 6 General Delestraint, whom de Gaulle had just appointed to coordinate underground military activities, was arrested, along with his second-in-command. On June 21 Jean Moulin and seven of his associates were arrested near Lyons. I didn't learn about these blows to the leadership until later, but I knew what happened in my own circle: Antoine Geoffroy-Dechaume was arrested in Corrèze in mid-July, and as I wrote my sister on August 6, Anne-Marie Bauer "caught the itch" in Lyons.

I went to see Antoine's parents at Valmondois. M. and Mme. Geoffroy had not heard from him but thought he was imprisoned in Limoges. I decided to make a trip there with the vague idea of seeing what his chances were for release or escape. Sometime earlier I had adopted the old motto "I need no hope to act nor success to persevere."

After walking around the prison, I knocked at the door.

"Is Antoine Geoffroy-Dechaume here?"

They looked at a ledger. "Yes."

"May I see him?"

"No, he doesn't have visiting privileges."

"Can he be sent packages?"

"Yes, one every two weeks."

"Can his wife visit him?"

"We don't know. She has to ask permission."

I was told the prison was under the control of the District Administrator, so I tried to see him. The highest civil servant I could find at the Préfecture told me he was sorry but absolutely nothing could be done for a prisoner arrested by the Germans. That conversation didn't take long.

However my little jaunt had not been a complete waste: we now knew where Antoine was; he would henceforth receive packages; and his wife, Grethe, would (as it turned out) be able to see him.

My father, who had heard that Laval's son-in-law, M. de Chambrun, wanted a seat in the French Academy, wrote him a letter pleading for Antoine's release in the name of French music. Georges Duhamel, also a member of the Academy and a friend of the Geoffroys, did the same thing. It was all useless. Antoine was deported to Buchenwald on January 20, 1944.

My father, feeling stifled in the oppressive atmosphere of Paris, left to catch a bit of sea breeze in Port-Blanc. He went alone. My mother stayed behind, forbidden to travel.

There was one thing I was pleased about: my former student Ginette Janin was eager to "do something." While she was in Collège Sévigné I had turned a deaf ear to her entreaties, urging her to concentrate on her final exams. Now they were over; she was eighteen and had gotten her parents' permission. I took her to see Marie-Hélène Lefaucheux. I had known Marie-Hélène since childhood in Port-Blanc. When we were children, she had always been held up to Antoinette and me as a model of intelligence and good behavior, so naturally we avoided her like the plague. But lately I'd come across her again. She and her husband, Pierre, lived in Paris, a few doors down from my parents in a big apartment that was literally a crossroads of the underground.[2] In fact, it made me a little nervous—what a haul for the Gestapo! But as soon as people appeared, Marie-Hélène, who never lost her head, tucked each of them into a different room to wait their turn to be heard—which meant they never saw one another. Her caution and discretion were all the more remarkable because these qualities were rare among young resistants.

The Lefaucheux's apartment was also the headquarters for an aboveground organization that prepared packages for political prisoners and helped their families, many of whom were destitute. On certain days the place swarmed with people moving about amid heaps of clothing and provisions. What better alibi could there be for comings and goings and furtive conversations?

I introduced Ginette to Marie-Hélène, who turned her over to Philippe Viannay, a philosophy student and founder of the underground paper *Défense de la France*,[3] the epigraph of which was Pascal's "I only believe in stories if witnesses are willing to have their throats cut." Ginette began doing typesetting and secretarial work for the paper.

And was there anything *I* could do? Marie-Hélène suggested I help with her above-ground work, which was increasing as arrests increased. In August, through the Red Cross, her organization sent about 400 of its own packages and 120 packages from relatives and friends to prisoners held in Paris. I started carting packages on a wagon behind my bike between the Lefaucheux's and the Red Cross. Part of my work was to get family messages to a German chaplain at Fresnes who kindly passed them on to prisoners.

As for Jacqueline, she was now working for Alain, whom I was soon to work for, under the code name Benjamin.[4] Alain assigned her to find lodgings in Paris for the new agents arriving from Lyons, London, and Algiers. Paris would henceforth be the new headquarters of the CNR[5] because Lyons, after the arrests of Jean Moulin and other underground workers there, was totally burned; the Gestapo, under Klaus Barbie, controlled the city, making it almost impossible to hide. Paris was vaster, safer—a Maquis in itself.

Jacqueline carried out her task brilliantly. Who could resist the young and beautiful Comtesse de Lorne d'Alincourt? Since BCRA was financially very generous, prices were never a problem for her. The greater her success, the more her services were in demand. She never refused. She had friends everywhere and lived in a whirlwind.

Some of her friends gave her RAF pilots to look after, and when she couldn't manage them all, she asked me to see to their welfare and entertainment—which I did gladly when I had time. These airmen were big athletic fellows next to whom I felt like a pygmy. They lived crammed together in small rooms without any of the amenities. They had a hard time waiting days, even weeks, for their turn to go home. (A whole chain of people had to be set up to shelter them during their clandestine journey to the coast or Spanish border.) While in Paris, they were dying to get out and walk the streets, but they weren't allowed to unless accompanied by a native French speaker, because if they'd had to say anything at all, their accent would have immediately betrayed them. As it was, just taking them out was a bit risky because they contrasted so sharply with our own underfed population. But I admit the danger added to the fun of being with them. Thank heaven we never had an incident!

"The pace of Jacqueline's life makes me dizzy. I'm worried about her," I wrote my sister on September 14:

> She is completely exhausted, more exhausted than I have ever seen anyone before—even at the Blanc.[6] She sets no limit on her energies. . . .
> In addition to work there are sentimental entanglements, as you can well imagine. She is so sweet and the men in her life so despotic! She needs someone to look after her.

Jacqueline finally decided to go to her mother's for three or four days, much to my relief, and asked me to take over some of her duties.

21 *The Gestapo on the rue de Grenelle*

SEPTEMBER, 1943

Toward the end of September, the Rigals returned to Paris for the start of school. Véronique Rigal, who was five months pregnant, arrived before everyone else, on the twenty-first, to get the house ready while I prepared to move on the twenty-fifth into the studio apartment Gautier had occupied. For some time Jacqueline had been using the apartment to store compromising papers.

On the twenty-third I went to spend the night with Lily Ferdinand-Dreyfus and her children at Montfort l'Amaury. A letter I wrote my sister the next day evokes the scene there better than anything I could write now:

> The weather is perfect and the garden is overflowing with vegetables and apples, and the roses are as beautiful as in springtime—white, yellow, red. Just now I am lounging in a deck chair gazing at butterflies and bees and little clouds very high in the sky. Claudine is stroking my hair with her soft, small, warm hands. Françoise is boning up on physics—I don't know how she can concentrate in the middle of all this beauty and sunlight! Lily is knitting and has almost regained her spirits. She isn't the same person I saw last time: she jokes the way she used to, and the atmosphere isn't as sad as I'd feared it would be. Geneviève is her usual gentle and austere self. She supervises what Françoise reads, who supervises what Renée reads, who supervises what Claudine reads! Geneviève gives almost 30 lessons a week, Françoise gives 19 (in addition to preparing her degrees in physics and astronomy), and Renée gives Greek lessons. An excellent postwar project would be a school run by the three Dreyfus sisters at Montfort! As usual, Alice, resident gendarme, reigns over the entire household.

Daniel was there also. He'd been in hiding for weeks, scarcely daring to leave the house, chafing at having nothing to do. When he begged me to find him some work, I said I'd talk to the Lefaucheux.

I returned to Paris that same day at about seven P.M., loaded with apples and vegetables. Should I take them to my parents on the boulevard Saint-Germain, or go directly to the rue de Grenelle? I decided to go to my parents', and they kept me for dinner. During the meal, the doorbell rang and I got up to answer it. As soon as I saw Ginette's face, I knew there had been a disaster and thought, "The Gestapo!"

I'd forgotten—oh, my legendary absent-mindedness!—that I had invited Ginette to lunch with me at the rue de Grenelle. She'd arrived and scarcely rung my bell, she said, when the door opened and an arm yanked her inside. She was surrounded by men in plain clothes. She'd only just been released from Gestapo headquarters on the rue des Saussaies and rushed over to warn me.

I was horrified. What about Jacqueline? And Véronique, who was expecting her seventh baby? And Anne Gondinet?

Ginette sat down, still out of breath. They'd immediately pushed her into the living room, she said, where Véronique and Anne were already sitting under guard. In the middle of the room was an enormous heap of books, evidence of a house search. Ginette's handbag was hurriedly searched and returned. At that instant she realized that her bicycle registration card in her handbag was not completely filled out, which made it look obviously counterfeit. What should she do? She racked her brain. Perhaps it hadn't been noticed. She sneaked the card from her handbag and threw it underneath a dresser. A long afternoon of silence followed, during which she strove to invent a good reason for not having the card. At five o'clock she was led into a nearby room and interrogated: identity, address, etc.

"And the phony bicycle card—where is it?"

"What?"

"Has it disappeared?"

Ginette had to return to the living room and ignominiously get down on all fours to retrieve it from under the dresser.

"How do you explain the fact that this card has not been filled in?"

Ginette told her story with a certain aplomb. When she'd finished, the Gestapo agent tore the card into little pieces, looked her straight in the eye, and said, "Let's hear no more about it."

Ginette thought he had deliberately saved her.

An hour later a soldier with a cocked pistol led the three prisoners single file, each to a different car. At the rue des Saussaies, Ginette lost sight of Véronique and Anne. She was again interrogated and then given the magic paper freeing her—after she had promised not to tell anyone about what had happened. Naturally, the first thing she did was to come and tell me.

About Jacqueline she knew nothing except that the Gestapo had taken her away from the rue de Grenelle before she, Ginette, arrived.

Now what should I do? I was completely thrown. I was certain of only one thing: I mustn't stay at my parents' and risk attracting the Gestapo there. I left about 9:30. Curfew was at midnight, which gave me a little time to make the necessary arrangements.

I was thinking, uneasily, that I might spend the night on the rue de Grenelle. (How difficult it is to break one's habits even in exceptional circumstances!) They couldn't find anything there to incriminate me, and after all I had gotten out of a similar scrape once before, over Gautier. But since I was passing the Lefaucheuxs' apartment anyway, I decided to go up and ask their advice. I had more confidence in their judgment than in my own.

"Really, Claire, you must be dreaming!" exclaimed Marie-Hélène. "Of course you can't go home—unless you have a special calling to be a martyr."

She couldn't take me in for the night, but she gave me the names of two friends of hers who she thought might. Before that, though, I was to hurry and warn the underground of Jacqueline's arrest.

Here compartmentalization showed its drawback. I knew only two underground addresses. One was Jacqueline's office on the rue de la Pompe, where I'd once carried a message and where I knew her contact Alain worked. The other, on rue Vaneau, was the room of a new arrival, Gustave.[1] I knew his address because I'd found him lodging during Jacqueline's recent absence. Rue Vaneau was closer so I ran there. Alas, Gustave was out, and his landlady gave me a suspicious look. Suspicious myself, I withdrew, leaving no message. (My stupid excess of prudence led to Gustave's arrest the next day and to his deportation to Buchenwald.)

At rue de la Pompe the door was closed. I was going to slide a message under it, but like an idiot I'd run off without pen or pencil. With my lipstick I wrote a few words in big letters on a piece of paper. The Gestapo found this odd piece of paper early the next morning and set a trap that caught Gustave and the whole office staff except for Alain, his boss Claude Serreulles, and a young secretary—and they barely escaped.

I rethreaded my way across Paris to the rue de l'Université. The first person whose name Marie-Hélène had given me wasn't home. However the visit proved lucky because I happened to run into a friend of Suzanne Hébrard's. My cousin Suzanne was the half-sister of Cécile who fell down the Métro stairs. I had been worrying a lot about Suzanne because several days before at my request she had agreed to let an important underground meeting take place in her apartment. I had been in a hurry as I was leaving for Montfort and had broken the rule by leaving her address in writing with Jacqueline. I told Suzanne's friend to tell her to disappear for a while, and when the Gestapo arrived to question her a few days later, she was gone. She stayed out to pasture for a month.

Finally, just before curfew, I made it to Paul Painlevé Square, near the Sorbonne, and was welcomed by Marie-Hélène's friends Annie Billoud and Elizabeth de Bie, lycée teachers devoted to the Gaullist cause. As I was getting into the comfortable bed they had ready for me (Marie-Hélène must have telephoned), the sunny afternoon in the garden at Montfort flashed through my mind: was it possible it had been today?

Waking up the next morning, September 25, I was aware that something terrible had happened. What was it? Ah, yes: Jacqueline had been arrested. And Véronique and Anne . . . I must get going. The first thing to do was warn Léon Rigal, who would be arriving from Lyons at any time. I had no desire to do it myself, for many reasons. So I went to see one of Véronique's brothers, Father B——, a Dominican. He received me kindly and agreed to tell Léon of his wife's arrest. You can imagine Léon's amazement and dismay when he was told about it on a platform of the Gare de Lyon, surrounded by his six children. He went straight to the Gestapo, rue des Saussaies, to reclaim Véronique. He insisted his wife was innocent, as was he, and nobly offered to be imprisoned in her stead—an offer that was declined.

Véronique, thank heavens, got out of Fresnes a few days later. Her fortitude never left her. We hoped that the child (it was Luc, born in February, 1944) would not suffer too much from this adventure.

Anne Gondinet had less luck and remained three months in Fresnes.

Of Jacqueline, we knew nothing.

Since returning from Fresnes I'd been doing some underground work, thanks to Jacqueline, but in an occasional, amateurish way. I now realized this work had become my chief interest in life, and I wanted to commit myself fully to it. However, because the Gestapo knew me and could easily keep watch over me, I had to "take the plunge": change my name, address, and whole way of life; I had to disappear. I chose the name Christiane Clouet,[2] looked for lodging in a far-off corner of the city, and resigned my job at Collège Sévigné. I also stopped liaisoning between the Lefaucheux and the Red Cross. I stopped visiting the Saint-Denis British internees. And I stopped sharing my parents' lives and going to Port-Blanc.

I contacted Jacqueline's boss Alain—whom I will henceforth call Benjamin, the new code name he was using since the Gestapo raid on the rue de la Pompe—and asked him for an assignment. He gave me the work I would do for the next year until the Liberation of Paris. He put me into the coding section of the Delegation in France of the CFLN, the French Committee of National Liberation (Comité Français de Libération Nationale), which was in Algiers under de Gaulle.

He said someone else, a Captain Drouot, would teach me the coding system. He said I needed a second alias for my work. I chose Anne.

We spoke of Jacqueline. Benjamin was very upset by her arrest, as I knew he would be. He said it had led to other arrests, and not only at rue de la Pompe. The Gestapo had staked out the rue de Grenelle for several days and had caught at least one other agent, Hugues Limonti.[3] They had also found a list of addresses in Jacqueline's room.

The rue de Grenelle had been raided and Jacqueline arrested because she had been betrayed by a landlady she met through a real estate broker. She knew it was risky going to a broker and only did it because after three months of looking for safe rooms she'd exhausted the leads she had through friends. The room she rented through the broker was for an agent just arrived from London. The landlady noticed that he had English papers—or clothes or cigarettes—and ran to tell the German police and get the reward that was her "due." The agent, Colonel Morinaud, was arrested but managed to swallow a cyanide pill. It was a magnificent coup for the landlady: she got a second reward for turning in Jacqueline's address.[4]

"If only we could get a message to Jacqueline," Benjamin said to me. I no longer remember the message he wanted to send. It had to do with what she should say or not say about one or two specific agents. "But it's impossible," he said. "She's in Fresnes."

Fresnes . . . I said I knew people in the women's building. I could try to get the message to them—through the window.

He was surprised at this suggestion, and interested. He said he was not asking me to take this risk, but I certainly knew the message would be useful.

That evening I went back to Fresnes, to my usual spot. I shouted: "Gi-sèle, Gi-sèle!"

A blond head came to the window. "How are you?"

"Fine."

That instant, looking around to make sure I was alone, I saw a German soldier behind a tree thirty yards away. He was watching me. I turned and started walking as quickly and calmly as I could across the open fields. I headed for the train station at Antony because it would have been too easy to catch me at the Fresnes station. After what seemed a long time—five, perhaps ten minutes—I began to feel safe. Then the dreaded call: "Halt!" I turned. The German, on a bike, was overtaking me on the uneven field. He was not more than twenty yards away. It was better to speak to him than to get a bullet in the back, so I waited.

He took me roughly by the arm and made me turn back toward the prison. We walked side by side for what seemed a terribly long time. Though I was aware of how ridiculous it was, I asked him in the sentimental way that sometimes worked with the Germans: "Haben sie keine Schwester?" (Don't you have a sister?)

He didn't respond.

Fresnes . . . I was going back to Fresnes!

By the time we got to the entrance of the prison, I had no hope. My despair was made worse by knowing that what had happened, and what was going to happen, was entirely my fault.

Several guards questioned me while we waited for the arrival of their superior. I gave them my true-false identity card[5] made out in the name of Christiane Clouet. I'd only received the card that morning, and as they handed it back, I noticed with horror that its serial number had been left off.

"Address?"

"45 rue Jean Jaures, Fréjus." (Fréjus is a little port on the Mediterranean. Perhaps they wouldn't go that far to verify an address.)

"Have you ever come to Fresnes before?"

"No."

"Why did you come now?"

"To get news of a friend."

"Who is your friend?"

"Gisèle Aillet," I said. I mentioned her because she had nothing to do with the underground. "She is my best friend—she's a friend from school."

They stopped the questions to wait for their officer, and I had time, two hours, to agonize over the mess I was in. They were sure to interrogate Gisèle, who knew me under my real name and who would tell the truth. They would find out my address at 86 rue de Grenelle and soon connect it with Jacqueline, rue de la Pompe, and the Delegation. Deportation would follow—for Jacqueline as well. My mother would fall ill. All obviously my fault.

The commanding officer, a giant of a man, finally appeared. He asked the guards about me and then, holding my false identity card in his hand, walked over to me. His questions were spoken with a strong German accent. I repeated what I had already said.

"And you really came all the way from Fréjus—so far south—to Fresnes?"

"Yes. I traveled all night and I'm very tired. Gisèle is my best friend. I haven't had any news about her at all."

He planted himself in front of me, crossed his arms, and said in a thunderous voice: "And you think it's *polite* to shout up at windows?"

I couldn't believe my ears.

"No, you're right," I said. "It's not polite. But it was the only way I could talk to her."

"But you could see her at her trial!"[6]

"Oh, I didn't know that. When?"

"That's for *you* to find out!" he boomed, thrusting my card at me. "And make sure, Mademoiselle, we never see you around here again."

I followed his advice and never again went to Fresnes.

Annie Billoud and Elizabeth de Bie had waited supper for me, very worried. How they exclaimed when I told them where I'd been! But the first thing to do, even before supper, was to write a number on my identity card!

My hosts were immensely enthusiastic. Though not part of any network, they "resisted" in their daily lives. In teaching history and French, what could be more natural than to speak of certain traditional moral values that were currently being infringed? What better way was there to influence public opinion than to start a conversation about current events with people standing in line near you and then give your own opinion? Everyone listened to Annie and Elizabeth, and no one had yet ventured to criticize them.[7] I would have liked to stay on with them, but because of my new work, I had to leave at the end of a week to set up in another part of the city.

Before leaving, I went to see my parents. Since Ginette's sudden appearance at dinner, we'd spoken only briefly on the phone. I knew that if the Gestapo linked together the arrests at the rue de Grenelle over the past months, they might come looking for me and question my parents. I didn't want my parents to know anything about my underground work so they could answer any questions without reservation. And I wanted to spare them anxiety. So I told them I'd decided that the best thing I could do was to get out of Paris until the end of the war (which we thought near). I said I'd arranged to live with a nice family not far from the city, taking care of their children. I said I would stay in frequent phone contact. They were relieved to know I would be out of danger.

And what should they tell the Gestapo if they came around? We decided I should write my parents a farewell letter, as though I were leaving for England. If the occasion arose, they would show it sadly to the Germans, saying they knew nothing more.

The war had at least taught me how to lie!

22 *Code Clerk*

OCTOBER, 1943–JANUARY, 1944

I found myself a room near the Porte Maillot in the far west of Paris and started on my new work. Nothing is more secret than code work. Had I been arrested and tortured, I might—who knows—have divulged the key to coded messages between the CFLN[1] in Algiers and its Delegation in France. To think of the consequences made one shudder.

The Delegation was extremely careful about my security. I was kept from any contact that might compromise me and vice versa. Thus I never saw my bosses. Until Paris was liberated, I knew them only by the style each one used in writing telegrams and by their bizarre aliases: Sophie and Scapin,[2] Cléante and Cadillac,[3] Belladone and Quartus.[4]

The only agents I saw were the couriers. I met them twice a day, morning and evening. From them I received messages that needed encoding or decoding and turned over the messages I had worked up. The coded messages went between the Delegation in Paris and "Merlin" in Algiers. The location for the courier drops changed each day. At first we usually met in cafés, but after several weeks word came down that we should avoid them because they were too often haunted by the Gestapo. We then began meeting in public gardens and churches. (Churches were especially good because they generally had several exits and you could wait in them a long time without attracting attention.) Toward the end, a sympathetic bookseller and a concierge served as our mailboxes, so after that I didn't even see the couriers on a regular basis.

The mysterious and powerful Merlin directing us from Algiers was— I learned this, too, only after the war—Emmanuel d'Astier de la Vigerie, the CFLN's Minister of the Interior and founder of Libération, one of the first and most important Resistance movements in France.

Benjamin put me in touch with Captain Drouot,[5] who taught me coding. Drouot had a stern and impassive air. His key words were "method," "patience," and "efficiency," and I quickly learned to trust and like him. The coding system looked complicated at first but turned out to be easy. For a long while it was based—how this would have astonished Alfred de Musset!—on some lines of his:

> Si je vous le disais pourtant que je vous aime,
> Qui sait, brune aux yeux bleus, ce que vous en
> diriez . . . ?

> (If after all I told you of my love,
> Sweet blue-eyed brunette,
> Who knows what you would say . . . ?)

Code work requires meticulous attention to detail, but with practice it becomes as automatic as driving a car. Soon after I'd begun, I thought I'd become quite skillful and was rather pleased with myself. But one day London (our telegrams went to Algiers via London) replied: "Telegram indecipherable." Surprise, shame, and consternation—but from Drouot, not a shadow of reproach. He simply asked me to come over to his place every day for a week so that he could give me a little more tutoring.

He lived near the Place des Vosges on the other side of town, and I remember those long bike rides through the empty streets. I discovered fine dilapidated neighborhoods I'd never seen before. I pedaled briskly, almost with joy. You may wonder how that could be. Great misfortunes had happened all around me, which I couldn't forget. But perhaps they made my fragile freedom all the more precious. This thought didn't occur to me at the time. I only knew that I was pleased to be doing what I was doing.

The work was draining; it was also irregular. At times I had nothing to do—other times I worked all day and into the night. Not being privy to what was happening higher up, I frequently didn't understand the messages I worked on. Sometimes they seemed unimportant, gabby, mainly concerned about the senders themselves. Without having realized it, I found I'd been passed from the Action and Information Section to the Political Section. People in it often gave the impression they were subtly pushing themselves forward. It was irritating to think that radio operators—the most often arrested of the Delegation's agents—were risking their lives for that.

I was terribly worried about Jacqueline, because she couldn't feign innocence like me—too much had been found in her apartment. Toward the middle of October I received a letter from her sister telling me Jacqueline was now receiving packages at Fresnes. This was important not only for her health but because, with luck, it offered a way to communicate. Prisoners would send their laundry home with messages written on toilet paper slipped into the hems of skirts or trousers. I cite a bit of Jacqueline's first letter to her mother:

> *21 Nov. '43.* Sept. 24 A.M. I was led to rue des S. and interrogated five days and nights, hands manacled behind my back, almost without food. Between interrog. a cell without windows. Not really bullied, just head banged against the wall. Sustained by ex. of Jo[6] and Father knowing honor worth more than life, decided to let myself be cut to shreds rather than talk. Seeing they could do nothing with me, they gave me the cruelest torture of all: you'd be taken hostage and my brothers and sisters sent to concentration camp. Evening, Sept. 30. Fresnes. Cell on first floor; solitary confinement. Oct. 6. Package. Joy! Oct. 7. Interrog. ave. Foch. Was told you were in Fresnes and would be kept there till I talked. Stayed silent, torn with anguish. Oct. 18. Communion. Inexpressible joy. Nov. 16. A package, but all food returned to senders as general punishment. End October was a little sick because of hunger, cold, but especially unbearable anxiety. Please use a suitcase.[7] When hunger doesn't prevent me, I sing to myself and all my sweet memories make me forget . . .

I myself received two messages from Jacqueline in December, which I still have, though they've become practically illegible. Even at the time I had difficulty reading them and so copied them over. She gave me news about our comrades, arrested and not. I transcribe here the parts that belong to this story:

> My dear, at interro. Dec. 7 saw Germain.[8] He says tell his friend[9] and S.[10] they are in great danger. Must get away if possible. Ask former send photos to Mother.[11] Ger. and I not ill-treated at interr. on 7. If possible, send packages and tobacco to Cl. Large.[12] Is with others in cell. Said he'd slept in my room Monday to Friday. When arrested had just gotten together all receipts and papers to report to Gustave.[13] The G.[14] seems to have given up trying to make me talk. They load me with imaginary responsibilities. I think Georges has told everything.
>   Your little Unicorn[15] who loves you.

Was so happy learning A.[16] not caught. My thoughts are with you all constantly.

Here is the second letter:

My dear Claire, heartfelt thanks for immense joy. . . . [17] From Large learned everyone in flat arrested. Gestapo told me: you're acting like a soldier—silent; you'll be treated as such, not like a woman. We'll never release you. Another said, "Up against the wall!" So many charming prospects. . . . But am at peace, my dear. Don't make too many efforts to get me out of here—useless, I'm sure! Am thinking and praying for everyone. Don't forget us. Not worried about anything, and advice unnecessary because I know you're there!

Your little Unicorn who loves you so much. Happy Christmas to all despite everything.

Jacqueline was deported to Ravensbrück on April 18, 1944.

In December Benjamin contacted me again. The disaster of September 24 had burned him too, and the Gestapo was on his trail. A British plane was to pick him up, as well as some others (among them my Collège Sévigné colleague Pierre Brossolette), and take them to London. But for a week before and a week after the full moon in November, December, and January, the weather was against them. They would gather near the landing field and await the BBC message confirming the operation—in vain. Storms and fog kept France in total darkness.

Benjamin wanted to learn English while he was waiting—a welcome distraction for me—and we met regularly in a tea room to talk about everything except the war. As it turned out, he did most of the talking. He was very intellectual and full of fire. I remember especially his holding forth about Pascal's being an unbeliever—in French of course. He couldn't have learned much English!

I had news of family and friends from Vivou Chevrillon, who sometimes joined me for lunch in a neighborhood crèmerie.[18] Her brother Rémi, seventeen, and a young friend had crossed the Pyrénées without a guide to avoid the risk of betrayal. Once across they were immediately arrested anyway and sent to prison, where they twiddled their thumbs for several months. Through great effort, my brother, Pierre, who was still in Barcelona got them released. They were half-starved and in a piteous state—Spanish prisons were notorious for being overcrowded and filthy. Under Pierre's care Rémi got back on his feet and became a cadet at the Naval Academy in Algeria. By the end of the war he was commanding a dispatch boat on the Aegean Sea.

We later learned that Pierre and Andrée's house had served as a way station for many French people in transit. At the time I'm talking about Andrée was painting a fresco in a chapel near Barcelona, and Pierre had written his first play, *Appollyon,* a visionary nightmare in which humanity was paralyzed by a monstrous tyrant—a mixture of Hitler and the academic dictator Pierre had told me about when I'd seen him in Lyons.

Vivou also reported that Marie-France Geoffroy-Dechaume had disappeared from view and was now working for an underground network escorting Allied pilots to the Spanish border or the Atlantic coast.[19] It was exacting, dangerous work: each of these pilots was a priceless asset in the conduct of the war. On occasion, Vivou's father, Louis, would shelter one or more of them—without hesitation but not without fear. Vivou said he had been very pale when he announced to his wife that he was going to take in pilots. He understood the risks better than young Vivou.

Vivou also brought news of my Aunt Adeline. I've scarcely mentioned her family, the Pelletiers, in this story despite the fact that we were close to them. Aunt Adeline was my father's sister and in ordinary times we saw them often. But times were not ordinary. We were living, as Francis Closon says in his book about his life in the Resistance, "au temps des passions,"[20] and the Pelletiers were Pétainists. Most of their friends were Pétainists. They thought it went without saying that all good French citizens were Pétainists. For us, the reverse was true.

Aunt Adeline and Uncle Henri had experienced the First World War very intensely, Henri as a volunteer in the trenches (he was too old to be drafted), and Adeline working for the Red Cross. Quite naturally, then, they put their confidence in Pétain. In the general collapse of 1940 he became for them the symbol of all those values on which they'd built their lives: patriotism, Christian acceptance of suffering, morality tied to work and discipline, dislike of anything revolutionary or disorderly. Out of loyalty they continued to believe in him. It was only at the time of the great roundups of the Jews in spring, 1942, that they began to see Vichy for what it really was. Yet even then they in no way blamed Pétain.

I rarely went to see Aunt Adeline. Each time I did, I left feeling unhappy with myself—whether we'd clashed or avoided discussion altogether. I was intimidated by her brilliant, mocking, somewhat autocratic mind, a reflex I'd stupidly kept from childhood. She had recently weathered personal trials with great fortitude. In October, 1940, Uncle Henri had been run over by a motorcycle, which dislocated his shoulder and broke his ankle. Immobilized for months, he died in 1942 at the age of ninety. Shortly before that Aunt Adeline herself, at seventy-six, weak and underfed, fell in the street and lay for hours without medical help. She had fractured a hipbone and despite her fragility was operated on. She learned to walk again, but then one day while strolling with her brother Louis, Vivou's father, in the forest at Fontainebleau, she suddenly found she couldn't take another step: her decalcified bones had given out. After that, she lived in an armchair, cared for by her daughters, reading, writing, embroidering, and receiving guests every afternoon—with never a complaint. Her spirit astonished everyone. In fact she wrote copiously—letters, articles, memoirs—and thus avoided brooding over the ruin of her body and the disasters of the day.

Vivou told me that during her most recent visit to Aunt Adeline's, my father, himself bent and shrunk, paid a call. Brother and sister had tacitly agreed not to talk about their physical condition or about the war. Instead, they discussed the Dreyfus affair—another "temps des passions." At the end of the last century, Adeline had taken quite some time to come around to André's view that a retrial was absolutely necessary. More than forty years later Vivou was amazed and amused to see the "passion" with which they still discussed the affair in all its details.

23 Code Service

JANUARY–JUNE, 1944

In early January I moved out of my grim little room near Porte Maillot and went to live with Eliane Frey and her husband, Jean Bichon, on rue Guynemer, near the Jardins du Luxembourg. They had invited me, and I knew I would enjoy living with them because Eliane and I had been close friends for years, sharing Scouting (we were at camp together, you may remember, when the war broke out) and a love of music. Eliane had just given birth to their first child, Anne. I'd met Jean only once, when I'd asked him to take Daniel Ferdinand-Dreyfus into the Protestant student house he directed.

At about this time I was put in charge of the Delegation's Code Service. Captain Drouot helped me assemble a team by turning over a recruit already trained in code work. He recommended Jeanne warmly, mentioning that her father and brother had been deported to Germany. She was young, unobtrusive, and sweet. We called her "Little Jeanne" and had no idea of the adventures she'd been through.[1]

Drouot suggested I add one or two others to my team. This was opportune because my former student Ginette Janin had recently come to me insisting that "no! no!" she could no longer spend her time dissecting earthworms and white rats, or even distributing *Défense de la France* at the medical school where she studied. "There are better things to do just now," she said. "Please tell me what." I presented her to Drouot, and soon Little Jeanne, Ginette, and I were gaily working away. We were later joined by a fourth coder, another of my former students at Collège Sévigné, Françoise Ferré.

Our usual schedule was this. The girls came to my house about nine in the morning, one of them having stopped by our mailbox to pick up the messages from Merlin that were to be decoded. The messages to be encoded—those from the Delegation to Merlin—I would have picked up the night before. We divided up the messages among ourselves and sat down at a big table to work on them. The messages were written on graph paper, one capital letter per box. As we worked, the table got covered with papers. We checked our work together and, at the end of a session, burned all the intermediate drafts in the fireplace. If the messages were urgent, I would work through the night, as would Ginette at her house.

Evenings I would meet a liaison agent from the Delegation, or sometimes one of the secretaries. I had a surprise once when the courier was Janine Daniel-Mayer, a cousin of the Ferdinand-Dreyfuses, and I learned that she typed the messages I coded.[2] A perfect place for our meetings, especially in the spring, was the Jardins du Luxembourg where we sat among all the mothers and babies. The Palais du Luxembourg at the north end of the gardens and the Montaigne Lycée at the south were both occupied by the Luftwaffe. The constant comings and goings of officers and men gave us a curious feeling of security.

Within three or four months BCRA changed the coding system to make it absolutely impossible to break. Small silk handkerchiefs were parachuted in for us, tucked inside ordinary items such as tubes of toothpaste and cigarette packs. These pieces of silk were as fine as they were tough. Each had 120 rows of tiny numbers,[3] and each row of numbers was the key to encoding or decoding one telegram. After using a row, I would take a scissors and snip it off. Then I would burn it, so that an encoded message could be deciphered only by BCRA's Intelligence Service in London, which possessed the only duplicate handkerchief.

There was a small complication with this system: the key to a coded message, rather than being in lines of a poem that we knew by heart, was now written on a material object that could vanish through loss, fire, theft, or Gestapo search. Consequently we were sent several different silk handkerchiefs at a time, each with a different code on it, and we kept these handkerchiefs in different places. I remember I kept two in the false bottom of a beautiful pig leather cigarette case—garnished with precious cigarettes, of course!—that had been parachuted in for this purpose. One was hidden in the organ of the Reformed Church of the Holy Spirit, and another among the hundreds of thousands of documents at the National Archives. Ginette remembers that a great-aunt of hers who lived in a retirement home hid one behind a picture above her bed. All this made our work seem like a game and, for my young colleagues as well as for me, added to the attraction of the good cause.

I recall very few of the messages I worked on because we threw everything away as soon as we were done with it. But I remember the messages got more interesting as the Allies moved to the offensive. A few stand out in my memory; Ginette recalls more. Here is a sample of what we remember:

- The BBC was asked to tell the French people to stop work and observe a minute of silence on a certain day at a certain time. Another time it was asked to request Parisians using the Métro to carry bags or suitcases stuffed with useless documents of all kinds in order to discourage searches.
- There were inquiries about Geneviève de Gaulle, the General's niece, who had been deported to Ravensbrück and whose release the Germans wanted to negotiate. (De Gaulle's response, naturally, was no.)
- Urgent appeals were made for money. The underground, its numbers increasing all the time, was now in desperate financial need: salaries and travel expenses for agents, supplies for the Maquis, publication of underground newspapers, etc.
- In April, 1944, many messages about the future French government. Everything needed to be in place immediately after the Liberation to prevent the Americans (who wanted to install an Allied

government in France as they did in all the countries they occupied) or the Communists (who predominated among the Resistance leaders) from assuming control.

- A request that Pierre Pucheu be sentenced to death.[4]
- A long exchange about whether or not the head of the Communist Party, Maurice Thorez, still in the USSR, should go to Algiers to work with the CFLN. The Communists wanted him to go; de Gaulle thought it premature. The CNR tried to insist—unsuccessfully.[5]
- We encoded news of two terrible Nazi massacres: eighty-six civilians killed in Ascq, a small city in the North, on April 2, and ninety-nine members of the Maquis hanged from the balconies, lamp posts, and trees of Tulle on June 9. (Word of the June 10 massacre of civilians in Oradour-sur-Glane did not go through us.) The BBC broadcast this information all over France.
- Throughout the spring we reported the disappearances, arrests, and deaths of Resistance leaders. I remember encoding the announcement of Brumaire's arrest on February 4 and, six weeks later, the news that the Gestapo, having discovered who he was, had tortured him, and that he, to keep from talking, had committed suicide by throwing himself from a sixth-floor window. (Five months later, after the Liberation, I learned that Brumaire was the ex-journalist Pierre Brossolette,[6] my colleague at Collège Sévigné.) Then Cleante (real name: Jacques Bingen), for whom we had encoded so many messages, disappeared. Later, word came—which we encoded and sent—of his arrest and suicide. It seemed to us the best people were disappearing, one after the other. Who would be left for the Liberation when at last it came?

Messages got longer and more frequent as D-Day approached. The loss of key people required reorganization of the networks, and Merlin had to be consulted about the changes—or perhaps I should say kept informed, because he often didn't answer our messages. If a message was long, it had to be cut into several, even a dozen, smaller telegrams (each one headed with the name of the sender, destination, message number, date, and code mark), because the dispatch time for a telegram could not be more than ten minutes. Otherwise, the radio operators were likely to be detected.

We were under such pressure that I tried to find other coders. I had kept in touch with Marie-Hélène Lefaucheux through a neighbor who worked with her, and that May she sent a friend of hers to me. Marie-Hélène said Mme. Girard needed distraction from agonizing worry about her husband and daughter, both of whom had been deported several months before.[7] Now her son, François, nineteen, had just been arrested.

Mme. Girard brought a new dimension to our group. Though she was obviously older than I, there was something girlish about her laugh, which rang out at the least provocation, and something very touching about her efforts to participate in our strange, brain-twisting work in which a mistake of one letter could render a message unintelligible. But whereas the younger ones were completely absorbed by their task, Mme. Girard was more distant. One could guess her feelings from the expressions that moved across her face—feelings she tried to conceal with her laugh.

Because she couldn't concentrate, Mme. Girard made many mistakes and slowed us down. She decided not to stay on, but our friendship continued long after the war. Dr. Girard, Anise, and François returned from concentration camp, but Dr. Girard's health had been so seriously affected that he did not live long. The Girards' elder daughter, Claire, twenty-three, who had not been arrested, suffered the unluckiest fate. She came to Paris just after the Liberation to celebrate with her mother and friends. Returning to the Oise where she directed a work farm, she was stopped on the road by German soldiers and, with the three young men who had given her a lift in their truck, was shot dead on the spot.

One incident that spring was so out of the ordinary that it remains engraved in my memory. The Bichons' doorbell rang, and I found a couple I didn't know standing there.

"We are Israelites," they said right away. (The Germans had succeeded in hanging so much opprobrium on the word "Jew" that the polite term now was Israelite.)

Were they *agents provocateurs?* I immediately found myself wondering. But the idea vanished as quickly as it had come because their anguish was so visible.

They told me the police had called them in for not wearing the Yellow Star. They had denied being Jews, saying they were Christians.

"Fine," they were told. "You have one week to prove it."

What to do? If convicted, they would be deported. They had to find a church that would certify that they had belonged to it for several years.

I went to see a Protestant minister I had known before the war when he was an especially intrepid Scout camp leader. To my surprise and without hesitation, he refused to lend his church's name to a lie.

"Even to save two lives?" I said.

"Yes," he said.

I next went to see the parish priest of Saint Sulpice. He listened with sympathy and perplexity. He considered the matter for quite a while. I thought perhaps the idea was working its way into his heart.

Finally he said, "But what if they check the records?"

The Bichons tried to help through their contacts—no luck. Every night the unhappy couple came to see if we had succeeded. At Eliane's suggestion we tried forging some certificates ourselves. The result was dubious.

Then suddenly we thought of Pastor Monod, who had given shelter to a code key in the organ of the Reformed Church of the Holy Spirit. That evening our smiling friends were holding indisputable proof of their Christianity—predated baptismal certificates stamped with the seal of the Holy Ghost!

In the beginning of June as the Allied landing drew near, our boss, Alexandre Parodi, whom I knew under the code name Quartus, divided the Code Service into two teams so that if he got cut off from one, he could use the other. I was to stay put, as was Little Jeanne, but I had to send two or three girls to Echarcon, a small village southeast of Paris. Ginette, my right hand, was one of them. From a letter to my sister written shortly before:

G. is my rock, my consolation. She makes me think of Rothery[8] because I can always count on her. She shows a warmth and joy in her work that is marvelous. I don't want to take advantage of her, but I'm on the verge of it most of the time, because everything I ask her to do she does as well as if I'd done it myself—even better. She won't stop until a job is completely done and her attention never wanders. To top it all off, the more I ask of her the happier she is!

But this was no time for regrets. It was D-Day.

Charles Ferdinand-Dreyfus before the war.

Sylvie Geoffroy-Dechaume
with Francis, Orgeval, 1942.

The children on the beach at Port-Blanc, 1942.

Jean Ayral, alias Gautier, code name Pal.

By November 11, 1942, the Germans occupied all of France. A German sentry stands guard in Lyons.
Photo: Document Gamet-Rapho.

Daniel Ferdinand-Dreyfus, alias Marc, before the war.

Geneviève (Ginette) Janin, alias Dominique, 1943.

Jacqueline d'Alincourt, alias Violaine,
shortly before her arrest.

Claire Chevrillon, alias Christiane Clouet, 1943.

The code on a silk handkerchief
(actual size 6 1/2 " × 9").

Pierre Brossolette in London.
Photo: Archives Documents Françaises.

24 *Elation and Sadness*

It was at first a rumor—in a phone call, I think, to the Bichons or to me. But very quickly even Radio-Paris was talking about it, saying of course it was doomed to fail. People on the street were excited and wanted to talk. No one had any details, only tremendous hope. The whole of France was turned toward Normandy.

In the Code Service there was a flood of messages—each urgent, essential. The process of coding accelerated. Bad luck: Jeanne got sick. The others were far away and, worse, burned for the time being by the arrest of a new agent in the Delegation. Again the work fell on me. I worked at the Bichons', my friend Eliane bringing me cup after cup of "coffee" made from grilled barley grain, and doing whatever she could to help. Little Anne, round and pink and calm, was nearby in a wooden cradle trimmed with blue cloth and red ribbons, a comfort for the eyes and spirit.

This time of tremendous elation was also one of worry and sadness for me. In May dear M. Geoffroy had had a double stroke. Despite the lack of trains to the suburbs (most stations had recently been bombed), I went to see him several times at Valmondois—by bicycle, I suppose. I wrote to Antoinette on June 1:

> He was in his deck chair in the courtyard, his face gray with fatigue. He spoke distinctly, despite some difficulty—if not with his usual energy, still with the same perceptiveness and confidence. He no longer torments himself about Antoine, but does about his other two sons. Denis, who is a Milicien,[1] has in fact been wounded.

Since Antoine's deportation to Germany in January, 1944, there had been no sign from him, and Geoffroy was terribly anxious. Then just a short while before, a card from Antoine had arrived, written in German,[2] thanking them for a package received. Though the card was three months old, it gave Geoffroy hope, and his anxiety was transferred to his other sons, Jean-Pierre, twenty-seven, and Denis, twenty-two, both with the Maquis in Corrèze. When Denis was wounded, his family decided not to tell Geoffroy. A letter to my sister, June 24:

I went to Valmondois and M. Geoffroy seemed much better. He was himself once more—all warmth and cheerfulness, increased by his sense of being out of danger. "My little Claire," he said to me, "*I am saved!*" I was so astonished I asked him to repeat it twice. One can't help hoping, but his fragility is frightening. . . . A visit from Jean-Pierre did him a world of good. It appears J. P. is in splendid form and happy with the way things are going. Denis is better now. His accident was nearly fatal, but he's been extremely well cared for. J. P. took care of him alone all through the first night.

A little later I learned that Geoffroy died June 24. "We mustn't forget he saw the Landing and that brought him tremendous hope and happiness," I wrote my sister on July 2.

I am wondering what to tell you about Mme. G. You know how she is—sad, but calm, and splendid in her simplicity and tenderness. It was beautiful weather, the garden full of flowers and fruit, and everything exactly as usual: the meal in the courtyard under the lilacs, everything.

At the end of June the order came through that it was my turn to go out to pasture—I needed some rest. I was transferred south of Paris, to Bures in the Yvette valley, to prepare a house in the village of Gif for Allied and French emissaries en route to Paris. (Why not for de Gaulle? I found myself thinking.)

My memories of this time are confused because I was continually shuttling between Bures-sur-Yvette, Paris, Echarcon, and Gif. Since public transport no longer existed and my bicycle had collapsed, the Delegation gave me a new one. What a blessing to spend long days speeding in silence through warm air!

I first went to a camp near Bures to teach two new girls the coding system. From a letter to my sister:

One of the girls was of noble birth, and a devout Catholic, her ideas narrow and conformist. But she has only good feelings, and she's unfailing in her duty. Actually, the girls are too good: they won't even take a walk unless they've finished all the household chores! And with the shorthand,[3] there isn't a minute free. If I don't toe the mark, they'll do everything for me.

Life at Echarcon in Ginette's group was completely different: tempestuous, the house a mess; we'd often skip lunch and eat twice as much at supper. We'd stroll through the countryside, read in the woods, fish for roach and swim in the nearby pond—and come back at nightfall, singing and carrying water lilies. Add to that homecoming picture some German soldiers watching us. They had taken over the mansion on the estate with the pond, and we couldn't get to our place without crossing in front of them. We had told them we were Parisians fleeing enemy bombs in our neighborhoods of Porte de la Chapelle and Porte des Lilas, both targeted by Allied bombers because of their railroad yards. They watched us pass—not, we thought, without pity and good feelings.

At Gif I lived in a rented house, preparing it for the agents in transit (who never came, such was the speed with which Général Leclerc's Second Armored Division moved to Paris). It was a fascinating place with an old red roof covered with vines and roses, and a wild garden. But inside it was a horror. A couple had lived there for forty years and then hobbled off to an old people's home. Filth was everywhere: mouse droppings, empty bottles, broken chamber pots, papers, debris. The walls were moldy under peeling paper. It took the labor of Hercules to make it ready. When I was finished, I spent a day or two luxuriating in the cleanliness and enjoying a raspberry orgy in the garden. A strange way to fight the enemy!

In Paris, the "little Lambkins"—as Antoinette and I called our parents in our letters[4]—vacillated between anxiety and optimism but always managed to be good-humored. That winter and spring I'd been to see them more often than I had at first thought possible. It seemed to me my mother kept taking on strenuous tasks in distant parts of Paris: ferreting out and standing in line for whatever Antoinette lacked in the way of clothing, books, and games for the children. My father liked to tease her about her efforts on the food front, which were more or less successful. Together, they tried to keep up with the changing military fronts in the USSR, Italy, and the Far East, but the electricity was increasingly cut off and listening to the BBC was difficult (radios with batteries didn't appear until after the war). They had many faithful visitors and, thank God, always a thousand things to say, which spared me having to talk too much about my own life. They still thought I was helping a large family in the country, and this meant I didn't have to explain my arriving with quantities of peas and strawberries, at that time of year the only food found in abundance around Gif.

My parents' anxiety naturally focused on those who were absent.

There had been no word of our cousins Charles and Jacques since their deportations in September, 1942, and July, 1943. I, on the other hand, had received infrequent brief cards in German from Jacqueline, Antoine, Mme. Roudier, Charles Baron, and Denise.

From Paul in his oflag near Dresden letters were rare but his news was good and full of detail. "Paul is always stunningly the same," my sister wrote. "He seems to stay completely himself, which I greatly admire." The thing that did not reassure us about his fate was the leveling of German cities by Allied bombs.

My brother, Pierre, now in Algeria, got a letter to us via the Red Cross. Andrée, his wife, had badly injured her spine while painting a ceiling fresco in Spain. She was flat on her back in a hospital in Blida. Pierre himself had experienced great difficulty finding work in Algiers.

News from Antoinette in Brittany often took as long as news from abroad: two to four weeks. Bombings and sabotage of the railroad lines were so heavy that by May the few trains running carried only German troops. After the Landing, the tracks were cut almost everywhere and nothing moved.

I returned to Paris for good on July 18. One evening shortly before, Suzanne Daniel-Mayer, Lily Ferdinand-Dreyfus's sister, was summoned to the police station for not having drawn a curtain in a lighted room. Because she was Jewish, she was handed over to the Germans and then deported. At the time we were still ignorant enough to hope. But not a word from her or about her ever reached anyone again. She simply disappeared.

Pierre Lefaucheux, who was doing important work for the OCM,[5] was arrested in June, and as I wrote my sister, "Poor Marie-Hélène is very much changed, wavering continually between hope and fear."

The Gestapo came to arrest my friend Grace Brandt at the Welfare Bureau where from the start she had been helping Jews in hiding. She narrowly escaped—she happened to be at the post office at the time. Since she was half Swiss, she was able to take refuge in Switzerland.

Our dear Daniel Ferdinand-Dreyfus was arrested the week before I got to Paris. As promised, I'd spoken on his behalf to the Lefaucheuxes, and thanks to Marie-Hélène he had been working for six months at *Défense de la France.* An underground contact told me he was in la Roquette prison, where visits were permitted. What happiness it was to see him, even in those conditions. I found him changed: he had lost weight and looked more mature. He wasn't worried about himself and was passionately following the progress of the war. The Allies were locked in hard combat in Normandy, but Daniel and I were sure of eventual victory. In fact, there were rumors of an assassination attempt against Hitler. (This was the July 20 plot, which failed.)

Daniel told me how he'd been arrested. On the morning of July 11 he heard that the Gestapo had learned the location of the office of *Défense de la France*. He ran to the office and started burning papers, of which there were many. He was finishing up when the soldiers burst in. He didn't think he'd be deported. "They have other fish to fry," he said, and we embraced with words of hope.

25 *Port-Blanc*

SEPTEMBER, 1943–JULY, 1944

Antoinette's life in Port-Blanc was, as I've suggested, far from easy. She had to make all decisions alone without any family to rely on; she had the care of children aged seven, four, and three who were often sick, sometimes seriously; she had the worry of her imprisoned husband and aging parents; and she had the constant responsibility of providing food for all these people and indeed for others. Her problems became more difficult as the Occupation grew more severe and the Germans sensed their approaching defeat. At this time, too, she had to contend with the meanness and greed of people around her, which was probably the hardest thing of all for her to bear.

Fortunately, she had some good friends and neighbors: the Louis Bougeants with their three teenage sons, who were always ready to lend a helping hand; the Stéphans and their young sons, Maurice and Paulo, in the Small House next door; Mme. Pellerin, on the far side of the garden, with whom Antoinette listened to the B B C; Marie Lelay, the Penvénan grocer and channel for my letters; the three Hamon sisters, one of whom took messages and packages between Port-Blanc and Paris; the Désiré Bellec family, who supplied milk and eggs for the children and bacon for Paul; Marie Perrot, in Tréguier, whose door was always open with real coffee and amusing tall tales told in a Breton accent;[1] and finally the remarkable Charles Fassier, an architect and painter in Plougrescant who never hesitated to walk the nine miles down the beach to give her advice and comfort.[2]

Of course her chief comfort was the children: their sweetness and high spirits, and particularly young André's deep, unspoken understanding way with her. I would also say, throwing modesty aside, that she had my letters, which kept her abreast of everything happening around us in Paris and enabled her to take part in our lives there. And to the list of good things let's certainly add the B B C. Antoinette lived for the news, and after June, 1943, the news was mainly good. The tide had turned: the Russians were advancing, Mussolini fell, the Italian army surrendered, Corsica was retaken, French and American soldiers were fighting side by side up the spine of Italy, Rome was freed. Then at long last came the landing in Normandy.

Rather than try to give the flavor of Antoinette's life secondhand, I prefer to quote passages from her letters.[3] I have taken out all mention of the packages of food—butter, potatoes, beans, eggs, and chickens— she sent to our parents and me and to my friends in prison (Denise, Charles Baron, Antoine). I've also left out her many requests for things for the children, which my mother and I tried to satisfy.

September 6, 1943:

The children have whooping cough, and I can't sleep at night—and then I get caught up in a kind of agony of physical tension that my mind can't control and I'm not good for anything the next day.

It's too bad they want to separate Denise's children, when she especially said she didn't want them to be separated.[4]

September 17:

The whooping cough is getting better. Soisette looked very small in my big bed, with her disheveled hair around her little face, all red from the fever. . . . You cannot imagine how much people's meanness weighs on me at this moment.

October [no date]:

Overjoyed to have your letter with the wonderful news about Sauvageon.[5] I'm so glad she's changed jobs. To tell the truth, I was thinking it was pretty obvious her life didn't mean much to her any more—so much so that I thought she might finally marry Gerard! . . . [6]

Imagine how surprised I was to find my little Ariel[7] running in the narrow gutter at the top of the house! I was so frightened I didn't dare call to him. When I later begged him not to do it again, he said calmly, "Why not? I'm not afraid to do it, and the others are. I just wanted to see if the drainpipe was blocked up with pine needles." He told me he'd done it several times before, and when I saw him way up there on the roof, he did seem perfectly at ease, even joyful. I'm sure just reading this makes you as dizzy as it does me. The next time the pipe's blocked, though, I think I'll let him go up again—like a Spartan mother! What do you say to that?[8]

October 19:

It is nine at night and I'm writing in little André's room. He is propping himself up, half-awake, on his elbow and saying, "Oh Mommy, if only Santa Claus could bring me a bird! I'd take care of it every day!" The two boys are in the same room now, and tomorrow morning I will find them both in the same bed, laughing like little monkeys.

November 4:

I'm swamped—swamped with things to do, and trying to make order out of disorder. A.'s schoolwork takes precedence.[9] I do everything I can to help him enjoy it—the drawers are overflowing with cut-outs and drawings done by my three monkeys. . . .

As for the authorization papers for sending things to Paris—when they finally arrive, they immediately get mislaid among all the other papers scattered around! To further complicate things, the forms they send are not accepted by the Lannion railroad people—that is today's No. 1 problem! And now the beans for Aunt Hedwige are in limbo somewhere—it's hopeless!

The children are in very good spirits; their noise and foolishness is incredible, especially at night. Titi is getting stronger and bigger and becoming quite witty—unhappily he knows it! A. is inundated with grammar and arithmetic homework. This grieves me because we can't do anything interesting as a result. With the best will in the world, he forces himself to concentrate—which is difficult for him. He and I together must make our peace with this system, which, alas, all French children have to go through.

January 2, 1944:

We had André's examinations before Christmas. What torment! Essays morning and night for three days! The spelling was outrageous: "Jewelius Seezher" for Julius Caesar. The feminine of rooster? "A roostress," etc.

[Undated]:

Little A. dropped from third to second grade. It is a great relief. Everything is now so much easier. Soisette is learning to read with irrepressible joy. She gloats over each new letter and laughs with pleasure at the words she understands.

January 9:

My dear Mother, what is going on now in Paris? I'm always afraid you're being bombed or that you'll fall down the Métro stairs in the dark. . . . [After a long recitation of domestic difficulties]: I wish I were up in a cloud and away from this country of grubbiness and gossip. . . . The fine weather compensates, and the children gather primroses and daisies. The gorse is teeming with promising buds.

January 18:

From what I can tell, Paul hasn't lost his taste for the joys of this world. He loves looking at the frost on trees, the sun setting, reading books, and the prospect of some things to come—chiefly the pleasures he can bring to others. . . .

Louise was married[10] and our three little ones led the procession, splendid in front of the whole world. Soisette was so proud! Titi was as red as a beet—and as proud as his sister. André, however, was unhappy and didn't want to be in front! It was Dutch treat, so we went only to "Max," as Titi says, meaning Mass, because at the banquet each of us would have had to pay 200 francs. Louise wore beautiful blue feathers and a little purple veil, which looked adorable in her red hair. The bridegroom didn't dare look at me. The mothers were very dignified in their grand shawls.

February 2 and 3:

After Friday there will be no more passenger service on trains to St. Brieuc. What will I do if something comes up and I need to get to Paris? Hopefully they will take me on a freight.

Then came the drama of little Maurice Stéphan's death. Yvonne, his mother, had been living in the Small House for several months and was in and out of Antoinette's life a lot. The father was basically absent, making upsetting drunken appearances every now and then. But he was always voluble about his patriotic exploits, whether or not they were true. For instance, one day—and this turned out to be true—he boasted that he put on his army uniform and picked up a knife to go kill two or three Boches at the Kommandantur's. He started by rushing over to our neighbors', the Marchands, and trying to enlist their oldest son, Charles. Charles was so horrified that he got another neighbor,

Joseph Jégou, and the two of them cornered Stéphan and led him back to the Small House by force.

Maurice, the Stéphans' five-year-old, caught cold, which developed into bronchitis, then pneumonia. The doctor decided it wasn't serious. Yvonne trusted him, but the illness rapidly got worse and the little boy died on February 9.

Antoinette felt very guilty that she had not been more forceful in urging Yvonne to get another doctor's opinion. The whole Stéphan family arrived from Quimper and stayed several days because they had no immediate way of getting back to their village. Antoinette put up a good front and took them all in.

February 18:

If you could see poor Yvonne, I wonder what you would say to her. She doesn't stop crying—doesn't stop. I never saw such sorrow. . . .

On New Year's Eve there was a tremendous migration over our heads—looking up from the garden, we counted 400 of them. Then one of them burst into flames and we realized what was going on.[11] It was too much for André. That and the death of little Maurice upset him very much, but his faith is complete and unshaken—quite marvelous.

André's schoolwork goes better and better. He had 12 A's in one week. What do you think of that?

March 6:

Many changes around here this week. They've mined the fields near the shore wherever the ground is level. The poor Pratts, who had just sowed a large field of potatoes, had it and another one as well taken from them. With great reluctance they've decided to sell their cows because they can't feed them anymore.

The Salious can no longer get water from their spring, and we don't dare walk the dog for fear he'll step on a mine. Everyone's talking about evacuation, but I'm worried about being caught on the road in the crowd. I think it's worth the risk staying behind—if they don't force us to go. We're better off here than anywhere else. Though lots of people are packing suitcases, no one is taking the first step. If you really think I should leave, telegraph "Yes." . . .

I'll be able to get the clogs[12] as soon as I get my hands on some mentholated spirits—an exchange.

March 13:

Paulo[13] has had a fever—over 104—and his father sent a telegram to Quimper: "All hope of saving second grandson gone." Yesterday, three relatives from Quimper arrived, and three from Pleumeur, and the little one was surrounded by six strangers. You know Paulo is Paul's godson, so I felt I could insist they not tire the child. . . .

Meanwhile, I've invited the Quimperois to meals. They have hundreds of stories to tell, many of them quite off-color. When I think of everything that André hears, I wonder what the effect on him will be. . . .

The little ones pretend they're grown-ups: "My husband is in Germany, Monsieur!" "Oh then, Madame, would you marry me? *My* wife is in prison!" etc. . . .

What a nightmare to think of little Kisse walking around with that open wound.[14]

March 14:

Doctor Cousin just left. Paulo has "an infectious type of 1918 flu." There is hope, but his life is in danger. They have created an abscess on his leg to get rid of the germs from the rest of his body, and the wound prevents him from moving, so he huddles in one position and howls. Oh darling, it is too terrible. You can imagine what Yvonne is going through. . . .

Obviously, this is an epidemic, and I'm afraid for the children. I don't want to desert Yvonne, but I also want to get away. There are several other new cases started, so there's no doubt the terrible microbe is here among us. I know of course that travelling one might catch something worse and risk carrying it to Lily,[15] so I won't go, finally. I'm telling you this because I tell you everything that goes through my mind. . . .

Quite a few Russians have arrived at Penvénan and here, at the Grand Hotel on the beach. They are wearing blue uniforms. They are not prisoners—they're armed.[16]

March 24:

The house is still full of sunshine from the surprise of the week. . . .[17] The arrival of such a great package has changed my life! All that I hope is that it didn't seriously deprive anyone of anything.

March [later]:

I'm writing you, sheltered from the west wind on a moor covered with gorse and smelling of apricot; the weather is splendid. Paulo is *fine*, and all goes well. He got through the critical moment—the lancing of the abscess did the trick—but a six-year-old boy died of the same thing the day before yesterday.

The mining has stopped with the Goasmeurs.[18] The Russians sing as they ride along on their low carts pulled by frisky horses, little foals following behind.

March [no date]:

Marie Lelay is here; she arrived the day before yesterday after four months in the hospital. I had the pleasure of drinking a coffee with her. She was standing, but much changed—bent, shrunk, her eyes very large, her hair white. It pained me to see her like that. The doctor told her, "It is your morale that has saved you." She said, "It is my faith."

Aside from that, life is always the same: gossip and more gossip!

April 1:

Paulo had a terrible relapse during which he changed completely. There was suddenly nothing left of him except eyes and a very weak voice which said "Mama."

April [no date]:

[Antoinette caught the flu herself.] After five days of high fever, I'm still a little "drunk"—but that's all. Cupping glasses administered by Jean Stéphan (!!) saved the day. I was in a state of complete collapse. André came in often to see if I wanted anything. Soisette brought flowers, pictures, and pretty handkerchiefs—everything she could think of. Titi felt sad at seeing me but never thought—never—of coming to see me! Together, the three did all the shopping.

April 23:

We're having a spell of bleu léger.[19] The mist comes and goes, cold and penetrating. The woods are icy. Paulo is cheerful; he plays, moves his leg, but still is painfully thin and has no strength to talk except in a very low voice. "Why are you talking so low, Paulo?" "Because I'm hungry."

Rumors abound.[20]

April 27:

We had a fierce naval battle behind Saint-Gildas[21] the other night. All Port-Blanc went out into the fields (we didn't).[22] It's not advisable to eat fish just now!

April 29 [letter from André]:

My dear Grandpapa, I wish you a very happy birthday and the coming year with you know what.[23]

Charlotte and Albert had a big contest with tennis balls and Charlotte won hands down. Mommy supervised their play.[24] Will there be much fruit at Montfort this year?

1 great big hug for Granny and for you 190,000 kisses.

André. Happy Birthday!

May 12 [Antoinette again]:

I am writing you with the sound of saws sawing.[25] Every now and then there's a big whoosh of air: it's artillery being fired from Ile Marquer. Poor Rik hides his tail between his legs and Soisette turns white.

There is still the evacuation question, and I'm hesitant, fearing panic on the roads at the last minute. Our trench is splendid—it has become a real contest around here. Ours is covered with tree trunks, branches and soil. The children will have fun playing in it later.

May 20:

I'm running all the time now. I'm having a trailer made in case we evacuate. And I'm reluctantly giving trees to the local people. I vacillate, and then they take advantage of my weakness. X told me he had to bring four trees to the occupying army, but then he sold them to a woman living near the Semaphore for 1000 francs. I wonder if there are two honest people in Port-Blanc.

[About Jacqueline d'Alincourt's deportation.] It is magnificent that she's managed things so that her mother isn't anxious. What letters she writes! I only have to think of her to put things in their proper perspective and make all the annoyances of life in P. B. vanish.

May 30:

I don't know how it is that I can't find a minute in the day to write; at night, of course, I'm plunged in darkness. Our electricity has been completely cut off. Are you really going to spend all summer in the stifling, half-starved city? . . . And Mother without an elevator?[26] Charlotte doesn't come! We have no news. The mail arrives only three times a week—if that. Time passes slowly. But I've met two Italian prisoners[27] who come over here to cut wood, and I reminisce with them about our trips to Italy: Portofino, Porte Vecchio, Santa Margarita, Firenze, San Giminiano, not forgetting Bellagio, the blue lake—they know it all. They are fine young men, gallant and charming. One of them is so good-looking, with olive skin and fine features. He makes advances, but is spurned! These poor souls have a lot to complain about; their position is impossible. Naturally, they've gotten to know the Café Gérard in Penvénan and they love going there.[28]

Soisette thinks only of work and reads all alone, two or three times a day. She is so good! Titi becomes lazier and lazier and is incapable of putting on his coat right side out. But his cheerfulness is a tonic.

Antoinette then told a long story about a shiny object that several people had seen fall from an Allied Mosquito into the pine woods. On the night she wrote her letter André had walked the undergrowth looking for it until 11 P.M. Such objects were seen falling from the sky several times. Were they messages? Army secrets?[29]

Quite a story, isn't it: shiny things falling from the sky! And typical of the country. Rumors, rumors—what doesn't one hear?! A week ago, Rome was taken! The Allies had landed on the Channel Islands! They'd landed in Belgium! An armistice was on the verge of being signed! . . . But all this talk doesn't impress me. I don't believe anything anymore. Real news arrives despite the rumors.[30]

June 15 [nine days after the Normandy landing]:
I've just learned I can try to write you—they're putting together relays of bicycles to carry the mail. . . .

I won't hide from you the fact that I'm very anxious about our parents. I'm sure that in this heat Mother will simply give up going into crowded restaurants, where she might find something to eat, and Father will be reduced to wandering around the apartment looking for crumbs. Except for that worry, everything is fine here—the weather, the beach, dips in the sea, André and Soisette's work, which is going well. We can hear the battle, not quite 120 miles away as the crow flies. It's far off, but continuous. We heard it right from the first day, and could distinguish between attack and counterattack. It is very exciting, of course, but not at all frightening.

There's a great deal of air traffic overhead. People are telling more bunk than ever. . . . I've done nothing but talk about us, but what else could I do besides repeat the daily chatter? My heart is too full to speak of all that's happening, or going to happen.

July 15:
I cannot describe to you the relief your little letter of June 12 brought me! It took a month to come. I've also had a very courageous letter from Mother, but I gather they eat only vegetables and a bit of fruit. . . .

Poor dear Geoffroy. I loved and admired him with all my heart. I thought of him so often during the war and always with a surge of desire to see him. . . .

Mme. Auffret is well, but there are some bad typhoid cases in her region—worse than Jacqueline's.[31]

We had a card from Paul dated June 8 with very good news. He is avidly following the communiqués. . . .

I would give anything to embrace you and send you a pound of butter! I confess I scarcely dared open the letters from you and Mother because I was so afraid of bad news! What patience we must have.

26 *Liberation in Brittany*

JULY–AUGUST, 1944

It wasn't until the first half of August that Brittany and with it our little towns of the north coast—Tréguier, Pleubian, Plougrescant, Penvénan, Port-Blanc, and Lannion—were liberated. Since I wasn't there, and since Antoinette didn't write for a long while because there was no mail service, I'm going to report what local people who lived through that time told me about it while I was gathering notes for this chapter in 1985.

These people,[1] now well along in years, were eager to talk about things that had happened when they were young and that are forgotten today. The events they describe are typical, I think, of what occurred throughout the countryside in France at the time.

In most of these events the central role was taken not by our liberators, who usually kept to the main roads, but by the Maquis.

The Breton Maquis were small groups of young men who, since 1943, had been hiding in the hills and forests of the interior of the province (the coast was too heavily patrolled), fleeing the conscription that would have sent them to work in Germany. They were untrained, badly provisioned and scarcely armed, so their actions—ambushes, arms seizures, sabotage of the railway—were sporadic and strategically unimportant. In addition they lived in constant danger of betrayal, because any neighbors suspected of helping them were exposed to German reprisals that ranged from the burning down of their houses, to deportation, or even execution. So while the Maquis were supported by many people, they were by no means popular with all. And when caught, they were treated as terrorists: summarily executed or tortured to death. Here are several examples of what happened in our neighborhood:

In early July, a month after the landing in Normandy, someone betrayed the 120 Maquis who were hiding on a large farming estate in isolated Coat-Nevenez, and 800 German troops launched a surprise attack against them. Fortunately, as the Germans were approaching the manor house, their vehicles got stuck in the mud, and a great uproar of shouting and swearing ensued. Somebody ran to warn the Maquis. The Germans were met with heavy gunfire. In the battle that followed, many Germans and eleven members of the Francs-Tireurs Maquis were killed. Most of the young Bretons managed to escape, carrying their wounded. The old manor house burned for three days.

At about this same time, six young Maquis near Plougrescant were also betrayed. They disappeared, their bodies later found between Penvénan and Camlez. (A monument in Beg-Vilin commemorates their deaths.)

Among those betrayed that month, perhaps the most innocent was Louis Maillot, twenty-one, the brother of a Penvénan grocer we knew well. Louis had just graduated from a school for children of sailors lost at sea and won a scholarship to prepare for the Naval Academy. While home on vacation, he decided to help some of his boyhood chums who belonged to a neighboring Maquis. On July 26 he was making bread for them at a farm near Lanvollon with a baker and another young man when the Gestapo came to the door. Louis and his two associates were tortured, then thrown into the oven. Their screams were heard for a very long time, his sister Yvette Guélou told me.

After General Patton's forces broke through at Avranches on August 1, the German units stationed in Brittany, fearing they'd be cut off from the rest of the army, began to retreat east. This was the moment for which London had been saving the Breton Maquis: they would help the Allies turn the German retreat into a rout.

On the night of August 3 British and French staff officers parachuted onto a moor near Kerien to provide liaison between the Maquis and the Allies. (A monument in Kerien commemorates this event.) Among the officers was our çousin Claude Boillot, alias Major Drinkwater,[2] and welcoming them was our friend from Plougrescant, Charles Fassier,[3] at the head of his own Maquis.

The Maquis were given the battle plan. The Americans, in tanks and armored cars, would move forward with all possible speed, through Rennes and across the peninsula. The Maquis would harass the Germans on foot: take out train tracks, dynamite roads and bridges, ambush trucks, and mop up the stragglers.

The American divisions roared across the Breton peninsula while the Germans attempted to slip through the American lines, harassed on all sides by the Maquis. Thousands of Germans were captured. The Allies were stopped only at the port cities of Brest, Lorient, and Saint-Nazaire, which served the German fleet, especially the dreaded U-boats, and were heavily fortified. Brest surrendered only after a three-week seige during which the whole town was leveled by American bombs and artillery fire. People still speak of the worst misfortune: 350 French civilians burned alive on September 9 in the Sadi Carnot bomb shelter. At Lorient and Saint-Nazaire, the Germans didn't surrender until the end of the war.

In Port-Blanc, when it became obvious that the German occupation was going to end, tension and danger increased. People stayed home unless they absolutely had to get food. Most of the stores were closed, including the bakeries, so there was no bread. My sister biked to the mill on the Guindy River to buy flour. Breton crepes and potatoes replaced bread as the staple—according to the children, a distinct improvement.

As always, Antoinette kept the young ones cheerful. She burrowed through chests of drawers and unearthed some old blue, white, and red material. She and the children made it into a superb flag they hid in the false bottom of a dresser.

That July, the Germans forbade the Port-Blanc fishermen to put out to sea. Their boats were tied up in an inlet at the bottom of a nearby field. Eventually all the boats from the villages between Bugueles and Trestel were towed there, anchored, and disarmed—forty boats in all, the fisherman Jean Tanguy remembers. Then the fishermen were told not to go near the harbor. A machine gun was set up on the rock overlooking it.

One day the fisherman Jean Ollivier rushed into my sister's house to tell her "they" were throwing grenades at the boats and had set them on fire. Antoinette was horrified. In fact little damage was done. The Germans, in their haste, were careless. They threw grenades at the boats from the shore, but the sea was high and some of the boats sank quickly, extinguishing their fires, while the boats farthest out were not hit at all. Young Louis Bougeant watched the whole thing from the distance and ran to put out the fires as soon as the Germans turned their backs. He was able to save several boats, among them the one belonging to Jean Tanguy on which he was cabin boy.

What was going to happen next? Would the houses and woods be burned? Antoinette sent her children to the Désiré Bellecs, whose farm was off the beaten track. The children were delighted at this turn of events and carried their little bundles as if going on a holiday.

Antoinette's neighbors Viviane and Ginette Hamon, also warned by Jean Ollivier, took their very old and very sick father, a few necessities, and their most precious possessions to a quarry at the bottom of the garden, saying they would live there until things quieted down.

But the night after the burning of the boats the Germans decamped, noiselessly. They blew up only one house—a big one on the Pointe du Royau used for stocking ammunition. By morning they were completely gone. When people realized this, there was an explosion of joy. They ran through the village making sure their friends knew. The church bells rang. Flags appeared. The Hamon family had made an enormous flag, and a young boy climbed up to hang it from the mast on the Semaphore Lighthouse. People rushed into the buildings the Germans had occupied for the last four years: the Grand Hôtel, the Hôtel de la Plage, the large private house that had served as the Kommandantur, and the houses they'd lived in. The portraits of Hitler hanging everywhere were torn up with fury and joy, and burned with piles of German papers. Excitedly, people retrieved their confiscated radios and furniture and other belongings.

A box of ammunition turned up. People decided it should be carried to Penvénan, three miles away, and given to the Patriot Maquis. The next morning a joyful throng started off. Captain Guillou, a school teacher, had arranged a celebration banquet for everyone at a Penvénan restaurant. Jean Tanguy and a friend carried the ammunition box. Mr. Rabache, a refugee from another part of France and little known in town, was wearing a belt of machine-gun bullets. The party was halfway there, when—stupefaction, horror, a sudden wavering in the ranks—a column of German troops appeared before them, marching toward Port-Blanc! The Germans were returning because the Maquis had done its work too well: the bridges along the route had been destroyed.

Total chaos. Port-Blanc's people ran every which way. Mr. Rabache was immediately shot dead. Jean Tanguy slipped down a side path and hid the ammunition box under a bush.

The citizens of Penvénan already knew the Germans were back—to get to Port-Blanc from the southeast you have to go through Penvénan—and they had rushed home, bolted their doors, and watched from behind curtains while the Germans tramped up and down the streets, shirts open, shouting and pointing guns at the windows. Since no one did anything to stop them (including the armed Patriots, later criticized for hiding rather than fighting), the Germans took over the restaurant and boisterously ate the celebration meal.

In Port-Blanc the flags disappeared, and everyone lay low, fearing reprisals. There were reprisals, but not in our district.

The Germans soon left for good.

A day or two later news spread that an "American landing" was taking place in the bay of Saint-Michel-en-Grève, and Antoinette and André biked the twenty miles to see it. It was a radiant summer day, not a cloud in the sky, and the vast stretch of sand swarmed with strange vehicles and young Americans—black for the most part—unloading arms, supplies, and food for the American army in amazing quantities. Huge warships bringing more of everything steamed tranquilly in and out of the bay.

The entire countryside had come out to watch and rejoice. The French and the Americans exchanged shouts, laughter, embraces, pidjin language, eloquent gestures. The very air was euphoric.[4]

But the bad times were far from over. Antoinette would have another hard winter in Port-Blanc waiting for the war to end and her husband to come back.

27 The Liberation of Paris

LATE JULY–AUGUST 24, 1944

I returned to Paris from Gif in mid-July and as the Liberation drew near had more coding than ever. Little Jeanne was well again and looked refreshed, but she was still fragile and so worked at home. Ginette Janin stayed in Echarcon near a transmitting team until just before the Liberation. Thus I was working alone, going out only for lunch at a neighborhood crèmerie, to meet liaison agents, and occasionally to drop in on my parents.

We didn't really know much about the Allied advance. The German communiqués printed in the French press rarely mentioned it, and the BBC was of course silent for security reasons. Despite this and despite shortages of all the necessities—food, electricity, transport, mail—optimism prevailed. Hope united us. We felt a joyful complicity, a feeling of connectedness, even with strangers in the street.

The fierce battle in Normandy had lasted almost two months, until the Americans broke through at Avranches. After that they came quickly across the plain, taking Rennes, Le Mans, Alençon, Chartres, then splitting their forces and taking Melun and Orléans to the south of Paris, and Dreux and Mantes to the west. From the Caen-Falaise area, the British advanced more slowly toward Rouen. The largest Free French unit, Général Leclerc's Second Armored Division, renowned for having crossed the Sahara from Chad to the north of Libya, landed in Normandy August 1 and was fighting under Allied command. By August 12, the Germans were everywhere in retreat.

When would liberation come to Paris? Our hopes were at a desperate pitch. Rumors had it that the Allies were very near; rumors confirmed these rumors. But Eisenhower didn't want to use his forces fighting for the capital and then have to stay on to keep order among the factious and excitable French. He would skirt Paris to the north and south, and pursue the fleeing enemy to Berlin.

Of course we knew nothing of Eisenhower's plans. But we could see the "Verdigris"[1] were getting ready to pull out. I remember trucks stacked with furniture and packages lined up in front of the Hotel Lutétia. People stopped to look mockingly at the pillage.

"The Exodus is beginning again," someone muttered. "In reverse. Now it's their turn."

A few irritated Krauts leveled their guns at us. Slowly we moved on.

The same thing was happening in front of most of the other fine buildings in the city.

Two or three days later German trucks, covered with branches of dead leaves and full of stone-faced soldiers, rattled down the boulevard Saint-Michel. Many of the trucks were rolling on their rims. They were followed by German ambulances crowded with the wounded. Heat, dust, din. Next came the tanks, also covered with branches and bristling with guns pointed in every direction. As these behemoths advanced, the boulevard emptied.

Were the Germans going to be allowed to depart unmolested?

The story of the Paris insurrection has been told many times. I saw less of it than most people because I was usually shut inside, coding. I kept (though I wasn't supposed to) the texts of about fifteen of the last messages I coded, and they give an idea of the situation in Paris that August. But you will need to use your imagination to appreciate the exaltation and anguish, the bloodshed and death, that lie beneath their telegraphic brevity.[2]

August 17:

Belladone[3] to Interior,[4] COMIDAC[5] and General Koenig.[6]

Paris situation is as follows: all police on strike, railway strike spreading, post office strike beginning.[7] Strikes in certain essential services, water and gravedigging, to be stopped or reduced.

CNR, deliberating today, unanimously favors strike extension. . . . At my request, CNR will meet every day. . . . Hope thus to contain situation and gain time. Serious threat of bloody reprisals.

Electricity mainly off, Métro stopped, streets continuously full of people, gas suspended, food supply difficult. Population excited by expectation of immediate liberation. German looting of occupied buildings obvious from endless passage of overloaded vans. All this creates dangerous situation if liberation not at hand.

Essential . . . to appeal for calm . . . to emphasize that order for national uprising given to one part of France does not yet apply to Paris and suburbs. . . . Despite more and more difficult conditions, population should not . . . take part in any irresponsible action.

August 17:

Oronte[8] to BCRA for Interior, Massigli[9] and General Koenig.

Agreement between Nordling,[10] Swedish Consul General, on behalf of several neutral countries, and Militarbefehlshaber[11] in France with Commandant of Greater Paris.[12] Nordling, assisted by French Red Cross, to take immediate charge of all political detainees in prisons, hospitals, concentration camps in Paris region, and of all evacuation trains going to all destinations.

Almost certainly there was an additional telegram, which I have lost, that set forth the counterpart agreement: all German soldiers in French hospitals were to be released and not considered as prisoners.

August 18:

Belladone to COMIDAC.

Situation in Paris as follows: rioting last night with gunfire at various points in city. Situation generally tense. CNR deliberates tonight on insurrection order proposed by CPL.[13] Strikes continue and spread. Resistance opinion and large majority of population will be humiliated if German troops leave Paris without participation of Paris FFI[14] in battle. Because of situation created by strike of police and public services, I urge General Koenig hasten Paris occupation.

August 18:
Belladone to COMIDAC and General Koenig.
Highest Priority.
Commando operations in Paris started at night. Uprising may break out any day. Situation requires occupation by French or Allied troops as soon as possible.

August 18:
Belladone to COMIDAC and General Koenig.
Immediate.
More details Paris situation: many bloody incidents provoked by excitement of population, nervous German troops, and Gestapo provocations. Sporadic shooting last night, notably Place Odéon, Place Médicis, in front of Gare du Nord, Boulevard de la Chapelle, Boulevard Barbès. Place de la République SS fired machine-guns, anti-aircraft guns. Shots fired at German troops on Boulevard Bonne Nouvelle; latter burned house . . . and café. . . . All those trying to flee were machine-gunned. Numbers of other victims rue Saint-Denis and Faubourg Saint-Denis. Rue Rivoli this morning, for no reason, German truck opened fire killing woman. Towards noon in front Hotel de Ville, demonstration by postal clerks on strike, marching, singing Marseillaise, International, carrying French, English, American flags.

August 18:
Delegation to Interior.
Rail workers Paris region on strike since August 12 . . . lying on tracks, unbolting them, thus preventing drivers, electricians from working.

August 19:
Belladone to COMIDAC, General Koenig.
Absolute Priority.
This morning police on strike occupy Préfecture[15] and police stations. General unrest having started, CNR and CPL have given the insurrection order. . . . Préfecture under German attack since afternoon. . . . Tonight Militarbefehlshaber threatens to bomb district. . . . Have asked Colonel IS[16] to cable Allied Command requesting immedi-

ate Allied occupation Paris. Same urgent request sent by messenger. I request it again directly from you now to avoid possible reprisals. Believe mood of population would not have allowed delay of insurrection order. Would have caused break between population and Delegation. Present situation dangerous.

August 20:
Belladone to General de Gaulle.
Absolute Priority.
CNR Board meeting yesterday unanimously asks you come immediately to Paris soon as capital liberated.

August 20:
Belladone to COMIDAC. 8 A.M.
Overnight reports favorable. Attack on Préfecture has ended. Hotel de Ville, Interior Ministry occupied by Resistance. Many Germans left last night. Fewer German troops in evidence this morning.

August 21:
Belladone to General de Gaulle.
Very urgent.
Again I ask occupation Paris soon as possible. Insurrection launched Saturday, now slowed for two days by truce[17] very favorable to Resistance, which can't last beyond tonight. Battle seems to me unavoidable tomorrow all over Paris with tragically disproportionate means.

Undated:
COMAC[18] to General Koenig.
In view of imminent violent battle in Paris, COMAC, H.Q. of PL region,[19] in agreement with Belladone and Arc,[20] extremely urgently request that you:
    first, have Allied aircraft mount all-out attack on German columns heading to Paris;
    second, send airborne troops as close to Paris as possible with anti-tank weapons to support FFI in Paris;
    third, drop parachutes with manageable containers of weapons, all kinds, especially anti-tank. Drop even in middle of Paris. Immediate retrieval by FFI certain;
    fourth, a nucleus of 35 to 50 thousand men[21] armed and fighting with improvised weapons. Hundreds of thousands men ready to fight awaiting arms.

August 22:
Oronte to BCRA.
Parachute drop urgently needed on Célestin barracks Fourth Arron-
dissement, corner Boulevard Henri Quatre and Morland. Direction of
drop south-north. Distance Notre-Dame 1000 yards east. Drop possible
by day.[22]

August 22:
Belladone to General de Gaulle.
Very urgent and important.
Fear preceding cables about Paris situation not received. After three
days fighting Resistance occupies all public buildings. Representatives
Vichy regime arrested or in flight. Authority of Provisional Government
completely recognized by population. Fighting continues. Despite magnificent Resistance victory, fast arrival Allied troops still imperative because insufficient weapons. Paris population disappointed to hear no
echo this great success on BBC.

As is obvious, Parodi put great emphasis on getting the Allies to Paris
before the Germans could crush the insurrection. What may not be
quite so obvious was his fear that the Communists, under cover of the
uprising, would seize power before de Gaulle arrived. As Delegate of the
Provisional Government, Parodi had to maneuver in such a way that
the unity of the Resistance—which meant the unity of France under de
Gaulle—was preserved. No less important, he had to try to save Paris
from German bombs and artillery. He could not prevent the insurrection from starting before he wanted it to, but at least he could try to
slow it down and thus gain time for the Allies and de Gaulle to arrive.
The truce Parodi mentioned to de Gaulle on August 21 did just this.
It had been worked out on August 19 between him and the German
Commander in Paris, General von Choltitz, through the mediation of
Swedish Consul General Nordling. At first it dealt only with the Paris
Préfecture, which the police, who had been on strike since August 15,
were holding with very few arms against a threatening German tank
and artillery attack. The next day, August 20, the truce was extended to
all of Paris.
The truce meant that public buildings occupied by the FFI would
not be attacked; that captured FFI members would be treated as prisoners of war (until then they'd been considered terrorists and immediately
executed); and that French fire trucks, confined to their stations by the
Germans since the start of the insurrection, would again be allowed to

operate, which meant they could put out fires caused by the fighting or those deliberately started by the Germans. In return, German troops would not be attacked until they had completely evacuated the capital. The truce was announced via loudspeakers on cars that cruised the streets all Sunday afternoon, August 20.

I learned about the terms of the truce first-hand that day when I saw a car of exuberant FFI brandishing their arms, followed by a car of impassive German officers. I was both surprised and relieved because the messages I'd been coding over the last three days had given me terrible forebodings of violence.

That same evening, I had a rendezvous with a courier in Bon Marché Square to pick up the cables I was to code. The courier was Mozart, a Delegation secretary whose real name was Jeanne Boitel. At the time a well-known actress, Jeanne was a cheering sight: beautiful, gay as a lark, and often boldly dressed in blue, white, and red—as though she were an incarnation of the French Republic. No one ever would have believed her to be an underground agent.

I remember I sat on a bench a long time waiting for Jeanne. I looked forward to her explanation of the unexpected truce. When she finally appeared, she was very upset. Parodi—de Gaulle's personal representative in France, the number one man in the Delegation—his sister, and two assistants had been arrested. There had been a brief phone call to the Delegation reporting this. Then silence. Everyone was in anguish trying to imagine what so big a loss would mean at this crucial moment.

The next day we learned—with what relief!—that Parodi had talked his way free of the Gestapo. Here is what happened. About 2 P.M. Sunday, while Parodi was driving around to verify the truce, a group of German soldiers standing in front of the War Ministry stopped his car and forced everyone out. The car was searched and Resistance documents found. The car's occupants, hands raised, were led inside the Ministry. Parodi decided to play his trump card. "We are the leaders of the Resistance," he said. "I am the Delegate of General de Gaulle's government and a minister of that government. A truce with General Von Choltitz was drawn up this morning. I demand to see him. I refuse to be arrested."

A confused trip across the city brought them first to a nondescript villa in Saint-Cloud that had been transformed into a military court, and then to von Choltitz's headquarters in the Hotel Meurice on the rue de Rivoli. A long argument, polite but tough, followed. About 7 P.M.

the prisoners were set free and, with Consul General Nordling, who had been present at the interview, drove off in a car flying the Swedish flag.

But that Sunday evening Mozart and I knew none of this. We sat on the park bench stunned by the magnitude of the arrest. It was getting late; there were only a few minutes left before curfew—not enough time to get back to Eliane and Jean Bichon's.[23] I suddenly remembered I'd heard that Evelyne Garnier—our friend who alerted my mother whenever there was to be a roundup of Jews—had just moved in nearby, and I quickly went to knock at her door.

As soon as Evelyne saw me, she understood that something bad had happened. Of course I could spend the night. Half of it we spent talking. Evelyne was a member of the NAP,[24] which had launched most of the strikes, and she had a great deal to tell me, including her own near-miss with the Gestapo one morning just before seven—the usual time for arrests at home. She was saved, she told me, by the Virgin Mary, whose statue she seized and pressed to her heart while the Gestapo kicked at her door, demanding that she open it. When she didn't, they dashed down the stairs to get something with which to force it (this according to the concierge who saw the whole thing). At just that moment the air raid siren began to scream, and the street filled with people running for shelter. Evelyne stole down the stairs, found the entrance to her building empty, and, slipping out, mingled with the crowd. Some moments later the Gestapo returned, broke down her door, and ransacked the apartment. Evelyne had not been back since.

Early the next morning when I arrived at rue Guynemer, I was amazed to find Parodi's sister, Jacqueline, and to hear about what had happened to them. She told me her brother was now waiting for me at the Préfecture. She gave me an FFI armband with the cross of Lorraine and told me to wear it when I reached the Ile de la Cité, which was almost entirely in the hands of the FFI. Thrilled at the prospect of going to the center of everything, I left immediately. Along the way I saw public notices with two crossed tricoleurs: *Call to arms! Stand and fight! Victory is ours!*

I passed windows pierced with bullet holes. Near Place Saint-Michel the streets were deserted. At the bottom of boulevard Saint-Michel was a large well-made barricade consisting of paving stones, sacks of earth, rails, broken furniture, wire netting, etc. There were also one or two machine guns[25] and many young FFI standing around in shirt sleeves, some of them wearing helmets. They sported every variety of weapon. I slipped on my armband and crossed the Pont Saint-Michel—quickly, because several bullets crackled on the quay. (But what about the truce? I thought.)[26]

At last I got to the Préfecture. Its windows were blocked almost to the top with sandbags. Resting on the sandbags were leveled rifles, and above them I saw the tense motionless faces of the Fifis. Inside many other Fifis were standing around in the large courtyard. Carelessly dressed, unshaven, their eyes shining, they were obviously both exhausted and exhilarated. They had hardly slept that night or indeed the previous nights. Perhaps they had also found a supply of wine in the cellars of the Préfecture. To right and left were stacks of rifles, neatly arranged. Fires burned under enormous quarters of meat and smoking pots.

They led me into a vast reception room to wait for Parodi. I'd never met him. At last I would!

He was short in stature, aloof, impeccably dressed.

"Ah, Anne, it is you," he said. "Hello. You can work in the other office. You have your code, don't you?"

"No . . ."

His face froze. "What! You don't have it?" A slight pause. "But I have no need of you without your code!"[27]

I suggested I bike home to get it—someone would loan me a bike.

"No, no," he said. "It's not worth it. But go get your code, and then go to Place Saint-François Xavier. Wait there, because we may need you outside this small FFI island."

And that is how I missed the most glorious moments of the Liberation: the arrival at the Hôtel de Ville of Captain Dronne with his three French tanks on August 24 at 8 P.M., the arrival later that night of General Leclerc, and the arrival the next day of General de Gaulle.

Instead I went to the address I'd been given. I stayed there alone, waiting and depressed. To make another mistake was of course out of the question. How long did I wait? Twelve hours? Thirty-six? Forty-eight? I'm no longer able to say. As one gets further away from such empty hours, they become impossible to measure. In any case, I heard nothing from anyone and finally decided to end my vigil myself—probably when I heard the BBC triumphantly announce that Paris was liberated.[28]

The outskirts of the Bichons' quarter were barred by Feldgraus,[29] and I had to show my papers. The Jardins du Luxembourg was now an entrenched camp, every gate locked, blockhouses all along the high railings. An enormous German tank camouflaged khaki and green stood at the corner of rue Vaugirard and rue Guynemer. Men in combat uniforms were running about inside the park.[30]

As I was nearing the Bichons' house on rue Guynemer, Ginette Janin appeared, sunburned and perspiring, with an array of typewriters and food supplies strapped to her bike. The Americans had reached Echarcon! There had been no fighting, but there were casualties. The Germans had set fire to the chateau and, to get the villagers out of the way, made them hide in their cellars. Were the Germans going to burn everything, as they'd done elsewhere? When the villagers dared venture out, they found Echarcon intact, deserted, silent. The Boche had gone. Quickly everyone got out the flags they'd prepared beforehand and ran to meet a column of vehicles glittering in the sun. Yes, it *was* the Americans! There were embraces and tears of joy. The son of the people Ginette had been staying with had watched the enemy's movements those last days. He hopped into a jeep to show his new American friends around the area. Scarcely had they taken off when an explosion shook the town. They had driven over a mine. One GI was killed, and the young boy's leg was torn off. (He was well taken care of by the Americans.) The GIs immediately set about demining the streets.

That evening I learned that the Gestapo had come looking for me at rue de Grenelle—some ten months too late! They'd spoken with the concierge, who of course feigned ignorance. I rushed over to the boulevard Saint-Germain and up the stairs to my parents' apartment. Exclamations all around—we had not seen one another since the start of the insurrection. No, they'd had no visit from the Gestapo. Phew!

"Our little parents," I wrote in my first letter to my sister after the Liberation,

> never went out, or practically never, and tranquilly ate their little supplies of food at home. In one stroke I told them I was not coming from Gif, where they thought I'd been for two months at a holiday camp, but from the Bichons' on rue Guynemer. I told them everything, perhaps a little too quickly because I was in a hurry. But a little later that evening I came back and told them everything, everything, everything that has happened since November 1942! That took till midnight. They

forgave me (my deception) at once, although their readjustment must have been a bit difficult. But now they are very happy and proud!

The next day the entire city was on edge. For several days a crowd of people had gathered at the Porte d'Orleans, where they sat on the sidewalk.

"What are you waiting for?" someone asked them.

"We are waiting for History to happen," someone else replied.

Standing on my parents' balcony overlooking the boulevard Saint-Germain, I also waited for History to happen. The boulevard was empty, not a barricade in sight, though many had been put up around Paris in the last two days. The weather was fine, the sky cloudless except for black smoke rising in the west where the Grand Palais had been burning since the day before. It had been rumored that the Germans were going to blow up the Palais du Luxembourg and the Palais Bourbon, and also bridges and factories.[31] From time to time you could see FFI running along the walls and hear sporadic gunshots and bursts of machine gun fire, as there had been on previous days.

But that day there was a new sound—a distant rumbling. Was it the battle drawing near? the Allies arriving?

My parents and I were listening to FFI announcements on the radio, since the electricity was back on. Radio-Paris had been silenced several days earlier. What a relief after four years of poisoned air waves! News bulletins were coming thick and fast, listing the results of street fighting, the number of captured men, arms, and vehicles; repeating that General de Gaulle had landed at Cherbourg (August 20), that the Allies were approaching Corbeil, Melun, Fontainebleau, Versailles, that the First French Army, landed in Provence on August 15, was rapidly advancing northward.

At one point my mother, without saying anything, left the apartment, despite the fact that the radio had warned civilians who were not fighting to stay at home.

A short while later she returned, wearing an ambiguous smile, half-ashamed, half-proud.

My father, coming out from his study, was scandalized. "What? Have you been out?"

She pulled a loaf of bread from her basket. "It's been so long since we've had any bread," she said. "I thought today might be just the right day. And I got it without standing in line! As I was coming back, I heard a soldier shout several times. I didn't see him because he was standing in the porch of a house. I had no idea he was shouting at me, and by the time I realized it, he looked angry—in fact, he was pointing his gun! I quickly made him a *no, no, no!* sign with my finger, and showed him my bread. And he kindly lowered his gun!"

My father raised his eyes to the ceiling and turned towards me. "Your mother is unbelievable!" he said.

The next day, August 24, I spent the evening with my parents again. The windows of the apartment were wide open. Toward nine or ten o'clock there was a great hubbub on the radio. A voice cried out:

"Paris is free! French troops have arrived! Tell everyone! Spread the news!"

We were so stunned that we were speechless—even though this was exactly what we had been waiting to hear.

There was a clamor outside. I ran onto the balcony. It was growing dark. People were at their windows. They were shouting, they were calling out, they were rushing into the streets. A confused *Marseillaise* was beginning. Was it coming from the radio or from the street? From both.

And then another sound, at first scarcely audible, suddenly swelled and seemed to come from everywhere at once. The bells, all the bells of Paris, were pealing forth together. They had been silent since the beginning of the Occupation. We had even forgotten they were there.

Then—crowning folly—the whole city sprang to light.

For a brief moment we believed the war was over.

Epilogue

In fact Paris was not yet completely liberated. General Leclerc's army fought against German resistance the whole of the next day, August 25, and it would be another eight months before Germany finally surrendered. But I've chosen to end my narrative at this point because the details of the following days, so often described in books, have been wiped from my memory by the jubilant crowds in the sunshine, and even more by a personal anxiety and grief I will speak of in a moment.

I want to offer here a brief account of what became of some of the people in this book who were not present at the Liberation. I will discuss them in the order in which they entered my pages. Many of these people were deported—simply vanished into a world the rest of us knew nothing about. I'm not going to try to describe what they lived through in the concentration camps, because that cannot be told second-hand. It was difficult to tell *first-hand:* those who came back were dismayed by the enormous gulf between what they had experienced and what they were actually able to say about it. As Robert Antelme has written,

> We wanted to talk and to be understood at last. We had just come back with our experience still alive and burning within us; we had a frantic desire to tell our friends exactly what we had lived through. But we couldn't. What we had to say was already becoming *unimaginable,* even to ourselves.[1]

Charles Ferdinand-Dreyfus

Charles died after being deported from Drancy in September, 1942. We never found out how or when he died, and never knew the concentration camp he was sent to. We think it was probably Auschwitz-Birkenau, where most Jews from Drancy were sent. The last word we had from him were two letters he wrote before leaving Drancy; they are reprinted in the Appendix.

I must add that I have always thought he probably didn't survive long after he left France. His courage, his sense of outrage, his perfect German, his strong sense of responsibility for those around him, and his natural authority would all have driven him to protest the dreadful conditions of the journey—with consequences that can easily be imagined.

Jacques Ferdinand-Dreyfus

Jacques also died after being deported, and about him too we never heard anything again. He was fifty-eight, malnourished, and in poor health. We think he most likely died during transport.

Daniel Ferdinand-Dreyfus

Daniel, twenty-five, died during the Paris insurrection—exactly how, we never knew. On August 28 a phone call from his friend Simone Morizet informed me that he'd not been seen for a week. Twelve days before, on August 16, he had been released from la Roquette prison (I think it was already under French control) and had hurried over to Simone's house and borrowed her bicycle. He then re-established contact with the leaders[2] of *Défense de la France*. Some days later Simone received a scribbled note from him, dated the 21st, written from the Hôtel-Dieu Hospital on the Ile de la Cité, saying that he'd been slightly wounded. After that, nothing.

Between August 19 and 24 there had been a great deal of fighting on the Ile de la Cité around the Préfecture de Police, and many wounded French and Germans were treated at the hospital nearby, the Hôtel-Dieu. When I went there on August 28 or 29, the staff, which was still working day and night, had no time for my questions. To my surprise, though, I stumbled upon my cousin Monique Chevrillon, Vivou's older sister, who'd been working as a nurse. She helped me find the notation on Daniel's entry into the hospital. There was no mention of his departure.

Two days later I got hold of a car so I could go to Montfort-l'Amaury to tell his mother, Lily, what I knew. I shall always remember the terrible anguish of that trip. For weeks Lily had been devoured by worry, knowing nothing of Daniel, not even that he had been freed from prison. She came back to Paris with me, and together we began a search that lasted until September 9.

We looked everywhere, in all the hospitals and clinics of Paris. Most responses were negative, a few unsure. Sent from one place to another, we lost hope as the days went by. Or at least I did—not Lily. She thought it possible that in the general pandemonium Daniel might have been evacuated to a hospital in the suburbs, or given an assignment in the provinces, and not been able to tell her because the mail wasn't being delivered and telephones weren't working outside Paris.

Finally I learned that the FFI and Germans killed in the Hôtel-Dieu neighborhood had been buried in the cemetery of Pantin, a suburb north of Paris. There was no trace of Daniel in the cemetery register. I was ready to leave when the name of the friend who'd loaned him the bicycle caught my eye. It had been converted to the masculine: Simone to Simon Morizet. There was no doubt that Daniel was buried there. According to the medical report that accompanied his body to the cemetery, he received a bullet in the back that passed through the carotid artery. As I wrote my sister at the time, "Apparently, in such cases, the loss of blood is so great that one instantly loses consciousness."

Impatient to take part in the Liberation, Daniel must have left the hospital on his own, gotten on the bicycle registered in Simone's name, and been killed outright sometime that day.

This long quest and Lily's despair, first over her husband's deportation and then over the search for Daniel, largely obliterated the joy of the Liberation for me.

Paul Fabre

Being a man of few words, Paul didn't say much about his captivity. But he was pleased when someone showed an interest in what he and his friends had experienced in POW camps. The deportees in German concentration camps had been treated so outrageously that people tended to overlook what our prisoners of war had gone through.

In telling you about his experience at the end of the war, I will again make use of Bernard Auffray's *Sur mon chemin j'ai rencontré . . .* I will also draw on two long retrospective letters Paul wrote me from Port-Blanc in June, 1945, while I was helping with refugee repatriation in Germany.

In February, 1945, prisoners in Oflag 4D, some forty miles northeast of Dresden, could hear the roar of artillery in the distance as the Red Army struck with tremendous force through Silesia. A feverish excitement seized the camp, and the Germans decided to evacuate it. Six thousand men, Paul among them, were sent out westwards in groups of about 150, guarded by Hungarian police under German command. (When the Soviets entered Hungary, many Hungarian police had been moved to Germany.) The prisoners, who hadn't received packages from France for several months, were weak from malnutrition. Their food actually improved a bit along the route because they could barter with peasants, but there was never enough. They advanced painfully in intense cold, either carrying their personal belongings or pulling them on little sleds they'd made themselves. Those who lagged behind were encouraged by rifle blows and roving police dogs. Paul's group covered about ninety miles in eight days.

At the beginning of March, they arrived in Colditz and were put into a medieval fortress with fifteen-foot-thick walls. A very small courtyard was the only space in which two thousand prisoners could stretch their legs. As Paul wrote in June:

> *Early March, 1945:*
> This was the month of Hunger—and what hunger!—but of feasting for our spirits. We met some 300 British and 20 Gaullists and it was very exciting to have news of France in '44 and '45—and to be able to speak to Englishmen, all exceptional characters; they'd been sent to Colditz as punishment for their conduct in prisoner of war camps. We learned a tremendous amount from them.

Late in March, the French POWs, about two thousand men, were transferred to Zeithain, east of the Elbe, to a big camp already crowded with Russians, Italians, and Poles. There was a German garrison close by.

> *Beginning of April:*
> The food situation was better, thanks to bartering cigarettes for wheat and rye flour and thanks especially to an American relief package. My pulse went up from 45 to 60. We managed to make our barracks just about habitable.

> *April 15–22:*
> The German garrison was bombed by the British and Americans. Munition depots flared and exploded—magnificent!

> *The morning of April 22:*
> There were no more Germans around the camp, but they were still nearby, a few kilometers away. We salvaged some reserves of food and could have lived on them for three or four weeks, especially since we had some cows that German refugees had left behind.

> *End of April:*
> On April 23 we woke to the sound of Cossacks galloping down the road, a hundred yards from us. It was our first—but astonishing— view of "modern" warfare! The whole day we saw nothing but Mongolian cavalry. . . . At 8 in the evening General Baranov came to warn our Colonel that we should leave the camp immediately: German artillery

were zeroing in on us. By 9 we were moving hastily to the east.[3] We were supposed to reach Silesia, 155 miles away, in 15 days. For three days we marched in columns, like an army. Then we rested a few days. When we started walking again, it was in small groups, camping where we liked, knowing only at approximately what point we were to rally. This was because the Russian army was no longer feeding us and we had to live off the land. The first days we lived royally because the countryside hadn't yet been exploited, but suddenly there were no more chickens, no more cows to be milked. Fortunately the Russians were very generous, and we were often favored with bread or meat. But a Russian might decide he wanted your watch and would rummage through your things using that marvelous tool, the machinegun, which made you quite inclined to "give" your watch to the friendly scavenger. He would do the same for a belt, pen, chocolate, sugar. Indeed, the Russians used their guns for just about everything. However, none of us was ever killed or even mutilated!

May 7:
We settled down in a beautiful house (already well looted), thinking we might live there two days or two months.

Pentecost Monday and after:
Orders to travel west! At last! We were 57 per train car intended for 40 men or eight horses[4]—in other words, overcrowded. Three days and two nights. Then a disagreeable surprise: the train came to a halt and we had to continue on foot some 25 miles to the Elbe (we passed 500 yards from Zeithain, where we'd been a month and a half before). Finally, American trucks picked us up and took us to a camp near Leipzig in the American Zone. Able to eat normally again. Two days later, departure at 4 A.M. Three days on the train, fed the first day, hungry the second, very hungry the third. May 30 we were at Sarrebourg. The 31st in Paris, Gare de l'Est!

Paul had returned home. On June 3 my mother wrote me in Germany:

He arrived May 31, having phoned us the night before that he was coming. I opened the door—I was the first friend he'd seen, he told me later. He is in good shape. Of course he has grown thin, his face is gaunt, and his eyes look larger and sad. But he's still charming and lively, and completely himself—always thinking of others.

My parents had a special affection for Paul. The last weeks before his return had seemed endless to them, and increasingly worrisome: it seemed as if all the prisoners had come home except for Paul.

Then an incident occurred that still makes me shudder. Replying to Paul's telegram announcing his arrival, Antoinette wired back, among other things: "Prière rester encore une semaine" (Please stay one more week). What? How could that be? Amazement, dismay, embarrassment. My parents were greatly puzzled at this strange demand. Paul racked his brains trying to think up things to do his last three days in Paris—going to see people he wouldn't have otherwise seen. Meanwhile, Antoinette bicycled the eleven miles to the Lannion station several times, bursting with impatience. When Paul finally arrived, it took only a minute to clear up the mystery. Antoinette had telegraphed: "Pierre reste encore une semaine" (Pierre is staying one more week). Our brother was visiting Port-Blanc.

At the end of the summer Paul and Antoinette moved to Boulogne, just outside Paris. Paul gave up his position at Maurice de Broglie's Center for Physics Research to follow his true vocation, teaching. He taught physics for more than thirty years at the Lycée Condorcet.

Anne-Marie Bauer (Claudine)

Anne-Marie was arrested and interrogated by the Gestapo in Lyons on July 24, 1943. She refused to give them her address until she knew that a friend who'd seen her arrest would have time to go to her house and put a pot of parsley in the window—a signal to her underground contacts that she had been caught. She calculated how long it would take to get the pot in place and decided not to talk until 5 P.M. She could see a watch on the table.

Klaus Barbie, head of the Lyons Gestapo, presided over the interrogation. Anne-Marie's hands were handcuffed behind her back. She was slowly hoisted by the handcuffs up the wall until the whole weight of her body hung from her wrists. A newspaper was set afire under her feet. When the paper burned out, another one was lit.

At five she revealed her address. She then told her torturers of a meeting she had scheduled for the next day. This meeting she invented in the vague hope that she would be taken to it and be able to escape. At least the meeting might give her a respite from the interrogation.

The next day while waiting for the fictitious Victorine at their supposed rendezvous, Anne-Marie was so closely watched that escape was unthinkable. After a long time she told the guards that Victorine had passed by earlier and, receiving a signal from her, had immediately understood the situation and gone on. By now, she told them, all her comrades would be warned. She thought saying this would bring an end to the interrogations.

The Gestapo was furious and led her to a cellar where they told her she was going to be executed. They faced her up against a wall. After some minutes, when nothing happened, she realized the whole thing was a sham. She has told me she was unspeakably wretched at *not* dying—which gives you an idea of what she had gone through the day before.

After six months in Fort de Montluc, two of which were spent in solitary confinement, Anne-Marie was deported to Ravensbrück, and then to Holleischen, Czechoslovakia. Life there was not so terrible because Holleischen was a work camp, not an extermination camp. She worked in a factory and at building roads. On May 5, 1945, anti-Nazi and anti-Soviet Polish and Czech partisans liberated the camp.

Later, Anne-Marie published a collection of poems, *La Vigie aveugle* (The Blind Watchman),[5] and a novel, *La Route qui poudroie* (Naught But the Dust),[6] attempting to convey the strange mixture of dread, horror, and brotherhood in concentration camp life that a straightforward account could not give. I don't think she ever overcame her remorse at returning from the camps alive when so many of her comrades, including her brother Michel, died in them.

In the late 1980s she was going to testify against Klaus Barbie during his trial, but was too ill to do so.

Jean Ayral (Robert Gautier, Pal)

After Jean Ayral made his extraordinary escape from the Hotel Cayré in April, 1943, he lay low for several months and was then flown to London. There he was well taken care of and underwent brain surgery for the injury he had suffered during his parachute landing in 1942. While convalescing, he recorded his experiences in his unpublished "Carnets de Guerre," from which I have seen only a few excerpts. He was impatient to get back to France, but BCRA opposed this for security reasons. So he received PT boat training and was sent to Algiers as a member of an elite corps of commando parachutists in the Free French Navy. He took part in missions from Corsica to the Italian islands and coast.

On August 12, 1944, three days before the landing of the First French Army in Provence, he and four other commandos were parachuted about thirty miles from Toulon with instructions to enter the city from the north. He marched his little group across the hills. They came upon a car, an Opel, attacked and took possession of it. A few nights later, his group—now reinforced and numbering about thirty—fell into a hard fight in a burned-over woods next to a large German training camp. Ayral and his men shot and captured many of the Germans and ran off the rest. Next day, from high rocky hills in the area, they fired at a German column heading toward Marseille and dispersed it.

On August 21, Ayral arrived at a crossroads and seeing a group of French soldiers ran toward them, his arms raised, shouting, "France! France!" He was holding a Colt pistol in one hand, however, and the commanding officer mistook him for a German. He fell under a volley of bullets.[7]

Antoine Geoffroy-Dechaume

Antoine began his underground work in late 1942 by finding a landing field in Corrèze that met BCRA's specifications. He then recruited a local team to receive parachute drops and supervised several receptions until he was arrested in July, 1943.

In 1985 Antoine told me how much he admired the audacity and skill with which the British pilots executed the drops. They were flying small, unarmed planes—usually Lysanders—with little fuel to spare; they had to fly low enough to avoid radar; and they flew at night over country unlit except by the moon until they spotted the three little flares in a triangle that marked the drop site. Those on the ground had no radio contact with the plane and could never be sure that a drop would be made. When it was, it seemed a miracle: the far-off purring engine became, in a few seconds, an enormous roar, followed by dozens of parachutes blossoming in the night sky. The plane would then turn away and disappear, and the ground team would quickly gather up the parachutes and containers before any Germans, drawn by the noise of the plane, arrived.

Antoine was not arrested for his BCRA work. Indeed, he was arrested almost by accident. As the administrator in the Limousin region charged with food distribution, he took it upon himself to supply the Limousin Maquis. This became known in the countryside, and the French police started an investigation. He had to leave his house and hide, at first with some hospitable farmers. Not wanting to compromise them, he moved on, and then moved on again. Everywhere he was tracked.

He ended up taking refuge with his friend Bertrand de Jouvenel, who owned a chateau in the neighborhood. Jouvenel was away, and an old caretaker received Antoine and took him under her wing. This gave him a welcome rest after days of stress. But at the end of a week, on July 14, the chateau was suddenly surrounded by German troops. The Gestapo was looking for Jouvenel for reasons that had nothing to do with Antoine. The chateau was searched from top to bottom, and Antoine was discovered in a small room filled with old furniture. He told the Germans he was hiding from the French police. He had remembered to bury his revolver in the seat of one of the armchairs, and might have escaped arrest had he also remembered to hide a paper he was carrying that had to do with the Maquis. Interminable interrogations followed. Twice he was savagely beaten. He revealed nothing.

He was taken to prison in Limoges and after four months deported to Buchenwald. From there he was sent to work in a salt mine that had been transformed into a Luftwaffe factory.

After the war he went back to music. He is a specialist in the music of the seventeenth and eighteenth centuries.

François Briant (Charles Baron, Pal W)

After his arrest in April, 1943, François was interrogated and tortured. He refused to talk. He spent ten months in Fresnes—three in solitary confinement—maintaining a close communion of spirit and prayer with his comrades, both free and interned. During this part of his imprisonment we were able to send him food and books. In January, 1944, he was deported to Buchenwald and from there to Dora, in the Weimar region, where conventional and experimental weapons were manufactured in a complex of underground factories occupying two-mile-long parallel tunnels inside a mountain. Prisoners at Dora worked twelve-hour days.

François was liberated in April, 1945, and returned home to live near his family in Lannilis (Finistère). He rested for three months and then resumed his novitiate with the White Fathers in Algiers. But his health, undermined by the war, prevented him from completing his studies. Convalescence took two years. In July, 1948, after a week of preparation, he joined two friends in climbing the Aiguille du Gouter, one of Mont-Blanc's peaks—something he'd dreamed of doing for a long time. He climbed with joy. Fifty yards from the top he stopped to fill his gourd from a trickling spring while the others continued their ascent. As François was waiting for the gourd to fill, loose stones fell down on him from above. Trying to duck, he lost his balance, bounced on the layer of rock beneath him, and disappeared into the fog.[8]

Jacqueline d'Alincourt (Violaine)

Jacqueline was a prisoner in Fresnes from September, 1943, to March, 1944, and then spent three weeks at Romainville, a transit camp for those about to be deported. She was one of thousands of women prisoners deported on April 18, locked in crowded cattle cars.[9] She traveled that way for about a week to Ravensbrück, beyond Berlin.

More than a year later—fifteen days before the Germans surrendered—the women still alive in Ravensbrück were saved by the Red Cross, which took them to Sweden. There they received intensive medical care until they were well enough to travel. Once back on her feet, Jacqueline decided to stay on and help with the repatriation of other prisoners. She would be the last of the women at Ravensbrück to return to France, which she did on August 15.

Later that same day, she knocked at my parents' door on the boulevard Saint-Germain, on the chance that, though it was summer vacation, someone might be there. My parents were in Brittany, but I had returned from Munster, Germany, one hour before!

The next day she visited the Hotel Lutétia, which had become a welcome center for returned deportees. She ran into our B C R A friend Gustave, who had resumed his real name, Pierre Péry.[10] He had been repatriated from Buchenwald three months before and so helped her through the paces of a returned deportee.

Three months later they were married and lived for some time in New York, where one of their two daughters was born. Pierre Péry died in 1966. Jacqueline now lives in Paris and has recently begun lecturing at American universities about her experience in the Resistance and at Ravensbrück.

Geneviève "Ginette" Janin (Dominique)

After the Liberation of Paris, Ginette joined the Corps Auxiliaire Volontaire Féminin (C AV F). She thus simultaneously acquired a uniform decorated with the cross of Lorraine, of which she was very proud, and a room in a grand Paris hotel that had been converted into a women's barracks. She worked in a C AV F office helping prisoners liberated from French camps, mostly Jews and Communists so recently arrested that Vichy hadn't had time to hand them over to the Germans.

Later she joined an auxiliary branch of the famous "2ᵉ D.B." (Leclerc's

Second Armored Division) and was responsible for finding wounded Division troops lost in Paris hospitals, contacting their families, and, in every way, helping them get back on their feet again. A high point of her brief military career was a dinner for four, with General Leclerc one of the four!

In October, 1946, she resumed her medical studies, which were followed by five years of pediatric specialization. She eventually chose to be a public health doctor in a Paris suburb and devoted thirty-two years to this career.

Assistant Police Commissioner Terrier

One day, just after the Liberation of Paris, I arrived late for lunch at boulevard Saint-Germain and was greatly surprised to find Assistant Commissioner Terrier seated at the table with my parents. The summer before, after leaving Fresnes, I'd gone to thank him and Commissioner Guichard for having saved me by burning the incriminating letter in my file before the Germans took me away. Guichard was absent, transferred to Toulouse, and Terrier could see me for only a moment. He said he wanted to talk, though, and made an appointment to meet me later at a café. There he recounted several complicated stories that had nothing whatever to do with me.

"And you," he said suddenly in a confidential tone, "you're not telling me much."

The phrase struck me as odd and I avoided seeing him again. Yet here were my parents warmly welcoming him at their table.

"For the last two weeks," he said, "I've been hunted by hoodlums[11] and hiding with friends."

"What can we do?" my mother said.

"You can't do anything now, but perhaps later . . ."

A little while later I heard he was in prison. I went there with a package and tried to learn something about him—in vain.

Then I received a letter from his wife. He had hanged himself in his cell. She had seen marks of torture on his body.

Police Commissioner Guichard

Guichard was also arrested after the Liberation. He wrote me from prison, and I sent a testimonial letter describing what he'd done for me. My father, who had seen him while I was under arrest, also sent a letter.

Guichard was condemned as a collaborator and deprived of his civil rights. Then, in December, 1944, he was removed from his position as chief of police and stripped of his pension. After his release from prison, he came to see me and thank me for my testimony. He did not accept the judgment of the court, he said; it was unfair. If he had worked against the Communists, it was for France. He and his wife were moving to the country, where he would look for work.

In October, 1949, he sent me a copy of the Conseil d'Etat's decision that canceled his removal from office, "because," the document said, "he was convicted while in prison without being informed of the charges brought against him, and was therefore unable to defend himself." I concluded from this that he'd be taken back into the police force, but in 1959, after years of effort, another court ruled that "the cancellation of his removal from office had no practical bearing in his case," since he had been condemned as a collaborator before being expelled from the ranks.

Shortly thereafter I received an announcement from his wife that he had died.

Mme. Roudier

Mme. Roudier, who had been so brusquely torn from our cell at Fresnes in June, 1943, spent the rest of the war in Germany. She was moved from prison to prison—seven times, if I'm not mistaken. Her sister received some news of her through infrequent postcards. She reappeared in May, 1945, very much thinner but still valiant. We were each impatient to see the other, she because she wanted to return—as if it were a treasure—the cape I'd given her as she was taken away.

She lived for several years with her sister in a small house in the Paris suburb of Arcueil. I always enjoyed my visits with them.

She died in the 1950s.

Renée Mirande-Thomas Laval (Denise)

When I returned from Germany in August, 1945, I learned with joy that Renée had survived the camps. I wanted very much to see this remarkable person whom I knew only by voice. Did she recognize mine on the phone? It was probably my imagination. But I can still hear her exclamation and burst of laughter when I entered her beautiful salon: "My chimney fairy!"

Her daughter, Jeannette, was there, looking shy and amused and much more reserved than her mother. The latter radiated energy and good health. Of course, she had been back for four months, well cared for, even overfed. But what hadn't she been through since the Fresnes period, which we now talked over with affection. She said little about her time in concentration camp, but gave me a copy of a speech she had made on May 5, 1945, a few days after her return, at a reception given in her honor by her colleagues in the legal profession. It is from the speech that I know the broad outlines of her experience.

She had been arrested in March, 1943, by a French police officer,[12] who interrogated her in vain for a long time. She was sent to la Roquette Prison, and finally handed over to the Gestapo. At Fresnes she was placed in solitary confinement and allowed no books or exercise. It was after three months of this regime that we got to know each other during my last two weeks.

In December, 1943, she was condemned to deportation as an "N.N."[13] She was one of the last people to leave for the East as an individual. After that, deportees were herded like livestock into cattle cars and shipped in massive convoys. Her journey east was interrupted, thanks to repeated Allied bombing of the rail lines, and she spent two months in the fortress at Aix-la-Chapelle, underfed but relatively calm and among French women. Then came a twelve-day journey in a Black Maria that stopped at many checkpoints to squeeze in more prisoners. She arrived at Ravensbrück on February 6, 1944, was tattooed number 28,176 (one year later, the number would have been 124,000), and put in the N.N. section.

By March, 1945, the Russians were within twenty miles of the camp. The commandant, unwilling to see the N.N.s liberated, sent them on to Mauthausen to be exterminated. There followed six weeks of nightmare, during which Renée saw her comrades "die like flies." Then, incredibly, a caravan of Red Cross trucks arrived and saved them by taking them on a frantic, weaving ride through Germany (the war was not yet over) that brought them to the French border on April 24, 1945.

Renée and I met several times, then lost sight of each other. She went back to being a full-time lawyer, but despite that and her family life helped found and direct the Society of Former Ravensbrück Deportees (Amicale des Anciennes Déportées de Ravensbrück). Later, until her death in 1979, she was president of the Ravensbrück International Committee, whose purposes were to support camp survivors and the families of those who had not returned, and to keep alive the facts about what happened in the camps so that such crimes would never be committed again.

Pierre and Marie-Hélène Lefaucheux (Gildas and Isabelle)

Pierre Lefaucheux, who headed the FFI in and around Paris, was arrested and imprisoned at Fresnes in June, 1944. He was to be deported on August 15, on the last convoy of prisoners going to Germany—twenty-two hundred men and four hundred women. This was just the moment when everything was coming to a head: the Allies approaching Paris, the insurrection imminent, the Germans under pressure to pull out. On August 14 Swedish consul Raoul Nordling began negotiations to get General Dietrich von Choltitz to sign a truce handing over all political prisoners still in France (Pierre one of their number) to the Red Cross.

Marie-Hélène knew of these tricky negotiations. She was keeping a vigil at Fresnes with Claire Girard,[14] a young friend whose brother was slated to be part of the August 15 convoy. In despair the two women watched as, one after another, the trucks were filled with prisoners and sent off. They got on their bikes and followed the trucks to the Gare de Pantin, where they saw the prisoners loaded into railroad cars. Who at this point would not have given up all hope of saving them?

Claire managed to find a car, a driver, and some gas, and she and Marie-Hélène followed the train's progress across France—FFI sabotage was causing many delays. At each stage of the journey, they phoned Paris: had the truce been signed yet? On August 17, phoning from the station at Bar-le-Duc, they learned that the truce had at last begun. They ran to tell the officer in charge of the train. He said he would do nothing without an order from higher up. The train pulled out.

Perhaps, Claire and Marie-Hélène thought quickly, they would be able to find some influential person in Nancy who could help. . . . In Nancy they found Laval and his entourage fleeing toward Germany—no help there. The train with its human freight moved out of Nancy heading east. Marie-Hélène and Claire returned to Paris; their efforts had failed.

Two or three weeks later I heard a rumor that Pierre and Marie-Hélène were once more receiving friends on the boulevard Saint-Germain. I couldn't believe it—rumors were certainly wild, I thought. Except it turned out to be true. Marie-Hélène had gone right up to Buchenwald and extracted her husband.

What she had done was to find another car and more gas, and off she'd gone again, crossing the American and German lines, the latter in total confusion. Back in Nancy, she ferreted out a high-ranking Gestapo officer who was trying to slip back into Germany. She let him know that both money and gas could be provided were he to agree (1) that her husband had been arrested by mistake, (2) that he, the Gestapo officer, would take her in his official car to Buchenwald, and (3) that, once there, he would himself seek out the commandant and order him to release Pierre Lefaucheux. Simple, wasn't it?

Several months after Pierre returned he became director of the Renault Factories. At Port-Blanc, where Pierre and Marie-Hélène also spent their summer holidays, we often met while canoeing. We would glide in silence in the sunlight between the islands of St. Gildas and Iliec. The water was transparent, and at the bottom we could see pebbles and sand and the shifting seaweed. Neither we nor they would want to break the spell, and so we made only a small sign of the hand as we passed.

Pierre was killed in a car accident on an icy road in 1955. Several years later Marie-Hélène, then a member of the French delegation to the United Nations, was killed in a plane crash in Louisiana on her way back to New York from a mission in Mexico.

Simone Lemoine (Jeanne)

In March, 1982, my telephone rang: "Hello, Anne, is that you?"

"No, Madame, you've made a mistake."

"But, Anne, I recognize your voice."

"I'm sorry, but you have definitely got the wrong number!"

"But, Anne . . ."

In a flash I recognized Little Jeanne's voice. We had not seen each other for thirty-eight years.

A few days later we met in a café, and Jeanne told me what had happened to her in the war before I knew her. It was an astonishing story that took her four hours to tell. Compared with hers, my version will be pale, stripped not only of details but of her intense delivery, which conveyed such urgency that you felt everything she said had taken place the day before.

In the fall of 1940 Jeanne's father, Léon Lemoine, owner of a gas station and mayor of Saulchery (Aisne), found a suitable landing field near his town for BCRA's air operations and became head of a team that received men and arms. His son Jacques, fifteen, was soon helping him, and nineteen-year-old Simone (whom I will call Jeanne because I never called her anything else) did the liaison work with Paris. Among the agents parachuted in from London was Captain Drouot[15] who would later be Jeanne's contact in Paris, and later still my coding teacher.

A member of Lemoine's team became dangerously talkative after too much drink, and Lemoine eased him out of the group. The fellow was furious and denounced Lemoine in a detailed letter to the Gestapo; the letter included a map of BCRA's landing field. Lemoine, Jacques, and two others from the team were arrested on July 23, 1943.

Jeanne and her mother were now alone, in despair and very frightened. The Gestapo would surely come back for Jeanne. Six days later they did. She played the little girl role—one that suited her—and said she knew nothing about anything; her father never spoke to her about his business. They took her to the Kommandantur at Chateau-Thierry, where she waited all day to be interrogated.

Meanwhile, the Germans searched the Lemoines' house and garden. In the garden they discovered a cache of weapons that Jeanne had buried after her father's arrest. She had intended to get rid of them by throwing them into the Marne River, which ran along the bottom of their garden, but they were too heavy for her to manage by herself.

The Gestapo interrogated Jeanne all night. She was insulted and brutalized. She was terrified when told that if she didn't talk, her mother was going to be arrested. Her father had already been executed, they said, and her younger brother had told everything, making her silence pointless. But when Jeanne's father had asked her and her brother to help with the parachute drops, he'd made them solemnly promise never to say a word about what they knew, no matter what happened. Jeanne clung to this oath as if to a life raft.

The Germans told her that if she continued to say nothing, she would be executed at 6 A.M. Was it possible they could, would . . . ? She spent the rest of the night in anguish. At dawn they led her outside. She was going to die. She prayed intensely. They stood her with her back against the wall. At that moment a great peace descended on her. Was this all there was to dying? She waited for the shot. Nothing happened.

They stopped their charade and led her back to the police station. She thought the interrogation was going to start all over again and, overwhelmed with despair and exhaustion, she burst into tears.

Several days later she was transferred to Fresnes. There, on one of her "walks," whom did she see? Was it even possible? Yes! In a split second she was clasped in her father's arms. They were able to say only a few words in front of their dumbfounded guards, but enough for Jeanne to learn that Jacques and the two other team members were also at Fresnes. She was unspeakably happy to know now that they were all alive and that she was no longer alone.

A little later there was another joy: all five were led away to a train together. Where were they going? They would know when they arrived, they were told. Meanwhile, traveling together, they were free to talk.

Alas, as soon as they arrived at their destination, Saint-Quentin Prison in Aisne, in northern France, they were separated. Jeanne was locked up in a filthy little black cell full of bedbugs. Fresnes now seemed like a lost paradise. She was given almost no food, and in the long solitude of her dark cell she became ill and, uncared for, got worse. The illness reached a crisis and she howled with pain. Her cries were heard by the president of the Red Cross, a Mme. Cadot, who was visiting the prison at that moment. Mme. Cadot insisted on seeing whoever was in such pain. A French prisoner who was a doctor was then called to the cell. He said Jeanne was gravely ill and ordered an immediate stomach operation, while a sympathetic German guard went to get her father. That brief interview was the last time Jeanne saw her father. Neither he nor Jacques returned from concentration camp.

Jeanne was operated on for peritonitis in the town hospital. A German soldier came to the hospital every day to make sure she was still there. Her recovery was not good. She stayed in the hospital for a month, and finally her surgeon, Dr. Drain, said she needed to convalesce elsewhere.

"She can recuperate perfectly well in prison," responded the German in charge.

That same evening Dr. Drain told Jeanne to get up; he was going to hide her, as comfortably as he could, in a small alcove off his office. The next morning Jeanne's hospital bed was empty. The staff looked everywhere. There was a great to-do, much shouting, and long, fruitless interrogations. After a while it was officially admitted that she had escaped.

Dr. Drain and Mme. Cadot closely watched over Jeanne in the doctor's cubbyhole, bringing her food and surrounding her with care and encouragement. But she couldn't stay cramped in her hiding place for long, and she begged them to let her out. A few days later they brought her some clothes, and in the afternoon, as visiting hours ended, she left the hospital by the front door like everyone else.

Once she was alone and free on the street, she panicked. She was sure she was being followed. She thought she'd forgotten the route she'd been told to follow to the train station. But she wasn't followed and hadn't forgotten; she arrived at the station, where she immediately fell into Mme. Cadot's arms. Mme. Cadot led her into a room where her mother was waiting and then gave mother and daughter two first class tickets to Paris. The date was November 30, 1943. Jeanne and her mother stayed hidden in Paris until the Liberation.

Jeanne never found either Mme. Cadot or Dr. Drain to thank them for having twice saved her life.

In January, 1944, Captain Drouot sent Jeanne to help me in the code service. After the Liberation of Paris, B C R A sent her to London to work in their photo service. Today she is a grandmother and works for the Charles de Gaulle Institute.[16]

Charles Fassier (Grégoire)

Fassier, who at age sixty-four recruited and led a Maquis in Brittany, had been a practicing architect until 1933, when his son was killed in a military plane crash. Deeply affected by this death, Fassier decided to retire to a place where he could paint and live out the rest of his days with his wife and mother-in-law. He found such a setting in the village of Plougrescant in an old farmhouse, the last in the region to have two large thatched roofs. The house was tucked into a fold of the land close to a little hill of pines and sheltered from wind and passers-by. A few minutes' walk uphill from the house, there was a vast view of the open sea and, to the west, the outline of the rugged coast with its many rocks and islands. Fassier set up a studio inside the barn and gradually filled it with canvases (mostly seascapes) and a jumble of papers, books, and newspapers that no one, not even his wife, dared touch. When his right arm, which had been wounded in the First World War, grew too tired to hold a paint brush, he would prop it up with his left.

In June, 1940, the idea that the Germans would ever be allowed to reach Brittany did not occur to him. As they drew near, however, he quickly got hold of some weapons, equipped a group of young men with them, and waited for the enemy. When he realized the futility of his action, all he could do was take back the guns, bury them in the hill behind his studio for use "at the first opportunity," and encourage the young men to flee to England.

The Germans set up in town, and because Fassier had a reputation among the local people for not being shy about expressing himself, he became their representative to the authorities. The Germans received his visits at the Kommandantur and visited him on the farm. Relations were polite.

One day, though, Fassier was kept waiting longer than usual, his presence apparently ignored. Suddenly the officer on duty turned to him

Antoinette doing homework with André.

Breton maquis assembled for U.S. Army
photographers near Brest.
Photo: U.S.I.S.

186

Welcoming the Americans in Rennes,
some of the liberated even coming out in pajamas.
Photo: Keystone.

Barricades, Paris, August, 1944.

Unknown German general at the time of surrender
of all German forces in the French capital.

The victory parade, Champs-Elysées, August 26,
1944.
Photo: Keystone.

General de Gaulle (*left*), with General Leclerc,
in front of the Arc de Triomphe, August 25, 1944.

Simone Lemoine, alias Jeanne, pre-
pares I.D. photos for secret agents
parachuting into France, at BCRA
in London, 1944.

Charles Fassier, alias Grégoire, after
the war.

and said in a chilly voice, "Well, Mr. Fassier, it appears you've been hiding weapons at your place."

Fassier was silent a moment. What could he say? Someone had obviously denounced him. Fassier then exploded as only he could—as he did again when he told me about it after the war. I can still see him, his arms folded, his face flushed, the great lump on his forehead (I never knew whether it was a birthmark or a war wound) turning purple, his magnificent blue eyes flashing. I can still hear his thunderous reply:

"Of course I hid weapons, lots of them! And what of it? I'm a Frenchman, aren't I? What do you think you'd do if we French were invading your country? You'd do exactly the same."

"Mr. Fassier," said the German, "you will hand over these weapons immediately. And you are under arrest."

"Wait a minute!" Fassier said. "You can do what you like with me, but you can't do anything about the guns, because they're at the bottom of the sea." He was so convincing the Germans never bothered to check up on him.

That was the first of several close shaves Fassier had. Another time, when he heard that a young man was telling everyone that he, Fassier, had helped people get to England (which was true), he immediately went to the courthouse in Lannion and filed a slander suit. Contrary to all expectations, he won the case, and his accuser spent a month in prison, "learning," as Fassier said, "to hold his tongue."

In early 1942 Fassier was recruited by BCRA's Intelligence Service and given the name Grégoire, from the well-known Breton song "Prends ton fusil, Grégoire . . ." ("Take up your rifle, Gregory . . ."). He spent most of his time striding across the countryside, even into Finistère, gathering information for the maps, photos, and detailed reports on German military installations along the coast[17] that he regularly passed on to his contact, "Marcel." His architectural skills proved very useful in this painstaking work, which he did in his studio for long hours at a stretch.

The Germans kept coming to see him with questions about local goings-on, so he bought a large German shepherd and put gravel on the path in order to hear the sound of boots approaching. He thus had time to shove whatever he was working on into a drawer, take up a brush, and go back to painting his current landscape with a serene expression on his face. He was never caught.

All this time he was recruiting and training a group of Maquisards near Kerien, a village some forty miles inland. His team had several successes, among them the elimination of a division general and two colonels.

One night at the beginning of August, 1944, Fassier's team received the Anglo-French general staff—including Colonel Eon and Major Drinkwater (real name: Claude Boillot)—who had parachuted into France with orders to coordinate the battle to liberate Brittany (see chapter 26). The officers were billeted with friends of Fassier's team in Kerien. During the night, one of Fassier's scouts reported a German column heading toward the village. Fassier readied the team for ambush. They were young and few in number. Fassier set the example and fired the first shot. It was a hard fight, but all the Germans were killed, captured, or run off.

As a result of this outstanding bravery, Private Fassier, sixty-six at the time, was promoted to captain by Colonel Eon. He joined the general staff of the Forces Françaises de Bretagne (Free French Forces of Brittany) and worked first for Major Drinkwater and then as assistant director of the FFB's Intelligence Service, the 2ème Bureau. Commenting on his work later, Major Drinkwater wrote the British War Office that Fassier

> circulated among the Germans and Russians, providing us with precise information about gun emplacements, mine fields, and manpower. . . . The quality of information he obtained at the risk of his life . . . was considered first class by Generals Ernest, Task Force A, and Middleton, G.O.C., 8th Corps. . . . His services were also inestimable as a member of the 2ème Bureau. Thanks to him I was able to provide the 8th Corps with a complete plan of the Crozon peninsula, showing the exact emplacement of German batteries, radar installations, headquarters, antitank defenses, etc.
>
> I would add that this 66-year-old man (who from 1924–33 was a member of the Conseil d'Etat)[18] could always be found in the midst of our fighting. I can certify that he killed at least three Germans in the attack of August 6–7, 1944. Colonel Eon has recommended him for the Légion d'honneur.

Fassier worked with the FFB in the mopping up of what were called the Atlantic Pockets: the heavily fortified coastal cities of Brest, Lorient, Saint-Nazaire, La Pallice, and Royan. In these cities some ninety thousand soldiers and sailors were trapped by the Free French Navy on the sea and by Maquisards and colonial regiments on the land (the regular French army was helping the Allies pursue the Germans eastward). Captain Fassier took part in the siege of Brest, and when it fell he took part in the FFB's siege of Saint-Nazaire and Lorient, which continued until the end of the war. When Fassier finally returned home in May, 1945, for the first time since before the fight at Kerien, he was at the end of his strength. In fact, he never completely recovered.

The last two or three years of Fassier's life were burdened by physical deterioration and illuminated by an intense surge of religious faith. He died in June, 1958, at age eighty.

Appendixes

Charles Geoffroy-Dechaume's letter to Dr. Bernard Ménétrel,
Advisor to Marshal Pétain, Premier, Vichy [1940]

Dear M. Secretary:

I greatly appreciated your frank response to my letter and your suggestion that I reply. Don't think for a moment I don't recognize how desperate the situation is. We've been beaten by naked aggression and treason, and what remains for us is to try and survive by guile.

You tell me the Marshal is completely disinterested. Who could doubt that? Indeed, it's his shining honesty that worries me in this situation, where his own personal delusion can be interpreted as heroic sacrifice. His rectitude seems to me utterly defenseless against Hitler's duplicity and Machiavellianism.

Defeat is not dishonorable; to collaborate with an unprincipled enemy is dishonorable. Hitler's victories have been won by cheating and lies. He lied to us at Munich; he swore friendship and peace with Denmark, Belgium, Norway, and Holland. He invaded Holland without declaring war, and in Rotterdam killed 30,000 civilians in three hours. This is a man who rose to power in his own country through the murderous tactics of his secret police. When he began extending these Gestapo methods to all of Europe, that was the time to stop him—even if we were badly prepared.

Is it possible now that a few spineless politicians, for short-term advantage, are ready to irreversibly dishonor France? Never in our history have we suffered such disgrace. Collaboration! Perhaps after the war, but not now, when France's shoulders are pinned to the ground, and the aggressor's knee at our throat.

France won't go along with collaboration because France isn't like Germany, which has made a vice out of obedience. France won't go along with the politicians. The name of France will not be defiled by a policy that brings only shame to those who promote it. There are enough French people who want to protect France's good name.

I implore the Marshal not to give in to traitors, no matter what material benefits are offered. There are things more important than eating well and living comfortably. We are ready to die, if we must. But spare us the shame of collaboration.

At the time of the Armistice, didn't the Marshal say that we wouldn't ever agree to act against our Allies? That is the bottom line. We've been beaten, but our Allies are continuing to fight and they will win. They are our brothers-in-arms. They are *our* soldiers. And quite a few of us have joined them. Happy are those who can fight in these decisive days!

We've denounced the Italians for knifing us in the back when we were down. That's exactly what we'll be doing to England if this odious policy continues. I'm ready to shout "Go back where you came from!" to the million British soldiers buried in France.

It's not only the fate of France that hangs in the balance; it's the fate of all mankind. In this crusade against the common enemy, I hope it won't be said that France repudiated her faith.

May I count on you to tell the Marshal about my letter?

APPENDIX B
Two letters written by Charles Ferdinand-Dreyfus before his deportation:

To Edouard Paulian

September 20, 1942

Sunday Evening

My friend, pass this letter on to Roger[1] and my family. If, as I fear, Lily and her daughters suffer our fate, go see my aunt[2] at 197 bd St Germain. I'm separated from Jacques: he leaves for the East tonight.[3] Without doubt, I'll be going tomorrow. Monod[4] has been to see me. Get in touch with her, if you can. I know Roger just had a daughter. My blessing on this child. For my companions and me, here begins the last phase of our great adventure: in the old days some came back from Siberia; others didn't. So with us in six months. One of my blankets, cut as a cape, will protect me this winter, since I don't have a coat. The enormity of this violence goes beyond us as individuals. I'm staying absolutely calm; I'm being of some use to a few good companions—intelligent, courageous men, valiant women, fearless children. Whether I return, whether Jacques returns, is not the question. Deportation will find me worthy of my past, I swear it. I've had dozens of years of complete happiness. I've created happiness. My fate now is of little importance. Everyone who loves me must be brave when you have no news of me, and be sure that wherever I am I will do what I have to do. I will often be thinking of Patrice[5] whom I love like a father. Jacques has enough clothes and, like me, several days of food for the trip, which we'll be making in unspeakably filthy conditions. I keep repeating the last verse of the "Mort du Loup."[6]

Family, friends, children, I'm carrying in my heart the comforting feelings of your affection. I love you and bless you. If Bel-Air survives, bravo! I will embrace you all after the winter.

To his sister-in-law Lily Ferdinand-Dreyfus

September 22, 1942

9 PM

As you must know, Jacques left Pithiviers Sunday night direct for the East. I was brought back here to be part of the next convoy. I leave tomorrow. Maybe we'll meet each other in Lorraine or further along—maybe not. He had his good woolens and food to last several days. I also have some food and was given sweaters, a coat, and extra blankets. I hope I won't be separated from some good companions who find me helpful. Jacques is in very good form and very courageous; he promised me he'd share the cooking with a young fellow who's resourceful and attentive. I know that the cruelest thing of all for you, as for us, will be the total absence of news. Be patient, be brave. We will see each other again. I hope Julien[7] didn't have to move. My spirit is with you and Clarisse and the young ones and Bel-Air—to all, please transmit my last thoughts of France.

I love you, I clasp you in my arms. France will live.

APPENDIX C

Two letters from Jacqueline d'Alincourt to her family written before her deportation in April, 1944:

We're leaving tomorrow morning—destination unknown. Getting up at 5. This may be the last time I can write. Tonight I'm thinking of all my beloved ones—where will we be tomorrow? Oh sweet France! Leaving her, we know how much we love her. And our dear home, and all those we've known. . . . They're all there, we see them, we're speaking softly to them. We're crying thank you for their love, their friendship, for everything they've given us, crying forgiveness for what we should have been for them, and weren't.

We're going to put on a smile and leave singing. This evening we said the compline together and ended with the Magnificat. We prayed for France, for our dear ones, for all who have given their lives that France may live . . . and we *swore to be worthy of them.* I don't want to worry about what's to come. You pray so much for me that I have the grace of renunciation and inner peace I need. Be at peace, too, my dears, because those who truly put their treasure in Heaven can't be troubled.

Very few of us here are not leaving tomorrow. Much nonsense is rumored about our destination and the way we'll get there. I'm returning my suitcase with some clothes in it, because we're told they'll take everything from us at the border. I'm still doing very well—you know I've decided to hold out at all cost.

We are intensely united in Christ, and all that you pray for, pray for me, too. Courage, my dear ones. Papa and Jo[8] are protecting me, giving me strength. *"Ce n'est qu'un au-revoir, mes frères."* [9]

Yours tenderly

April 18

Past Epernay, rumbling along in sealed boxcars towards . . . ?

Got up at 4 this morning. It must be 6 in the evening. . . . They tell us 36 more hours of travel. Morale magnificent: all fired up. Practically no voice left from singing the Marseillaise and the "Chant des Adieux."

Even if you don't hear any news, don't worry. Whatever happens is under God's guidance. I would like so much to be your lightning rod. . . . [10]

I don't want you to be consumed by worry, but instead to trust God and surrender to His Will. I wish you could see how fervent we are and how stout of heart.

No sacrifice is too great for France, for all her souls.

Aside from those who are sick, no one allows themselves to cry. Smiling is de rigueur. It appears the packages that arrived Monday are following us.

Au-revoir, my loved ones.

APPENDIX D

Letter to Jean Ayral's father from Doctor Cécile Dubost, in whose house Jean Ayral spent his last night:

Signes
November 13, 1944

Dear Sir:

Your unexpected visit moved us so much I'm afraid I didn't tell you everything I should have. . . .

We met him [Jean Ayral; alias Gautier] the morning of August 19, the day Signes was liberated. He was the first Frenchman we saw, the first of General de Gaulle's soldiers! You can imagine what that meant to us! He arrived from out of the blue—although we'd been waiting for him for four years. He was tired from spending several days and nights in the hills. . . . After refreshing himself, he shared our meal, and from that moment on Jean Ayral was at home and knew it. . . .

After lunch, he left us quickly, taking his parachutists and the marines billeted at Lauzière over towards a camp where the Germans were numerous, had reinforcements arriving, and seemed to want to fight. He returned late that night, exhausted and blackened from fighting in recently burned-out woods, but vibrating all over from the excitement. Marie-Claire, Martine,[11] and their little friend Mireille threw themselves on his neck, embracing him. He ate quickly while telling us about his day—he was very keyed up by the fighting. At one point, he said he and some of his men had found themselves surrounded, but managed to disengage and fall back. "My marines were fantastic—I didn't have to think about them. They were always there," he said. "I knew I could count on them to follow me. We were fighting in the dark, in undergrowth, and we'd see silhouettes rushing by—and have to hold fire to see if they were friend or foe. I saw that spoken orders, however brief, gave away our positions, and so we—and the Germans—ended up giving orders by hand signals. At one point I realized I'd shot at a civilian—fortunately I think without hitting him." Then he added, laughing, "But what was he doing in the middle of a battle?"

It was at this point in his story that the incident occurred Marie-Claire told you about: his strangling a German with his hands to avoid the noise of a gunshot. . . .

The next morning, I was to wake him early. Before getting him up, I watched him sleep for a minute. The feverish excitement of the fighting had worn off, his hair was tousled, his face very young and reposed—at that moment I saw your little boy. . . .

He left us promising to come back in two or three days.

We waited for him, but he never came. . . .

Notes

FOREWORD

1. Robert Laffont, 1947.
2. René Julliard, 1961.
3. Librairie Arthème Fayard, 1970.
4. Sarah Fishman, *We Will Wait: Wives of French Prisoners of War, 1940–1945* (Yale University Press, 1991), is excellent on this theme.

CHAPTER ONE

1. We Chevrillons were perhaps better acquainted than others with what was happening in Germany thanks to my father, André, and his prophetic book *La Menace allemande* (Plon, 1934) and because of the refugees, both Jewish and socialist, whom my parents took in.
2. The Phony War was, in French, the Funny War ("drôle de guerre"). It lasted eight months, September, 1939, to May, 1940, during which the enemy armies stood almost motionless, buried along the Franco-German frontier in their fortified lines, the Maginot and Siegfried, watching each other, hardly fighting at all.

CHAPTER TWO

1. In fact they were not able to board the ship. With Pétain's consent, the *Massilia* was commandeered to take political leaders to North Africa, where they would form a government in exile and continue the fight. But the armistice was signed before the ship docked in Casablanca, and on arriving the passengers were treated with suspicion. Four of them, including a future prime minister, Pierre Mendes-France, were thrown in prison for desertion.
2. A nationalist movement of the Right in the 1930s.
3. Affectionate term used by the family for my mother, whose name was Clarisse.

CHAPTER THREE

1. In 1939, the mark had been worth six francs.
2. We heard "Ja, Morgen" (Yes, tomorrow) in so many circumstances that we used it as a joking catchphrase meaning "Never! Out of the question!"
3. It was also very unusual. An American woman had begun building it in the 1860s, planning to receive her friend Napoleon III there in pomp. It wasn't quite finished with the 1870 war with Germany broke out, and the woman fled the country. She disappeared, and for years the house lay abandoned. Finally the government put it up for sale, and Claire's mother's father bought it at a bargain price to use as their country house. When Claire's grandparents died, Claire's parents kept it for its magnifi-

cent view of the west of Paris across the Bois de Boulogne. Her parents
lived there until the arrival of the Luftwaffe.—Trans.

4.   Ceremonial suit worn by members of the French Academy.

CHAPTER FOUR

1.   The term "émigrés" was used during the French Revolution to show contempt for those aristocrats who fled France, many of them joining the enemy army (Austrian).—Trans.

CHAPTER FIVE

1.   Collège Sévigné, founded in the late nineteenth century, was one of the
first high schools for girls in France. A private school subsidized by the
government, it went from kindergarten through preparation for the presti-
gious agrégation exam.—Trans.

CHAPTER SIX

1.   The Ferdinand-Dreyfuses were not related to Alfred Dreyfus, the French
military officer and Jew who was the center of the Dreyfus Affair.—
Trans.

CHAPTER SEVEN

1.   All these figures and those which follow come from a document I put together at the end of 1944 for lectures I gave in England. The main sources
I drew upon in preparing the document were my memory, the Consistoire
de Paris, and Madeleine Barot, founder of CIMADE, an organization that
helps foreigners in France.

2.   When Jews were ordered to wear the Yellow Star, Claire got a yellow cloth
flower and pinned it on the left lapel of her jacket. She wore it for several
days until two or three anti-Semitic activists came to her apartment and
rudely told her to stop it or she'd get into trouble. She later learned many
other people in Paris had done the same thing, among them a seventeen-
year-old Collège Sévigné student, not a Jew, who wore the Yellow Star out
of sympathy for a Jewish school friend. She was denounced, arrested, and
kept three months in an internment camp.—Trans.

CHAPTER NINE

1.   Unfortunately I don't know much about Paul's time as a prisoner of war.
He almost never spoke of it, and my memory of what he did say is un-
clear. He burned his letters to Antoinette after her death, and the letters
he received in prison were lost during his forced marches at the time he
was set free. He never wrote of his experience because he said he didn't
want such things to drag on.

2.   Bernard Auffray, *Sur mon chemin j'ai rencontré* (Klincksieck, 1979).

3.   Letter from Eugene Arnaud, September 8, 1984.

4.   Abbreviation of Poil d'Hérisson, Paul's nickname among the Scouts. He was given the name because he bristled (*se hérisser*) easily.

5.   Letter from R. Michel, March 16, 1985.

CHAPTER TEN

1.   The report, dated December 31, 1940, was signed "Some Alsatians expelled by the German authorities." I still have it.

2.   The full text of the letter is given in the Appendix.

3.   Ginette Janin, one of Claire's Collège Sévigné students, reports that she and her classmates learned the Geoffroys' song and, when they went to the cellars of the nearby Val-de-Grace Hospital during air raids, would sing it—"yell it"—hoping to be heard by the Germans occupying the building.—TRANS.

4.   I.e., the French.

5.   Charles Ferdinand-Dreyfus's letters appears in his *Quelques lettres* (published by his friends, 1950).

CHAPTER ELEVEN

1.   Denis, twenty-one, Sylvie's brother, was living in his father's painting studio, rue Roussin, Paris. He would later join us on the rue de Grenelle.

2.   For the bombing of the factories at Poissy.

CHAPTER TWELVE

1.   The Germans had occupied our Small House in the summer of 1940, then found more comfortable accommodations. They continued to walk in and out of our garden to use their observation post on the terrace.

2.   Jean Valjean is the hero of Victor Hugo's *Les Miserables.*—TRANS.

3.   Geneviève, Claudine, and Françoise are Renée's sisters. Daniel is her brother; he had gone south with the army, disappeared for a time, and then turned up in Avignon. Alice is their nanny.—TRANS.

4.   A transit camp in a Paris suburb.

5.   Claire Chevrillon, the author of this memoir.—TRANS.

6.   Julien Cain, former director of the Bibliothèque Nationale. See chapter 7.—TRANS.

7.   A social worker.

8.   It had been built before the war to house the families of gendarmes, but was never finished. In 1939 it was used to intern Communists and, after the Occupation, British, Greek, and Yugoslav civilians. By August, 1941, Drancy was a transit camp for Jews awaiting deportation. Over the next three years seventy thousand Jews, including pregnant women, children, and old people, stayed there, crowded together in abominable conditions. It was staffed by French police until July, 1943, when the Gestapo took over.

CHAPTER THIRTEEN

1.   Real name: Jean Ayral. I will call him Robert Gautier in this narrative because it was by this name that I knew him.

2. The eldest son of the Geoffroy-Dechaumes. See chapter 1.
3. A metropolitan force limited by the Armistice terms to those troops "necessary to maintain order." A few days later Marc joined the French Army of North Africa.

CHAPTER FOURTEEN

1. De Gaulle's speech was addressed to the French in North Africa. Its climax: "Officers, soldiers, sailors, pilots, government workers, colonists, now is the time to rise. Join the Allies! Help them unreservedly! Come, this is the great moment! This is the time when common sense and courage must prevail!"
2. On this subject, see in particular Charles de Gaulle's *Mémoires de guerre* (Plon, 1956), vol. 2: *L'Unité;* and Churchill's *History of the Second World War* (Houghton Mifflin, 1948–53), vol. 4: *The Hinge of Fate.*
3. On November 27, 1942, as the Germans approached, the fleet scuttled three battleships, eight cruisers, sixteen submarines, seventeen destroyers, sixteen destroyer-escorts, ten patrol vessels, and some sixty freight carriers, tankers, and mine-sweepers. Seven ships were not sunk and were later used by the Germans. Five submarines escaped. See de Gaulle, *Mémoires de guerre,* vol. 2, p. 63.

CHAPTER FIFTEEN

1. Gautier's BCRA code name was Pal.
2. Later, back in England, he would undergo brain surgery.
3. Code name: Max.
4. Real name: François Briant. His BCRA code name was Pal W.
5. Although the Germans had taken over all of France after the Allied invasion of North Africa in November, 1942, the frontier between the Free and Occupied zones remained in force until March, 1943.

CHAPTER SIXTEEN

1. Some dates and details of the following events are given in Paul Schmidt's article on François Briant (Charles Baron), "François Briant, lieutenant des FFL," *Gens de la lune,* no. 28, Apr.–May, 1950.
2. Real name: André Dewawrin.
3. Conseil National de la Résistance.
4. Real name: Paul Schmidt. He had participated in the Norway campaign in the Spring of 1940, been with the FFL in June, 1940, and then transferred to BCRA, where his code name was Kim.
5. The following conversation is quoted from Jean Ayral's unpublished "Carnets de guerre."
6. A town a few miles west of Paris.
7. Gestapo headquarters.
8. The rule for a BCRA agent was not to reveal anything for at least a week after being arrested. During that time all links in his network would be changed.
9. The operator was Louis Tolmé, who had parachuted into France just two

weeks earlier. We didn't know that he had in fact already been denounced by Gilbert and arrested. He was tortured, interned at Fresnes, and later deported. He survived and returned to France in May, 1945.

CHAPTER EIGHTEEN

1. *Schnell:* quick; *raus* (a shortened form of *heraus*): out. These were words I would hear again and again.
2. Easter morning I asked the guard who led me to my cell how many people were in Fresnes. "Ah, more and more," he said. "Seven thousand—maybe nine thousand."
3. Her real name was Renée Mirande-Thomas.

CHAPTER NINETEEN

1. Compiègne, thirty-five miles northeast of Paris, was a transit camp for those "political" prisoners to be deported. They were kept just long enough to fill a train. The difference between Compiègne and Drancy, also a transit camp, was that Drancy was mainly for Jews.
2. This number was confirmed by Paul Schmidt (Dominique). See Henri Nogueres, *Histoire de la Résistance,* vol. 3 (Laffont, 1972), p. 318.
3. Real name: Gilbert Védy. He was one of the leaders of Ceux de la Libération.
4. As things turned out, the book didn't get published. Father Riquet was arrested and deported to Dachau. In addition to his work for Témoignage Chrétien, he was directing an escape network for Allied pilots. He survived the deportation and came back to France at the end of the war.
5. An underground network in the North headed by Colonel Rémy (real name: Gilbert Renault-Roulier).

CHAPTER TWENTY

1. Evelyne was in touch with the police section of the NAP (Noyautage de l'Administration Publique), an underground organization that infiltrated the civil service.
2. I later learned that Pierre headed Maquis operations in and around Paris.
3. One of the most important papers of the Resistance. There were forty-seven clandestine issues, from July, 1941, to August, 1944. The forty-eighth issue, the first one openly published, was for sale in the Paris streets on August 22, 1944, in the middle of the insurrection.
4. Real name: Daniel Cordier; BCRA code name: Bip W. Cordier escaped to England in June, 1940, leading fourteen volunteers, and parachuted back into France in July, 1942, with Robert Gautier and Charles Baron, as a radio operator for Georges Bidault. Jean Moulin made him his secretary, giving him important work to do—encoding, decoding, drafting reports, liaison, etc. Since Moulin's arrest, Cordier had been working with Claude Serreulles (code name: Sophie), Moulin's temporary replacement.
5. National Council of the Resistance (Conseil National de la Résistance).
6. The annual Scout camp we attended in the years before the war. It was common for the leaders there to work themselves until they dropped.

CHAPTER TWENTY-ONE

1. Real name: Pierre Péry.
2. François Clouet was a French sixteenth-century painter Claire admired.— TRANS.
3. Alias: Claude Large; code name: Germain.
4. After the Liberation, the landlady was arrested and condemned to death. Her sentence was commuted to twenty years. She spent a few years in prison, then was released.
5. The "true-false" cards were forgeries made with completely authentic materials—printing, stamps, etc.—and were usually obtained through agents of the NAP working in municipalities.
6. The Germans always spoke as if those detained would be judged in court. They seldom were, except at the beginning of the Occupation. Detainees were either deported or released.
7. A few months later both Annie and Elizabeth were arrested for reasons I never knew. Elizabeth was sentenced to ten months in prison. Deported, she served time in fourteen different German prisons, three months being added to her term because she refused to work for the Nazi war effort. She escaped during a bombing attack in February, 1945, and tried in vain to reach the Russian lines. For a month she hid alone in an abandoned school before she was discovered by the village police. She was dismissed as a lunatic and wound up in Bavaria, where the Americans repatriated her at the end of April. She resumed teaching in Paris the following fall. Annie was imprisoned at Fresnes and not deported.

CHAPTER TWENTY-TWO

1. French Committee of National Liberation (Comité Français de Libération Nationale), de Gaulle's cabinet in Algiers. It became the Provisional Government, the GPRF (Gouvernement Provisoire de la République Française), on June 2, 1944.
2. Claudes Serreulles, sent by de Gaulle in June, 1943, to assist Jean Moulin. When Moulin was arrested on June 21, Serreulles took over his responsibilities and headed the Delegation until March, 1944.
3. Jacques Bingen parachuted into France from London in August, 1943, to assist Serreulles. He was arrested on May 13, 1944, escaped, was retaken, and swallowed a cyanide pill.
4. Alexandre Parodi, a former member of the Conseil d'Etat and a high official in the Ministry of Labor, refused to serve the Vichy government. In March, 1944, de Gaulle named him head of the Delegation, replacing Serreulles.
5. Real name: Georges Lecot. Lecot, a coder with the French Expeditionary Corps in Norway, arrived in London in June, 1940, and immediately put himself at de Gaulle's disposal. Before parachuting into France in 1943, he helped Colonel Passy create BCRA.
6. Her husband.
7. For her clean linen and, perhaps, hidden messages.
8. Code name of Hugues Limonti, a Delegation agent.
9. Benjamin.
10. Claude Serreulles.

11. Benjamin had taken several photos of Jacqueline just before her arrest.
12. Limonti's alias.
13. Pierre Péry.
14. Gestapo.
15. A name I once called her that stuck.
16. Benjamin, whom Jacqueline knew under his earlier code name, Alain.
17. Evidently a letter or package from me had reached her.
18. A shop selling mainly dairy products where one could sit and eat. We frequented crèmeries in those days because they were quicker, cheaper, and less conspicuous than restaurants.
19. Marie-France led at least one group to Guingamp, in Brittany, where, after dark, M. Kerambrun, a car mechanic friend of ours, drove them in his old truck to the Maison d'Alphonse, not far from Plouha, some fifteen hundred yards from the sea. From there, once they heard the okay on the BBC, they were led down a steep cliff (never watched because it was considered too dangerous) to the sea. They then waited in a cave for a British ship to send in dinghies to pick them up. Between January and August, 1944, there were eight such operations, which rescued 135 pilots. For more information, see Rémy, *La Maison d'Alphonse* (Librairie Académique Perrin, 1968).
20. Francis Closon, *Au temps des passions* (Presses de la Cité, 1974).

CHAPTER TWENTY-THREE
1. Jeanne's real name was Simone Lemoine. For her story, which I learned only forty years later, see the Epilogue.
2. Later, she had the immense pleasure of typing the surrender terms for German troops in Paris, which General Leclerc dictated to her and which General von Choltitz signed.
3. For an example, see the photo on page 136.
4. Pierre Pucheu had been Minister of Interior in October, 1941, when many French hostages were executed in reprisal for the killing of German officers. He was accused of asking the Germans to change a hostage list that included many military veterans for one in which Communists predominated. He had been arrested in Algiers by the CFLN and was executed in March, 1944.
5. In September and October, 1939, Thorez under instruction from Moscow had led a campaign against the "imperialist war" that resulted in the dissolution of the Party and the dispersal of its leaders. Thorez fled to the Soviet Union, where he was condemned in absentia by Vichy as a deserter. After the Liberation, he was granted amnesty and returned to France. He was named a member of the Assemblée Consultative and then Ministre d'Etat by de Gaulle.
6. Brossolette had waited for three months (November, 1943–January, 1944) to be picked up and flown to England, but bad weather kept planes from landing. Impatient, he decided to leave by boat from Brittany. Storms forced the boat back to shore. The car he was trying to get away in was stopped at a German roadblock and Brossolette was put in a Rennes prison for having tried to leave the country illegally. The police didn't

know they had Brossolette in their hands until March 19. He was then immediately transferred from Rennes to Paris, where he was interrogated and tortured (March 21). When his torturers left the room for a few minutes, he jumped out of the window.

7.   Dr. Girard and Anise were arrested in 1942, Anise, eighteen, for furnishing military information to BCRA's Intelligence Service, her father for having served as a mailbox for the same service. Neither had known of the other's activity.

8.   Miss Rothery, our English governess for two years, had impressed upon us that the most important character trait was "to be reliable."

CHAPTER TWENTY-FOUR

1.   The Milice was the national parapolice force of volunteers that helped the Vichy regime fight the Resistance, especially the Maquis. In our epistolary code Milicien stood for Maquisard.

2.   To make it easier for the censors, all other languages were forbidden in correspondence from concentration camps.

3.   "Shorthand" stood for coding.

4.   A pun on the name Chevrillon, which means little goat.—TRANS.

5.   Organization Civile et Militaire, a Resistance unit in the North.

CHAPTER TWENTY-FIVE

1.   A notorious Communist, Mme. Perrot later played an important part in the liberation of Tréguier. A street in the town is named after her.

2.   Fassier's remarkable career in the war is described in the Epilogue.

3.   The excerpts are in chronological order as best I can reconstruct it, given the fact that some of the letters are undated.

4.   Denise (Renée Mirande-Thomas) was still in Fresnes at the time.

5.   A childhood nickname that stuck to me. A *sauvageon* is a little savage.

6.   A letter I'd written after Jacqueline's arrest made Antoinette understand I was going to become a coding agent. To "marry Gerard" meant going to England.

7.   Light and nimble André.

8.   Like a fearful mother hen, I said no!

9.   André, working by correspondence, was in the third grade. Later, he transferred back to the second.

10.   Louise le Gall, a Breton girl, had worked for my sister until just before her marriage.

11.   They were probably Flying Fortresses come to bomb a German naval base at the mouth of the Trieux.

12.   These were for Charles Baron, who'd sent me a postcard from his concentration camp in Germany asking for them.

13.   Jean and Yvonne Stéphans' second son.

14.   Antoinette is referring to our mother's wearing the Yellow Star.

15.   Lily Ferdinand-Dreyfus had invited Antoinette and the children to Montfort l'Amaury.

16.   They were anti-Soviet Ukrainians serving in the German Army. They were much feared by the local population.

17. I'd gone to Port-Blanc for two or three days unannounced in answer to her distress. I couldn't tell Antoinette I was coming because Port-Blanc was in the Forbidden Zone.
18. The Goasmeurs were our neighbors on the coast; Antoinette was telling me that our property had not been mined.
19. A Chevrillon expression for a special kind of fine weather in Port-Blanc: east wind, light blue sea, and intermittent haze.
20. They were probably about local women sleeping with Germans. There were those who did it in Port-Blanc, as elsewhere—a good source for gossip.
21. A small island opposite the Port-Blanc harbor.
22. During a bomb attack, fields were safer than houses.
23. My father was eighty on May 3. André was of course alluding to Allied victory in the war.
24. The play was the naval battle off Saint-Gildas. Charlotte stood for the Allies; Albert, for the Germans. Though we never learned the outcome of the naval battle, no one doubted the Allies had won.
25. The Germans were cutting down trees for posts to stick in the beach to prevent landings.
26. Our parents were living on the sixth floor. There was an electric elevator, but more and more often no power.
27. When Italy surrendered, the Germans captured Italian soldiers to prevent their joining the Allies. They treated them with the greatest contempt.
28. In this café you could listen secretly to the BBC.
29. In 1985 André told me they were probably decoys made of bands of aluminum paper to trick enemy radar.
30. The real news was the BBC news that Antoinette listened to at Mme. Pellerin's, on the far side of the garden.
31. The typhoid probably refers to German reprisals against underground activity. Mme. Auffret was the wife of one of Paul's prison mates who lived near Langoat, where there had been some killings.

CHAPTER TWENTY-SIX
1. They were Mme. Lestic, Mme. Désiré Bellec, Ginette Hamon, Jean Tanguy, and Charles Marchand, of Port-Blanc, and Marie Savéan and Yvette Guélou, of Penvénan.
2. Attached to the British Army in 1940, he participated in the Libyan campaign. At Kerien he was working for the British War Office. He would soon become Chief of Staff, Second Division, FFT.
3. Alias Grégoire. See the Epilogue.
4. François Flohic mentions this landing in his *Ni chagrin, ni pitié* (Plon, 1985). Flohic, a young naval officer on board one of three French frigates escorting the American ships, writes that "the operation went off as if the enemy didn't exist."

CHAPTER TWENTY-SEVEN
1. Name commonly used for German soldiers because of the greenish-gray—vert de gris—color of their uniforms.

2. So far as I know, the messages given here have never been published. The last three, however, appear almost word for word in a dispatch General Marie-Koenig, recently appointed commander-in-chief of the FFI, sent General de Gaulle on August 22 at 11 P.M. See de Gaulle's *Mémoires de Guerre*, vol. 2, p. 705. Another message is referred to in D. Lapierre and L. Collins, *Paris brule-t-il?* (Livre de Poche, 1984), p. 328. I have added punctuation to make the messages clearer.

3. Alexandre Parodi.

4. Ministry of the Interior of the Provisional French Government.

5. Committee of Military Action attached to BCRA (London).

6. General Koenig was still in London.

7. Only the telephone—indispensable to resistants—would continue to function normally until the Liberation.

8. Roland Pré, Parodi's assistant.

9. René Massigli was a member of the Provisional Government.

10. Raoul Nordling.

11. German Military Command.

12. Major General Dietrich von Choltitz.

13. Paris Liberation Committee (Comité Parisien de Libération), a group with a majority of Communists, wanted immediate action. CNR, the national organization, preferred to wait for H-hour, the time for general insurrection, to be announced by Allied Command.

14. FFI: Forces Françaises de l'Interieur (French Forces of the Interior) were troops from metropolitan France—that is, the Maquis. Parisians often referred to these troops affectionately as "Fifis." The FFL (French Forces of the Liberation) were French troops from England or Algeria.

15. Paris police headquarters.

16. British Intelligence Service.

17. See explanation below, n. 26.

18. Military Action Committee (Commission d'Action Militaire) attached to BCRA and CNR. This was one of the few times COMAC sent a message through the Delegation code service.

19. Military headquarters of the Resistance in Paris.

20. Jacques Chaban-Delmas, national military delegate of the Provisional Government.

21. In his dispatch to de Gaulle, General Koenig reduced this figure to thirty thousand—still an inflated number, according to Adrien Dansette in his *Histoire de la Libération de Paris* (A. Fayard, 1946). It was impossible to determine the exact number of FFI because of secrecy and confusion.

22. I doubt any parachute drop took place in Paris.

23. I was on foot because I was afraid of losing my bicycle. The Germans were "requisitioning" them.

24. Noyautage de l'Administration Publique, an underground organization that infiltrated the civil service.

25. This was one of the best places in Paris to stage an ambush. Vehicles would come thundering down the boulevard at full speed and then look in vain, right and left, for a way to escape. More than forty trucks and cars were seized this way.

26. In fact, I learned later that the truce had provoked heated controversy

among Resistance leaders. Those on the left strongly opposed it as an intolerable show of weakness. Not everyone obeyed it.

27. Jacqueline hadn't mentioned anything about my needing a code. I assumed Parodi would have one or more at his disposal because carrying them about was strictly forbidden.
28. This announcement was premature and misled many Parisians.
29. A name used for the lowest-ranking German soldiers.
30. The Luxembourg Gardens and Palace, occupied by seven hundred SS, was the last garrison in Paris to surrender. It did so on August 25, having continued to fight for several hours after General von Choltitz signed the surrender of all German forces in the French capital.
31. In fact, those were Hitler's orders to General von Choltitz.

EPILOGUE

1. *L'Espèce humaine* (Gallimard, 1979).
2. By June, 1944, the editors of *Défense de la France* had started their own maquis, called DF, in the Paris region. They wanted to fight with arms as well as with pen.
3. The Russian army's battlefront line couldn't take care of the prisoners of war and so sent them to the rear.
4. All French freight cars were then labeled "40 men or 8 horses."
5. Mercure de France, 1957.
6. The title comes from the old tale of the wife-killing Blue Beard. The seventh wife, waiting in terror for her brother to rescue her, asks her sister over and over again, "Ann, sister Ann, seest thou aught a-coming?" Ann always answers, "Naught but the dust a-blowing." Anne-Marie took that sentence as a metaphor for her long wait for the Allies to liberate her camp. Librairie José Corti, 1957.
7. For more on his last days, see Dr. Cécile Dubost's letter to Ayral's father in the Appendix. See also André Vulliez, "La fantastique adventure de Jean Ayral," *Hommes et Mondes* 117 (April, 1956) and 118 (May, 1956). I am also drawing information from a talk I had with Ayral's father in February, 1945, which I described in a letter to my sister.
8. François's death was described by Marc Perrot, one of the men climbing with him, in a July 16, 1948, letter to François's friends. See also Paul Schmidt, "François Briant, lieutenant des FFL," *Gens de la lune* 28, April–May, 1950.
9. See the Appendix for two letters she wrote the day before she was deported.
10. See chapter 21.
11. He was referring to the FFI.
12. He was executed in April, 1945.
13. Nacht und Nebel—Night and Fog—was the designation the Nazis gave the prisoners they considered most dangerous; such prisoners were cut off from all contact with others.
14. Claire Girard was the daughter of Mme. Girard who'd joined our code service that spring. See chapter 23.
15. See chapter 22.

16. A research library containing all books and articles published in France and elsewhere about de Gaulle.
17. During these rambles he would often stop to see Antoinette and offer counsel and support.
18. There are eighty conseillers d'Etat in France. Their responsibility is to preserve the French constitution by acting as a kind of review board for the ministries.—TRANS.

APPENDIXES
1. Roger Louvet, a former student at Bel-Air, became its manager.
2. Clarisse Chevrillon.
3. Charles was mistaken. Jacques would go back to Pithiviers a few days later. He was deported July 31, 1943.
4. Mlle. Monod, a social worker.
5. One of Edouard Paulian's sons.
6. Famous Romantic poem by Alfred de Vigny. Its stoic last lines:

> Groaning, crying, praying are all equally cowardly.
> Do energetically the long and heavy task
> That Fate has given you.
> Then, like me, suffer and die without a word.

7. Julien Cain, Lily Ferdinand-Dreyfus's brother-in-law, then at Compiègne. He was later deported to Buchenwald.
8. Her husband, Joseph de Lorne d'Alincourt, who died in German captivity in 1941.
9. "This is just good-bye for now, brothers, we'll meet again"—a line from the "Chant des Adieux" (Song of Farewell), sung to the tune of "Auld Lang Syne.—TRANS.
10. The translation here is literal. Jacqueline means she hopes so much that her suffering will prevent those she loves from having to suffer.—TRANS.
11. Dr. Dubost's daughters.

Index

Abbeville, 9
Académie française. *See* French Academy
Aix-la-Chapelle, 179
Algeria, 18, 212
Algiers, 71, 77, 110, 116, 119, 120, 127, 173, 175, 208, 209
Allied pilots, 74, 123, 207
Allies, 194, 198, 212; in Normandy, 139, 155; in North Africa, 70–71, 77, 137, 206; in Paris, 158, 159, 160, 165
Alsace and Lorraine, 26, 51
American Academy of Arts and Letters, xi
American troops, 152–53, 164
American Zone, 171
Amicale des Anciennes Déportées de Ravensbruck (Society of Former Ravensbruck Deportees), 179
Antelme, Robert, 167
anti-Semitism, xvi, 56, 58; and deportations, xiii, xvi, 61–66, 77, 199; and laws, 33–35; and press, 25–26. *See also* Yellow Star; Vichy regime
Appollyon (Pierre Chevrillon), 123
Armistice (1940), 13, 52, 71; terms of, 17, 26
Armistice Army, 71, 206
Arnaud, Eugene, 40, 204
Ascq, 127
Atlantic Wall, 106–107
Auffray, Bernard, 40, 169, 204
Auschwitz-Birkenau, 59, 167
Au temps de passion (Closon), 123, 209
Avignon, 77
Avranches, 152, 156
Ayral, Jean (Robert Gautier), 68, 69, 72–78, 79, 80, 81–83, 86, 88, 93, 95, 99, 114, 173, 207, 200–202, 205, 206, 207, 213; arrest and escape of, 101–103

Barbie, Klaus, 110, 172, 173
Barcelona, 67, 122, 123
Baron, Charles. *See* Briant, François
Battle of Britain, 23–24, 31
Battle of France, xv–xvi
Bauer, Anne-Marie (Claudine), 67, 68, 69, 93, 172–73, 213; arrested, 109
BBC, 17, 18, 23, 24, 42, 51, 70, 122, 126, 127, 140, 142, 143, 155, 160, 163
BCRA. *See* Bureau Central de Renseignement et d'Action
Beaune-la-Rolande, 64, 66
Beauvais, 17, 20
Bel-Air School Farm, 10, 11, 54
Belgium, xii, 9, 13
Belladone. *See* Parodi, Alexandre
Bergson, Henri, 37
Bibliothèque Nationale, xv, 33
Bidault, Georges, 207
Bingen, Jacques (Cleante; Cadillac), xv, 119, 127, 208
black market, 23, 31
Blum, Léon, 62
BOA. *See* Bureau des Opérations Ariennes
Boillot, Claude (Major Drinkwater), 194
Boitel, Jeanne (Mozart), 161
bombing: Allied, 179; German, 3, 4
Bordeaux, 10, 11; French government in, 12, 14, 17, 24
Boulogne, 10, 37
Boulogne-Billancourt, xvii
Bourg-Dun, 4, 7, 8, 52
Brest, 153, 194
Briant, François (Charles Baron), 76, 79, 80, 81–83, 93, 100, 125, 126, 141, 143, 175–76, 206, 207, 210, 213
Britain. *See* Great Britain

British Army, 18, 156, 170, 211
British Broadcasting Company. *See* BBC
British civilians in France, 28
British Intelligence Service (IS), 158, 212
British pilots, 54, 111
British Secret Service 76, 78, 81
British War Office, 194, 211
Brittany, 11, 14, 15, 76, 94, 176; German navy in, 153, 154; German troops in, 14, 15, 18, 19, 20, 23, 106, 152, 210; liberation of, 151–55; military installations in, 193
Brossolette, Pierre (Brumaire), 79, 104, 122, 127, 209, 210
Brumaire. *See* Brossolette, Pierre
Buchenwald, 33, 70, 109, 175, 176, 181, 214
Bureau Central de Renseignement et d'Action (BCRA), 73–74, 78, 79, 80, 101, 102, 111, 125, 126, 173, 174, 176, 182, 184, 193, 206, 207, 208, 210, 212
Bureau des Opérations Ariennes (BOA), xi, 73–74, 75
Bures-sur-Yvette, 139

Cadot, Mme., 183
Caen-Falaise, 156
Cain, Julien, xv, 64, 199, 205, 214; anti-Nazi views of, 33–34; and Bibliothèque Nationale, 33; deported, 109
Casablanca, 203
Ceux de la Liberation, 79, 81, 207. *See also* Resistance groups
CFLN. *See* Comité Français de Libération Nationale
Chaban-Delmas, Jacques, 159, 212
"Chant des Partisans," 53
Charles de Gaulle Institute, 184
Chartres, 10, 156
Chateaubriant, 52
Chateau-Thierry, 181
Chevrillon, André, xi, xv, xvii, 15, 17, 30, 32, 59, 60, 70, 72, 86, 100–101, 106, 112, 123, 124, 140, 164, 177, 203
Chevrillon, Claire: arrested, 84–89; in Code Service, 124–28; goes underground, 115–16; imprisoned, 89–100; joins Resistance, 67–69; as teacher, 4–5, 37–38
Chevrillon, Clarisse, 15, 30, 32, 70, 72, 93, 100, 106, 112, 140, 164, 203, 213; and Yellow Star, 58–59

Chevrillon, Pierre, xii, 11, 12, 16, 47, 68, 86, 93, 100–101, 141, 211
Churchill, Winston, 13, 17, 24, 206
Cleante. *See* Bingen, Jacques
Clermont-Ferrand, 68, 69
Closon, Francis, 123, 209
Clouet, François, 208
CNR. *See* Conseil National de la Résistance
Coat-Nevenez, 152
Code Service. *See* Service du Chiffre de la Délégation Générale du Gouvernement Provisoire
Colditz, 170
collaboration, ix, 96, 197; and Vichy, 42, 67
Collège Sévigné, xi, 4, 22, 28, 33, 67, 79, 80, 83, 104, 105, 115, 122, 125, 127, 204
Collins, L., 212
Colonel Rémy. *See* Renault-Roulier, Gilbert
COMAC (Commission d'Action Militaire, attached to CNR), 159, 212
COMIDAC (Commission d'Action Militaire, attached to BCRA), 157, 159
Comité Français de Libération Nationale (CFLN), 116, 119, 127, 208, 209
Comité Parisien de Libération (CPL), 158, 205, 209, 212
Commission d'Action Militaire. *See* COMAC; COMIDAC
communists, 52, 87, 127, 160, 178; and Resistance, 127, 212. *See also* Franc-Tireurs-Partisans; maquis
Compiègne, 77, 100, 207, 214
concentration camps, 35, 167, 169, 173; in Paris region, 157. *See also* Auschwitz-Birkenau; Buchenwald; Dachau; Manthausen; Ravensbruck
Confrérie Notre-Dame, 104. *See also* Resistance groups
Conseil d'Etat, 178, 194, 208, 214
Conseil National de la Résistance (CNR), 79, 110, 127, 157, 158, 206, 207, 209, 212
Cordier, Daniel (Bip W), xv, 110, 112, 114, 115–16, 120, 121, 122, 207, 209
Corps Auxiliaire Volontaire Féminin (CAVF), 176
Corrèze, xviii, 68, 69, 109, 174
Corsica, 143, 173
Cours de la Civilisation Française, xii–xiii
CPL. *See* Comité Parisien de Libération
Croix de Berny, 105

Croix de Feu, xv, 14
Crozon peninsula, 194

Dachau, 207
Darlan, Admiral François, 36, 71
d'Astier de la Virgerie, Emmanuel (Merlin),
    119, 125, 127
D-Day, 127, 129, 138
de Bénouville, Guillain, xv
Défense de la France, 110, 125, 141, 148, 168,
    207, 213
de Gaulle, Charles, 13, 17; French attitude to-
    ward, 26–27, 42; and Pétain, 27, 36, 51, 70,
    71, 73, 76, 108, 116, 139, 159, 160, 161, 163,
    206, 208, 212, 214
de Gaulle, Geneviève, 126
de Jouvenal, Bertrand, 174, 176
de la Rocque, Colonel François, xv, 14
Délégation Générale, xii, xv, xvii, 117, 119–20,
    124, 125, 138, 139, 158, 159, 208, 212
Delegation's Code Service. *See* Service du
    Chiffre de la Délégation Générale du Gouv-
    ernement Provisoire
Delestraint, General Charles, 108
de Lorne d'Alincourt, Jacqueline (Violaine),
    76–77, 79, 80, 82, 93, 101, 103–104, 110–11,
    113, 114, 115, 116, 117; deported, 121–22, 143,
    149; letters from, 199–200; returned, 176;
de Lorne d'Alincourt, Joseph, 214
Demarcation Line, xvi, 29, 35, 76
de Musset, Alfred, 120
deportations. *See* anti-Semitism
de Vigny, Alfred, 214
Dewawrin, André (Colonel Passy), 79, 206,
    208
Drancy, xvi, 61, 62; conditions at, 63–66, 158,
    159, 167, 205, 207, 212
Dresden, 40, 169
Dreux, 156
Dreyfus, Alfred, 204
Dreyfus Affair, 124
Druon, Maurice, 53
Duhamel, Georges, xv, 38, 109
Dunkirk, 9, 10, 16

Echaron, 129, 155, 164
Epernay, 200
Exodus, xvi, 10–12, 37, 67, 69, 156

Fabre, Antoinette, xvi, 6–7, 9, 16, 20, 42, 57,
    59, 100–106, 140, 204, 210
Fabre, Paul, xii, xvi; in prison, 16, 20, 22, 23,
    39–43, 145, 204, 205, 211
Fassier, Charles (Grégoire), 142, 152, 184,
    193–95
Ferdinand-Dreyfus, Charles, xii, 10, 32; in
    Fresnes, 54–56, 60–66, 141, 167, 198–99, 204,
    205
Ferdinand-Dreyfus, Daniel, 16, 63, 65, 77–78,
    85, 93, 108, 112, 124, 141–42, 168–69, 205
Ferdinand-Dreyfus, Jacques, xii, xv, 16, 32,
    33, 34, 56, 59–60, 61–66; arrested, 77; in Min-
    istry of Labor, 107–108, 141, 167, 198–99,
    204, 213
Ferdinand-Dreyfus, Lily, 15, 16, 21, 34, 59, 61–
    66, 112, 147, 168, 169, 210, 214
Ferdinand-Dreyfus, Renée, 34, 60–65, 108,
    205
Ferdonnet, 5
Fez, xiii
FFB. *See* Forces Françaises de Bretagne
FFI. *See* Forces Françaises de l'Interieur
FFL. *See* Forces Françaises Libres
"fifth column," 11–12
"final solution," xvi. *See also* anti-Semitism
First French Army, 165
Flohic, François, 211
Fontainebleau, 124
Forbidden Zone, 26, 80, 210
forced labor in Germany, 53
Forces Françaises de Bretagne (FFB), 194, 195
Forces Françaises de l'Interieur (FFI), 158–
    63, 165, 168, 179, 212
Forces Françaises Libres (FFL), 51; training
    agents for, 73, 212
Fort de Montluc, 173
Fort du Ha, 77
Franco-German Armistice (1940). *See* Armi-
    stice
François, Louis, 104
Francs-Tireurs-Partisans (FTP), 52. *See also*
    maquis
Free French Navy, 194, 206
Free French units, 10, 156
Free Zone, 26, 29, 35, 51, 52, 63, 67–68; Ger-
    mans invade, 71, 75, 76; Jews and, 35, 63
Frejus, 117
French Academy, xi, xv, xvii, 21, 72, 109, 204
French anti-Bolshevik Legion, 95

French Committee of National Liberation (CFLN), 116, 119, 127, 208, 209
French Expeditionary Corps, 208
French Navy, 17, 18, 173
French police, 55, 84, 85, 175; and roundup of Jews, 59
French Provisional Government (GPRF), 159, 160, 162, 163, 208, 212
French Republic, 161
French troops, 158, 166
Fresnes, xvi, 55, 56, 89–100, 104, 105–106, 110, 115–17, 121, 175, 176, 177, 178, 179, 182, 183, 207
Freud, Sigmund, 3

Galsworthy, John, xi
Garches, 81
Gaullism, xviii, 75, 87, 115, 170; and Pétainists, 27
Gautier, Robert. See Ayral, Jean
General Commission on Jewish Affairs, 34
general mobilization, 3
General Union of French Jews, 61
Gensoul, Admiral, 18
Geoffroy-Dechaume, Antoine, 16, 69–70, 93, 109, 138, 143, 174–75, 177, 205
Geoffroy-Dechaume, Charles, 7–8, 52–54, 109, 138–39, 197–98
Geoffroy-Dechaume, Marie-France, 5, 6, 7, 8, 9, 27, 37, 38, 69, 75, 90, 123, 209
German propaganda, 18, 25; and Mers-el-Kebir, 18
German Relief Committee, 29
German troops, xvi, 174, 194, 209; in Bordeaux, 14; in Brittany, 14, 24; in Paris, 29, 156, 158, 160, 164, 167; in Port-Blanc, 18, 20, 31; in Soucy, 54–55
Gestapo, xvi, 9, 10, 11, 74, 83–87, 100, 101, 102, 103, 110, 111–13, 114, 115, 118, 121, 122, 126, 127, 141, 152, 158, 161, 164, 167, 170, 172, 175, 205
Gif, 139, 140, 155
Gilbert. See Goron, Marcel
Giraud, General Henri, 71
Goebbels, Joseph, 31
Goron, Marcel, 79, 81–83, 84–85, 88, 103, 207
Gournay, 102
Gouvernement Provisoire de la République Française (GPRF), 159, 160, 162, 163, 208, 212

GPRF. See Gouvernement Provisoire de la République Française
Gray Mice, 76, 91, 106. See also Wehrmacht
Great Britain, 73, 76, 198, 207, 212; enters war, 3; French attitudes toward, 12, 17; Pétain's attitude toward, 3
Gregh, Fernand, 13
Guichard, Police Commissioner, 85–86, 177–78
Guingamp, 80, 85, 209

Heine, 37
Histoire de la Résistance (Nogueres), 207
History of the Second World War (Churchill), 206
Hitler, xii, xvi, 52, 123, 197, 213; attempted assassination of, 141; and England, 19, 23; and foreign refugees, 34; and French fleet, 17; and Pétain, 36, 39; and Poland, 4; and Stalin, 4; and U.S.S.R., 52
Hitler Youth, 39
Holleischen, 173

Institute de France, 72
Intelligence Service of the Free French. See Bureau Central de Renseignement et d'Action
Interior, Ministry of, 87, 209
International Brigades, 52
internment camps. See Beaune-la-Rolande; Compiègne; Drancy; Pithiviers
Is Paris Burning? (Lapierre and Collins), xi, 212
Italian Occupied Zone, 26
Italy, 143, 211

Jews, xvi, 33; persecution of, 3, 33–35, 58–66, 107, 123, 176
Janin, Geneviève (Dominique), 84, 93, 97, 104, 109–10, 112–13, 117, 125, 129, 155, 205

Kerien, 152, 193, 194, 195
Kessel, Joseph, 53
Kim. See Schmidt, Paul
Koenig, General Marie-Pierre, 157, 158, 159, 212

Labor, Ministry of, 33, 60, 61, 108, 208
Lapierre, Dominique, 212
Laval, Pierre, 24, 60, 71, 109

Laval, Great Seminary of, 16; as prison, 20–21
Leclerc, General, 167, 176–77, 209
Lecot, Georges (Captain Drouot), 116, 120, 124–25, 181, 208
Lefaucheux, Marie-Hélène, 110–11, 112, 127–28, 141, 179–81
Lefaucheux, Pierre, 110, 114, 115, 141, 179, 207
Légion d'honneur, 52, 108, 194
Le Mans, 16
Lemoine, Simone (Little Jeanne), 125, 155, 181–82, 209
"Les Français parlent aux Français," 31
Liberation, ix, 13, 32, 119. *See also* Resistance groups
Liberation of Paris, 116, 126, 155, 163, 167, 176, 184
Libération Zone Nord, 75. *See also* Resistance groups
Libyan campaign, 211
Limoges, 109, 175
Limonti, Hugues (Claude Large; Germain), 116, 121, 122, 208, 209
Limousin, 174
Loiret, 59
Lorient, 153
Luftwaffe, 21, 30, 125, 175
Lycée Condorcet, 172
Lycée Racine, 62
Lyons, 67, 68, 79, 80, 109, 110, 123

Maginot Line, 8, 203
Maison d'Alphonse, 209
Maisons-Lafitte, 62, 210
Mann, Thomas, 37
Manthausen, 179
maquis, 126, 138; attitudes toward, 174, 175; Breton, 151, 152, 154, 184; Francs-Tireurs-Partisans and, 152; in Paris, 207; training for, 151
Maquisards, 53, 193, 210
Marseillaise, 13, 166, 200
Marseille, 23, 174
Martinique, 18
Massigli, 157, 212
Massilia, 13, 203
Maurice de Broglie Center for Physics Research, 192
Maurois, André, 37
Max. *See* Moulin, Jean

Mein Kampf, 53
Melun, 156
Memoires de Guerre (de Gaulle), 212
Ménace allemande, la (Chevrillon, André), xii
Mendelssohn, Felix, 37
Mendes-France, Pierre, 203
Ménétral, Dr. Bernard, 53, 197
Merlin. *See* d'Astier de la Vigerie, Emmanuel
Mers-el-Kebir, 18
Milhaud, Darius, 37
Milice, 210
Militarbefehlshaber, 157, 158, 212
Mirande-Thomas, Renée, 97–98, 105–106, 141, 143, 178–79, 207, 210
Montfort-l'Amaury, 59, 60, 77, 107, 108, 112, 114, 149, 168, 210
Montluçon, 73
Montoire, 36, 39
Morocco, xiii
Mort du Loup, 199, 214
Moscow, 209
Moulin, Jean (Max), xv, 73, 79, 80, 102, 110, 207; arrested, 108
Mussolini, 143

Nancy, 180
Nantes, 15, 52
NAP. *See* Noyautage de l'Administration Publique
Narvik, 7
National Council of the Resistance (CNR), 79, 110, 127, 157, 158, 206, 207, 209, 212
Nazism, 42, 53, 67, 127
Netherlands, xii
newspapers, 36, 51. *See also Défense de la France; Oeuvre, l'; Trait d'Union*
Ni Chagrin, ni pitié, 211
Nicolson, Sir Harold, 53, 104
Niort, 10, 11
Nogueres, Henri, 207
Nordling, Raoul, 157, 160, 162, 180, 212
Normandy, 3, 11, 138, 142, 143; landing in, 150, 152; battle of, 156
North Africa, xi, 13, 17–18, 26, 203, 206
Notre Dame de Paris, 7
Noyautage de l'Administration Publique, 162, 207, 208, 212

Nuit sans ombre, la (Vistel), xv
Nuremberg Congress, 39

Occupation, xv, xvi, xvii, xviii, ix, xii, 74,
142, 205, 208
Occupation Era, xv, xvii; conditions, xiii,
xvii, 166
Occupied Zone, 26, 29, 35, 51, 69, 75, 206
Oeuvre, l', 62, 126
Oise River, 57, 128
Oradour-sur-Glane, 127
Oran, 18, 57
Organization Civile et Militaire (OCM), 21.
See also Resistance groups
Orléans, 156
Oronte. *See* Pré, Roland

Pallice, la, 194
Paris-brule-t-il? (Lapierre and Collins), xi,
212
Paris Liberation Committee. *See* Comité Par-
isien de Libération
Parodi, Alexandre (Belladone; Quartus), xv,
119, 121, 129, 157, 158, 159, 160, 161, 162, 163,
208, 213
Pascal, Blaise, 95, 100, 105, 110, 122
Passy Colonel. *See* Dewawrin, André
Patton, General George, 152
Penvénan, 107, 142, 149, 151, 152
Périgueux, 14
persecution of Jews, 58–66; by Germans, 35;
by Vichy, 33–34. *See also* anti-Semitism
Péry, Pierre (Gustave), 114, 121, 176, 208, 209
Pétain, Marshal Philippe, 13, 17, 105; French
attitude toward, 26–27; as head of French
state, 24–25; and Hitler, 36, 39; and New
Order, 25–27, 36; speeches of, 62, 71
Pétainists, xvii, 27, 123
Phony War, 3, 5, 203
Pineau, Christian, xv
Pithiviers, 59, 62, 63, 64, 65, 199
Plougrescant, 142, 151, 152, 184
Plouha, 209
Poincaré, 25
Poissy, 205
Poland, 3, 4, 18
Port-Blanc, xii, 9, 10, 11, 14, 15, 18, 20, 22, 23,
57, 59, 68, 75, 80, 84, 85, 90, 100, 106, 109,
110, 142, 169, 181; liberated, 151–55

Pré, Roland (Oronte), 157, 160, 212
prisoners of war, 23, 26, 36, 40, 41, 76, 160;
daily life of, 39–42, 169–72
Provence, 165
Provisional French Government. *See* Gouvernement Provisoire de la République Française
public opinion, 27
Pucheu, Pierre, 209
Pyrenées, 72, 122

Quartus. *See* Parodi, Alexandre
Quimper, 146, 147

Radio Londre, 31, 102
Radio Paris, 24, 138
radios, 31–32, 33
rationing, 23
Ravensbruck, 122, 126, 173, 176, 179
Ravensbruck International Committee, 179
Red Army, 169
Red Cross, 10, 28, 60, 110, 115, 123, 157, 179,
183
refugees, 54; anti-Nazi, xii, 34; German Jew-
ish, 17
Reims, 17
Renault factories, xvii, 181
Renault-Roulier, Gilbert (Colonel Rémy),
104, 209
Rennes, 80, 85, 87, 152, 209, 210
Resistance, ix, xii, xiii, xv, xvi–xvii, 36, 51, 71,
159, 160, 183; communism and, 127; women
in, xvi–xvii
Resistance groups: Ceux de la Libération, 79,
81; Confrérie Notre-Dame, 104; Libération,
119; Libération Zone Nord, 75; Organisa-
tion Civile et Militaire, 210
Roosevelt, Franklin Delano, 71, 156
Roquette Prison, 141, 168, 179
Rouen, 156
Ruskin, xi
Russian troops, 143, 148, 179

Sacrifice du matin, le (de Bénouville), xv
Saint-Brieuc, 145
Saint Denis barracks, 28–30, 100, 115
Sainte-Gauberge, 4
Saint-Gildas, 211
Saint-Nazaire, 5, 153, 194, 195

Saint-Quentin Prison, 183
Salvation Army, 60
Scapin. *See* Serreulles, Claude
Scapini, 41
Schmidt, Paul (Dominique), 80, 81, 83, 93, 102, 206, 207, 213
Scouting, 3, 29, 74, 75, 78, 86, 95, 124, 207; in prisoner of war camps, 41
Seine River, 9, 57
Serreulles, Claude (Sophie; Scapin), xv, 114, 119, 121, 207, 208
Service du Chiffre de la Délégation Générale du Gouvernement Provisoire: code samples of, 157–60; code work of, xi, xiii, xv, 137, 138, 212; organization and method of, 119–20, 124–28
Siegfried Line, 203
Silesia, 64, 169
Simple vérité, la, xv
Siohan, Robert, 33
Smolensk, 89
Social Security Administration, 33, 108
Somme River, 10
Sophie. *See* Serreulles, Claude
Sorbonne, xiii, 115
Soucy, 10, 11
Soviets, 169
Soviet Union, 4, 52, 127, 209
strikes, 157, 158
Sur mon chemin, j'ai rencontré (Auffray), 169, 204

Taine, Hippolyte, xii
Taine; formation de sa pensés (Chevrillon, André), xii
Témoignage Chrétien, 84, 207
Terrier, Assistant Commissioner, 86, 177
Thorez, Maurice, 127, 209
Tolmé, Louis, 82, 206
Toulon, 72, 173
Toulouse, 68, 70, 177

Touraine, 67
Tours, 11, 12, 29, 36
Trait d'Union, 41
Tréguier, 142, 151
Triel, 105
Trotsky, 31
truce of Paris (August, 1944), 159, 160, 161, 212–13
Tulle, 69, 209

U-boats, 153
UGIF (General Union of French Jews), 61, 62, 63
United Nations Relief and Repatriation Association, xii
University of Strasbourg, 68
U.S.S.R., 140

Valcroissant, 3, 29
Valmondois, 53, 109, 138, 139
Védy, Gilbert (Médéric), 79, 103, 207
Vélodrome d'Hiver, 59, 60
Viannay, Phillippe, 110
Vichyites, 42
Vichy regime, xvi, xvii, 18, 19, 24, 37, 41–42, 60, 123, 160, 208; propaganda of, 25–26, 51; requisitions food, 31; persecution of Jews by, 33–35. *See also* anti-Semitism
Vigie aveugle, la (Bauer), 173
von Choltitz, General Dietrich, 157, 160, 161, 180, 209, 212, 213

Wehrmacht, 76, 91, 99, 106
Why Britain Is at War, 53
World War I, 10, 11, 17, 24, 25, 36, 52, 53, 108, 123, 184
Wuilleumier, Hélène, 104

Yellow Star, xvi, 35, 58, 60, 65, 128, 204, 210; purchase of, 59

Zeithain, 170, 171